The What's-for-Dinner

C O O K B O O K

D0118294

The What's-for-Dinner
C O O K B O O K

52 Weeks of Balanced Dinners for Your Family

Kathleen Botta and Claire Mendonca

Cumberland House Publishing
Nashville, Tennessee

Copyright © 2002 by Claire Mendonca and Kathleen Botta

All rights reserved. No part of this book may be reproduced or transmitted in any form or by any means, electronic or mechanical, including photocopying and recording, or by any information storage and retrieval system, without permission in writing from the publisher, except for brief quotations in critical reviews or articles.

Published by
  Cumberland House Publishing, Inc.
  431 Harding Industrial Drive
  Nashville, TN 37211
  www.cumberlandhouse.com

Cover design: Unlikely Suburban Design
Text design: Lisa Taylor

Library of Congress Cataloging-in-Publication Data

Botta, Kathleen, 1963–
    The what's-for-dinner cookbook : 52 weeks of balanced dinners for your family / Kathleen Botta and Claire Mendonca.
        p. cm.
Includes index.
    ISBN 1-58182-279-0
  1. Dinners and dining. 2. Menus. I. Mendonca, Claire, 1963– II. Title.
    TX737 .B68 2002
    641.5'4—dc21

2002005118

Printed in Canada
1 2 3 4 5 6 7 8 — 07 06 05 04 03 02

Contents

"What do you want for dinner?"

How often do you find yourself asking your family "what do you want for dinner?" *The What's-for-Dinner Cookbook* was created to take the hassle out of meal preparation. No more coming up with an idea only to find you don't have all the ingredients. Delicious well-balanced meals are now at your fingertips. Follow the weekly shopping lists and you're guaranteed to be prepared for the meals you will be cooking.

This book is the brainchild of best friends who were always asking each other, "What are *you* making for dinner tonight?" Both of us are busy moms with hectic schedules. Tired of repetitive meals, we came up with the idea to make a list of as many meals as we could think of that our families liked, and then we traded lists. This gave us several months of meals. Friends were jealous—they wanted the lists—and thus *The What's-for-Dinner Cookbook* was born.

These recipes are family favorites that require no longer than thirty minutes of preparation. We have numbered the days as 1–5 instead of Monday–Friday to allow you to decide which days of the week you would like to cook. We have planned only five days of menus per week because we all deserve a break from cooking or like to eat leftovers now and then.

The What's-for-Dinner Cookbook is organized according to the four seasons of the year, and the recipes call for fresh seasonal ingredients, saving you money by utilizing what is in abundance during a given season.

This cookbook was not written with any special dietary needs in mind. The meals are simple and well-balanced. Generally speaking the recipes yield enough for families of four to five, the national average. If your family is larger or eats the equivalent of more than four to five servings, then add to the recipes and shopping lists.

We have organized the meals so that the leftovers from a chicken or roast you prepare one day can be used later in the week—a time- and money-saving method. Meals that require marinating are noted the day before in the Time Saver section.

The shopping lists are divided into sections much like the supermarket in order to allow you to move quickly through the aisles. If you like to bulk shop, refer to the monthly bulk shopping lists for items commonly found in large discount centers.

Congratulations on never having to worry about dinner again! The planning is done, and the preparing is now up to you. We think you'll find the program so convenient that you will never want to use another cookbook again.

Time Saver Look for the Time Saver icon for time-saving tips. They are intended to make your week go more smoothly. For example, if chopped onions are necessary in several recipes for the week, we suggest you do all the chopping on Day 1.

Crock Pot
next day—read ahead! Several of the recipes in this book utilize a crock pot. The Crock Pot icon alerts you that the next day's menu requires slow cooking so you're never taken off guard.

ALTERING THE SHOPPING LISTS—A NUMBERED APPROACH

If you choose not to prepare a particular meal, changing the shopping list is easy. After each item on the list is a number that corresponds to the day of the week that item is required. You need only to cross off those items with the number that corresponds to the day you wish to skip. For instance, if you don't plan to make Day 4's menu of a given week, delete all items from your weekly shopping list that have a "4" next to them.

Remember when alternating the menus to review the Time Savers to see if the alternations will affect any other days. Feel free to substitute your favorite lasagna or spaghetti recipe for ours. These are family favorites and each family has their own special recipes. If you'd like a new recipe, try ours; they are all time-tested and delicious.

DOWNLOAD THE SHOPPING LISTS

The shopping lists in the back of this book are available on our publisher's website: www.cumberlandhouse.com. Just download the PDF file and print before your weekly shopping trip. It's easy and convenient!

CHECK YOUR STAPLES

The shopping lists specify which seasonings and staples are needed for the week. Quantities for basics such as salt and pepper and dried herbs are not given, so check your staples often and replenish when you're low.

BUTTER AND MARGARINE

Most of the menus in this book call for butter. Butter and margarine are interchangeable, so feel free to substitute.

SALAD AND VEGETABLES

When the shopping list specifies salad greens, purchase either your favorite lettuce or a bag of pre-washed salad greens. Toppings refer to any additions you might like such as mushrooms, tomatoes, or croutons. Choose whatever your family prefers. The side dish vegetables can be fresh, frozen, or canned based on your preference. In most cases, they are listed as either canned or frozen. Review the recipes and adjust the shopping lists accordingly.

CAN/JAR SIZES

When the shopping list calls for a certain size can, jar, etc., purchase whatever size your market carries that is closest to the size listed. Minor alterations like these will not affect the recipe.

TIME SAVING VERSUS MONEY SAVING

If a recipe calls for boneless, skinless breasts, you will save money if you purchase the chicken with bone and skin. This will add 15 minutes to your prep time. The cheese used in the recipes is usually grated. You can save time purchasing it already grated and in some cases the cost is the same as buying it in a block.

The What's-for-Dinner
C O O K B O O K

· FRUIT SALAD · CORN ON THE COB · STRAWBERRIES ·

· GRILLED VEGETABLES · BARBECUE PORK SANDWICHES ·

· FETTUCCINE WITH TOMATO BASIL · ORANGES · SCAMPI · CHICKEN &

HERB DUMPLINGS · FRUIT SALAD · GREEN SALAD · CORN ON THE COB ·

· TURKEY TETRAZZINI · ORANGES · BRANDIED ROUND STEAK ·

Spring

· SHRIMP CURRY · SPANISH RICE · CRANBERRY CHICKEN ·

· GARLIC SPINACH · STRAWBERRIES · ASPARAGUS WITH SAUCE ·

· CORN ON THE COB · GRILLED VEGETABLES ·

· RICE PILAF · GREEN BEANS · STRAWBERRIES ·

· GRILLED VEGETABLES · BARBECUE PORK SANDWICHES ·

HAM & CHEESE CREPES · ORANGES ·

SCAMPI · SHRIMP CURRY · FRUIT SALAD · GREEN SALAD ·

CORN ON THE COB · CHICKEN & HERB RICE ·

· SQUASH CASSEROLE · FRUIT SALAD ·

· CORN ON THE COB · STRAWBERRIES · GRILLED VEGETABLES ·

· ORANGES · SCAMPI · SHRIMP CURRY · FRUIT SALAD · GREEN SALAD ·

· GLAZED CORN BEEF · BRANDIED ROUND STEAK ·

· ASPARAGUS EGG CASSEROLE · GARLIC SPINACH ·

· ROASTED CHICKEN AND VEGETABLES ·

· STRAWBERRIES ·

WEEK 8

Day	Main Dish	Side 1	Side 2	Side 3
Day 1	Sicilian Meat Roll	Green Beans	Garlic Bread	
Day 2	Chicken Marsala	Egg Noodles	Dinner Rolls	
Day 3	Tangy Pork Chops	White Rice	Peas	
Day 4	Stir-fried Chicken & Vegetables	Peaches	White Rice	
Day 5	White Squash & Shrimp Casserole	Carrots	Dinner Rolls	

WEEK 7

Day	Main Dish	Side 1	Side 2	Side 3
Day 1	Barbecue Tri-tip Roast	Grilled Vegetables	French Bread	
Day 2	Herbed Chicken Casserole	Baked Zucchini	Rice	Green Salad
Day 3	Spinach Meatballs	Noodles	Apples	
Day 4	Baked Chicken Strata	Green Beans	Cheese Potatoes	
Day 5	Tuna-Sour Cream Casserole	Strawberries	Green Salad	Potato Chips

WEEK 6

Day	Main Dish	Side 1	Side 2	Side 3
Day 1	Baked Ham	Macaroni 'n' Cheese	Fruit Salad	
Day 2	Chicken & Rice	Spinach	Oranges	
Day 3	Quick Ham Barbecue	Green Salad	Corn Chips	Buns
Day 4	Grilled Turkey Breast	Corn on the Cob	Stuffing	
Day 5	Fettuccine with Tomato Basil Sauce	Green Beans with Oregano	French Bread	

WEEK 5

Day	Main Dish	Side 1	Side 2	Side 3
Day 1	Cranberry Chicken	Asparagus Casserole	French Bread	
Day 2	Lasagna	Spicy Garlic Bread	Green Salad	
Day 3	Blackened Fish	Potato Casserole	Steamed Cauliflower	
Day 4	Broccoli Soup	Crackers and Peanut Butter		
Day 5	Chicken Enchiladas	Spanish Rice	Refried Beans	

continued on next page

SPRING MENUS AT A GLANCE

WEEK 1

Day 1	Pork Roast	Carrots	Potatoes	Biscuits
Day 2	Smothered Steak	Mashed Potatoes	Green Beans	
Day 3	Pork Chimichangas	Mexican Rice	Green Salad	
Day 4	Stuffed Chicken Pasta	Broccoli	Breadsticks	
Day 5	Barbecue Pork Sandwiches	Carrot/Celery Sticks	Potato Chips	

WEEK 2

Day 1	Chicken Enchiladas	Mexican Rice	Refried Beans	Green Salad/Tortillas
Day 2	Hungarian Casserole	Carrots	Dinner Rolls	
Day 3	Clam Chowder	French Bread		
Day 4	Shepherd's Pie	Fruit Salad		
Day 5	Korean Stew	White Rice	Oriental Vegetables	

WEEK 3

Day 1	Rio Grande Pork Roast	Acorn Squash	Dinner Rolls
Day 2	Cheeseburger Pie	Salad	
Day 3	Chicken Tahitian	Green Beans Caesar	Dinner Rolls
Day 4	Chow Mein	Broccoli	Won Tons
Day 5	Tuna Vegetable Casserole	Dinner Rolls	

WEEK 4

Day 1	Baked Ham	Green Bean Casserole	Fruit Salad
Day 2	Roasted Chicken and Vegetables	Baked Potatoes	Green Salad
Day 3	Taco Beef Skillet Dinner	Hominy Casserole	Corn Chips
Day 4	Quiche	Green Salad	Garlic French Bread
Day 5	One Chicken Dish	Green Salad	

WEEK 13

Day 1	Glazed Corned Beef	Rolls	
Day 2	Chicken & Herb Dumplings	Green Beans	Green Salad
Day 3	Layered Supper	Fruit Salad	Dinner Rolls
Day 4	Chicken Puff Casserole	Asparagus	Dinner Rolls
Day 5	Cheesy Hash-Spinach Pie	Oranges	Green Salad

SPRING MENUS AT A GLANCE

WEEK 9

Day 1	New England Dinner	Dinner Rolls	
Day 2	Parmesan Yogurt Chicken	Asparagus	Baked Potatoes
Day 3	Barbecue Beef Sandwiches	Carrots	Potato Chips
Day 4	Brandied Round Steak	Green Beans	Pilaf
Day 5	Scampi Fettuccine	Green Salad	Garlic Bread

WEEK 10

Day 1	Roast Beef	Squash Casserole	Dinner Rolls
Day 2	Baked Pork Chops & Rice	Spinach & Orange Salad	
Day 3	Broccoli Chicken Roll-ups	Green Salad	
Day 4	Turkey Tetrazzini	Baked Stuffed Eggplant	Dinner Rolls
Day 5	Tuna/Water Chestnut Casserole	Asparagus with Sauce	

WEEK 11

Day 1	Spaghetti	Green Salad	Garlic Bread
Day 2	Chicken Supreme	Peas	Biscuits
Day 3	Barbecue Burgers	Baked Beans	Jell-O
Day 4	Smothered Pork Chops	Applesauce	Steamed Rice / Vegetables
Day 5	Fish Sticks	French Fries	Sliced Fruit Salad

WEEK 12

Day 1	Chicken Casserole	Garlic Spinach	Potato Chips
Day 2	Baked Ham	Broccoli-Corn Bake	Breadsticks
Day 3	Mexican Chili Con Carne	Tortillas	Corn on the Cob
Day 4	Ham & Cheese Crepes	Steamed Carrots	Green Salad
Day 5	Shrimp Curry	Rice	Peas

Pork Roast

BISCUITS

Prep Time: 10 minutes • Total Time: 6 hours or all day

2   large pork roasts
Garlic
Cumin
Salt and pepper
1   package dry onion soup mix
1/3 cup barbecue sauce
1   small bag baby carrots
6   potatoes, peeled and cut in half

PORK ROAST

Place the pork roasts on a large piece of foil. Season with garlic, cumin, salt, pepper, and onion soup mix. Pour barbecue sauce over and wrap very well, so that nothing leaks out. Put 1/2 cup of water in the bottom of a crock pot along with the carrots and potatoes. Place the foil pork roast package on top. Cook on low all day or at least 6 hours.

To serve take out only 1 of the pork roasts, reserving the other for Day 3 and Day 5's meals, along with any leftover juices from the roasts.

Note: If no crock pot use a large covered casserole in the oven all day at 200°.

1 to 2 cans large refrigerator biscuits
Butter

BISCUITS

Follow the directions on the can for baking. Serve with butter.

Time
Saver

Crock Pot
today!

One pot roast will be used on Day 3 and Day 5—store with leftover juices.

Smothered Steak

MASHED POTATOES · GREEN BEANS

Prep Time: 20 minutes · Total Time: 1 hour 15 minutes

1 to 1½ pounds round steak,
    tenderized
Salt and pepper
Flour
1 tablespoon oil
¼ onion, chopped
1 clove garlic, pressed
1 6-ounce can sliced mushrooms,
    undrained
1 10½-ounce can mushroom soup
2 tablespoons Worcestershire sauce
1 teaspoon catsup
1 teaspoon steak sauce

SMOTHERED STEAK

Salt and pepper the round steak. Flour the meat. In a skillet heat the oil and brown the beef. Add the onion and garlic and sauté. Add the mushrooms, soup, water, Worcestershire, catsup, and steak sauce. Cover the meat with liquid, add enough water to do so. Cook until tender on simmer, about 45 minutes.

6 to 8 potatoes
Salt and pepper
Margarine or butter
Milk (optional)

MASHED POTATOES

Peel and dice the potatoes. Place in a saucepan with 1 teaspoon of salt, cover with water, and bring to a boil. Boil for at least 10 minutes or longer until soft enough for mashing.

Drain off the water and add margarine or butter to taste (2 to 4 tablespoons). Mash, adding salt and pepper. For extra smooth potatoes add 2 tablespoons of milk or more after mashing and whip until fluffy.

Serve with gravy from Smothered Steak.

2 16-ounce cans cut green beans
2 slices bacon, chopped
Fresh diced onion, if desired

GREEN BEANS

In a large saucepan place the green beans, bacon, and onion. Cook according to the directions on the can.

Time Saver *Chop an entire onion and save the leftovers for Day 3.*

Pork Chimichangas

MEXICAN RICE • GREEN SALAD

Prep Time: 15 minutes • Total Time: 45 minutes

1	pound pork (3 cups), shredded
1	16-ounce jar salsa
1	can refried beans
1	4-ounce can diced green chilies
1	envelope taco seasoning mix
16	8-inch flour tortillas
4	cups grated Jack cheese

PORK CHIMICHANGAS

In a large skillet combine the meat, salsa, beans, green chilies, and seasoning mix. Cook on medium heat. Heat the tortillas in another skillet for 30 seconds on each side. Place ½ cup of meat mixture on the edge of each tortilla, top with cheese, and roll up. Should make 16. Set out those you wish to eat, wrap the remainder in foil, and place in the freezer. Bake at 350° for 10 minutes until crisp. If frozen bake for 30 minutes. (Great for a quick lunch.)

1	tablespoon oil
1½	cups long grain rice
2	cloves garlic, minced
¼	large onion, chopped
1½	teaspoons cumin
2	beef bouillon cubes
½	8-ounce can tomato sauce
3½	cups water

MEXICAN RICE

In a large skillet pour the oil. Add the rice. Heat to medium and brown the rice. Stir to brown all sides. Add the garlic, onion, cumin, and bouillon cubes. Add ½ can of tomato sauce. Simmer to mix in. Add water. Stir in; cover and simmer for 25 minutes.

1 bag salad greens
Favorite dressing (Catalina makes for a festive Mexican meal)

GREEN SALAD

Place salad greens in serving bowls and drizzle with dressing.

Stuffed Chicken Pasta

SPAGHETTI NOODLES • BROCCOLI • BREADSTICKS

Prep Time: 15 minutes • Total Time: 1 hour 30 minutes

---

4 to 6 boneless, skinless chicken breasts
1 pound sliced mozzarella cheese
1 large jar spaghetti sauce

STUFFED CHICKEN PASTA

Slice each chicken breast in the middle lengthwise and stuff with cheese. Place in a large casserole dish and cover with spaghetti sauce. Bake at 350° for 1 hour.
Serve over spaghetti noodles.

---

1 pound spaghetti noodles
Margarine

SPAGHETTI NOODLES

Follow package directions for the number of servings desired and start cooking noodles about 20 minutes before the chicken is due out of the oven.

---

2 heads broccoli

BROCCOLI

Place the broccoli in a steamer over an inch or two of boiling salted water. Cover and steam for 6 to 8 minutes or until bright green and tender.

---

2 cans refrigerator breadsticks
Butter

BREADSTICKS

Bake at the end of chicken baking cycle as directed. Serve with butter.

Crock Pot
next day—read ahead!

Barbecue Pork Sandwiches

POTATO CHIPS • CARROTS AND CELERY STICKS

Prep Time: 5 minutes • Total Time: 3 hours in crock pot or 50 minutes on stove top

Remaining pork roast
Remaining juices from roast
Barbecue sauce
1 envelope onion soup mix
6 to 8 sandwich rolls

BARBECUE PORK SANDWICHES

Shred the remaining pork roast (from Day 3) and place in a crock pot. Add any leftover juice from your roast, add the same amount of barbecue sauce, and the onion soup mix. This mixture should look very soupy. Add a little water, if needed. Cook in the crock pot on low for at least 3 hours or simmer on the stove over medium-high heat for 45 minutes. Serve over sandwich rolls.

---

1 bag potato chips

POTATO CHIPS

Carrots
Celery

CARROTS AND CELERY STICKS

Cut raw carrots and celery into sticks. Serve on relish tray.

Low-fat Chicken Enchiladas

MEXICAN RICE • GREEN SALAD AND TORTILLA CHIPS • REFRIED BEANS

Prep Time: 20 minutes • Total Time: 1 hour

4	boneless chicken breasts
3	tablespoons margarine
1	teaspoon minced garlic
1	medium onion, chopped
1	tablespoon flour
1	tablespoon cornstarch
1	14-ounce can chicken broth
1	4-ounce can chopped green chilies
1	14½-ounce can diced tomatoes
2	cups sour cream
2	cups grated mozzarella
14	small flour tortillas

LOW-FAT CHICKEN ENCHILADAS

In a large pot boil the chicken until cooked. Shred. In a skillet melt the margarine and add the garlic and onion; cook until soft. Add the flour, cornstarch, chicken broth, and green chilies; stir until bubbly and smooth. Add the chicken and remove from the heat. In a medium bowl combine the tomatoes, sour cream, and half of the cheese; add to the chicken mixture. Spoon the sauce onto the tortillas, roll up, and place in a casserole dish sprayed with cooking spray. Pour the remaining sauce over all. Sprinkle the remaining cheese on top. Bake at 350° until hot and bubbly, 15 to 20 minutes.

1	tablespoon oil
1½	cups long grain rice
2	cloves garlic, minced
¼	large onion, chopped
1½	teaspoons cumin
2	beef bouillon cubes
½	8-ounce can tomato sauce
3½	cups water

MEXICAN RICE

Pour the oil in a large skillet. Add the rice. Heat to medium and brown the rice. Stir to brown all sides. Add the garlic, onion, cumin, and bouillon cubes. Add ½ can of tomato sauce and blend. Add the water, stir, cover, and simmer for 25 minutes.

1	bag salad greens
	Favorite dressing
	Tortilla chips

GREEN SALAD AND TORTILLA CHIPS

Place salad greens in serving bowls and drizzle with dressing. Serve with tortilla chips.

1	17-ounce can refried beans

REFRIED BEANS

Heat the beans in the microwave or on the stove top.

Time Saver *Chop an additional 2 onions for use the rest of the week.*

Hungarian Casserole

COOKED CARROTS • DINNER ROLLS

Prep Time: 20 minutes • Total Time: 1 hour 10 minutes

8   large potatoes, boiled and sliced
1½   pounds smoked sausage, thinly
      sliced
8   hard-boiled eggs, sliced
1   large onion, sliced
1   pint sour cream
Salt, pepper, paprika, to taste

HUNGARIAN CASSEROLE

In a greased casserole dish place a layer of potatoes, a layer of sausage, a layer of eggs, a layer of onions, and some sour cream. Repeat layers in the same order 2 to 3 times. Season the final layer with salt, pepper, and paprika. Leave dish uncovered and bake at 350° for 40 minutes.

1   small bag baby carrots

COOKED CARROTS

Place carrots in a saucepan and boil until cooked. Serve with salt, pepper, and butter.

1   package prepared dinner rolls
Butter

DINNER ROLLS

Warm the rolls and serve with butter.

Time Saver *Boil an additional 8 potatoes for use on Day 3 and Day 4.*

Excellent Clam Chowder

FRENCH BREAD

Prep Time: 20 minutes • Total Time: 45 minutes

2 cups cubed potatoes
1 cup butter
1 cup chopped celery
2 cups chopped onions
2 cups chopped green bell pepper
¾ cup flour
5 cups hot milk
3 6½-ounce cans clams and juice
½ teaspoon dried thyme
Salt and pepper to taste

EXCELLENT CLAM CHOWDER

In a pot of boiling water cook the potatoes. In a separate pot heat the butter and sauté the celery, onions, and green pepper until the vegetables are soft. Add the flour and mix until smooth. Add the hot milk, clams, and juice. Cook for 10 minutes. Add the potatoes, thyme, salt, and pepper. Mix and simmer on low heat for a few minutes.

1 loaf crusty French bread
Butter

FRENCH BREAD

Serve soup with a loaf of warmed crusty French bread and butter. You could even buy the small loaves to use for soup bowls.

Shepherd's Pie

FRUIT SALAD

Prep Time: 20 minutes • Total Time: 45 minutes

4 to 6 potatoes
2   pounds ground beef
¼   cup chopped onions
2   cans corn, drained
Butter or margarine
Milk
Salt and pepper
¼   cup grated Cheddar cheese

SHEPHERD'S PIE

Peel the potatoes and place in a large saucepan. Cover with water and add salt. Boil for 10 minutes or until soft enough to mash. In a skillet fry the ground beef, adding salt and pepper to taste. Add the chopped onion and cook until soft. Pour the beef and onion mixture into a casserole dish, adding the corn. Mash the potatoes with butter, milk, salt, and pepper. Spread the potatoes on top of the beef and corn mixture. Sprinkle the top with grated cheese. Bake at 350° for 20 minutes.

4 to 6 pieces of fruit, any combination

FRUIT SALAD

Cut up favorite fruit, mix, and serve.

Time Saver — *Marinate meat for tomorrow's dinner.*

Korean Stew

WHITE RICE • ORIENTAL VEGETABLES

Prep Time: 15 minutes, plus marinating • Total Time: 25 minutes, plus marinating

1 pound round steak or sirloin	**KOREAN STEW**
1/2 cup oil	Cut the round steak into 1½-inch strips and marinate
1/2 cup soy sauce	with the other ingredients 2 to 3 hours, or do in the
2 to 3 chopped green onions	morning and marinate all day. Separate and place pieces

KOREAN STEW

Cut the round steak into 1½-inch strips and marinate with the other ingredients 2 to 3 hours, or do in the morning and marinate all day. Separate and place pieces on a cookie sheet evenly. Pour the marinade over all. Broil until done. Serve over White Rice.

---

2 cups water
2 cups instant rice

WHITE RICE

Bring the water to a boil. Stir in the rice; cover and remove from the heat. Let stand 5 minutes or until the water is absorbed. Fluff with fork.

Serves 4.

---

1 large bag Oriental vegetables

ORIENTAL VEGETABLES

Prepare according to the directions on the bag.

Crock Pot
next day—read ahead!

Rio Grande Pork Roast

STUFFED ACORN SQUASH • DINNER ROLLS

Prep Time: 25 minutes • Total Time: All day

1	4- to 5-pound boneless rolled pork loin roast
1/2	teaspoon salt
1/2	teaspoon garlic salt
1	teaspoon chili powder (divided)
1/2	cup apple jelly
1/2	cup catsup
1	tablespoon vinegar
1	cup crushed corn chips
4	peeled potatoes
8	peeled carrots

RIO GRANDE PORK ROAST

Place the pork fat side up on a rack in a crock pot. In a small bowl combine the salt, garlic salt, and 1/2 teaspoon of the chili powder and rub into the roast. Cook in the crock pot all day.

In a small saucepan combine the jelly, catsup, vinegar, and remaining 1/2 teaspoon of chili powder. Bring to a boil, reduce the heat, and simmer, uncovered, for 2 minutes.

Brush the roast with glaze and sprinkle with crushed corn chips. Add the potatoes and carrots. Roast 10 to 15 minutes at 325°. Remove from the oven and let stand 10 minutes. Measure the pan drippings and corn chips; add water to make 1 cup. Heat to boiling and pass with sliced roast.

Serves 8 to 10.

2	acorn squash
1/2	cup brown sugar
1/2	teaspoon cinnamon
1/4	cup chopped onion (optional)
1	cup sour cream
1/4	cup bread crumbs
1	tablespoon chopped parsley
1	tablespoon butter

STUFFED ACORN SQUASH

Split the squash, clean, and bake upside down in a baking pan until done. Scrape out the shell and mash the pulp. Mix with all ingredients except the bread crumbs and butter. Spoon back into the shells. Mix the butter and bread crumbs and sprinkle on the squash. Bake at 350° until hot and the crumbs are toasted.

Serves 4.

1	package prepared dinner rolls
Butter	

DINNER ROLLS

 Chop 5 onions for use throughout the week.

Cheeseburger Pie

SALAD

Prep Time: 25 minutes • Total Time: 55 minutes

Pastry for 1 9-inch pie
2 pounds ground beef
1/2 teaspoon oregano
1 teaspoon salt
1/4 teaspoon pepper
1/2 teaspoon Worcestershire sauce
1/2 teaspoon dry mustard
1 cup chopped onion
1/4 cup chopped green bell pepper
1/2 cup fine dry bread crumbs
4 ounces tomato sauce (1/2 can)
2 cups grated mellow Cheddar cheese
1 beaten egg
1/4 cup milk
Salt and pepper to taste

CHEESEBURGER PIE

If preparing pie shell from scratch, make the dough. In a skillet brown the beef; drain well. Divide in half, save half for Day 4. Add the seasonings, onion, green pepper, bread crumbs, and tomato sauce. Stir well and pour into the unbaked shell.

In a bowl combine the cheese, egg, milk, salt, and pepper, and pour over the meat mixture. Bake in a 425° oven for about 30 minutes.

Serves 6 to 8.

1 bag salad greens
Favorite salad toppings
Favorite low-fat or nonfat dressing

SALAD

Place salad greens in serving bowls. Add toppings and drizzle with dressing.

 Time Saver *Brown 2 pounds of ground beef and save half for Day 4.*

Chicken Tahitian

GREEN BEANS CAESAR • DINNER ROLLS

Prep Time: 30 minutes • Total Time: 1 hour 20 minutes

½ cup butter or margarine
1 envelope onion soup mix
1 tablespoon cornstarch
1 20-ounce can pineapple chunks, drained (save juice)
6 chicken breasts, boned, rolled and secured
2 tablespoons lime juice

CHICKEN TAHITIAN

Preheat the oven to 350°. In a small saucepan melt the butter; stir in the dry soup mix and cornstarch. Add 3/4 cup of the reserved pineapple juice and the lime juice. Bring to a boil. Arrange the chicken breasts and pineapple chunks in a 2-quart oblong baking dish; pour the onion mixture over the chicken. Bake at 350° for 45 minutes or until tender.

Serves 6.

Note: Chicken may be prepared with bone in, if desired.

1½ pounds green beans, cooked
2 tablespoons salad oil
1 tablespoon vinegar
1 tablespoon minced onion
¼ teaspoon salt
1 clove garlic, crushed
⅛ teaspoon pepper
2 tablespoons dry bread crumbs
2 tablespoons grated Parmesan cheese
1 tablespoon butter
Paprika

GREEN BEANS CAESAR

Preheat the oven to 350°. Toss the beans with salad oil, vinegar, onion, salt, garlic, and pepper. Pour into an ungreased 1-quart casserole. Stir together the bread crumbs, cheese, and butter. Sprinkle over the beans, and sprinkle with paprika. Bake uncovered for 15 to 20 minutes or until heated through.

With canned beans, use 2 16-oz. cans and bake 40 to 50 minutes.

Serves 6.

1 package prepared dinner rolls
Butter

DINNER ROLLS

Warm the rolls and serve with butter.

Chow Mein

STEAMED BROCCOLI • WON TONS

Prep Time: 15 minutes • Total Time: 45 minutes

1	pound ground beef, browned on Day 2
1	10-ounce package frozen peas, thawed
2	cups chopped celery
1	6-ounce can sliced water chestnuts
1	10½-ounce can condensed cream of mushroom soup
2	tablespoons milk
1½	teaspoons salt
½	teaspoon pepper
1	onion, chopped
1	3-ounce can chow mein noodles

CHOW MEIN

Place the hamburger in the bottom of a 2-quart greased baking dish. Over the hamburger, arrange layers of peas, celery, and water chestnuts. Mix together the soup, milk, salt, pepper, and onion. Pour this over the meat and vegetable layers. Top with the chow mein noodles. Bake at 350° for 30 minutes or until hot.

Serves 8 to 10.

2	heads broccoli
½	cup balsamic vinegar

STEAMED BROCCOLI

Place the broccoli in a steamer over an inch or two of boiling salted water. Cover and steam for 6 to 8 minutes or until bright green and tender.

Toss with balsamic vinegar.

1	box won tons

WON TONS

Tuna Vegetable Casserole

DINNER ROLLS

Prep Time: 25 minutes • Total Time: 1 hour 20 minutes

6   carrots
2   medium potatoes
1   large onion
2   stalks celery
4   turnips
1   14-ounce can tuna, flaked
Seasoned salt to taste
Garlic powder to taste
2   10½-ounce cans golden mush-
     room soup, undiluted

TUNA VEGETABLE CASSEROLE

Chop all vegetables into bite-size pieces. Combine with tuna and seasonings. Place in a large buttered casserole dish. Stir together the soups and pour over all. Bake covered at 350° until the vegetables are tender, approximately 45 minutes.

Serves 6 to 8.

---

1   package prepared dinner rolls
Butter

DINNER ROLLS

Warm the rolls and serve with butter.

Baked Ham

GREEN BEAN CASSEROLE • FRUIT SALAD

Prep Time: 10 minutes • Total Time: 1 hour 20 minutes

1	4- to 5-pound boneless cooked ham
¾	cup honey

BAKED HAM

Bake the ham in oven at 325° for approximately 30 minutes. Remove from the oven, score, and spread with honey. Bake an additional 30 minutes at 350°.

2	9-ounce packages frozen cut green beans, cooked and drained
¾	cup milk
1	10½-ounce can condensed cream of mushroom soup
⅛	teaspoon pepper
1	2.8-ounce can French fried onions

GREEN BEAN CASSEROLE

Preheat the oven to 350°. In a medium bowl combine the beans, milk, soup, pepper, and ½ can of French fried onions. Pour into a 1½-quart casserole. Bake uncovered at 350° for 30 minutes or until heated through. Top with the remaining onions and bake uncovered for 5 minutes or until the onions are golden brown.

Serves 6.

Microwave Directions: Prepare the green bean mixture as above, and pour into a 1½-quart microwave-safe casserole. Cook, covered, on high for 8 to 10 minutes or until heated through. Stir the beans halfway through cooking time. Top with the remaining onions and cook, uncovered, for 1 minute. Let stand 5 minutes.

2	apples, peeled and cored
18	grapes, cut in halves
2	oranges, peeled and sectioned

FRUIT SALAD

Place all fruit in a salad bowl and mix.

Time Saver *Reserve ½ cup ham for Day 4.*

Roasted Chicken and Vegetables

BAKED POTATO WITH CHIVES • GREEN SALAD

Prep Time: 30 minutes • Total Time: 2 hours 35 minutes

1	2- to 3-pound whole chicken
8	carrots, cut in 1-inch pieces
2	green peppers, cut in rings
8	celery stalks, cut in 1-inch pieces
4	onions, quartered

Salt and pepper
1   tablespoon butter, melted
Paprika

ROASTED CHICKEN AND VEGETABLES

In a large foil-lined pan arrange the chicken and vegetables. Season with salt and pepper. Wrap foil loosely around the chicken and secure the edges. Cook at 375° for 1 hour.

Turn back the foil and baste with juices. Brush with butter and sprinkle with paprika. Roast 45 minutes more.

6 to 8 potatoes
4   teaspoons chives
4   tablespoons butter

BAKED POTATO WITH CHIVES

Preheat the oven to 350°. Poke a hole or two in each potato. Bake the potatoes for 1 hour.

Cut the potatoes in half, score. Place ½ tablespoon of butter and ½ teaspoon of chives on each half.

1   bag salad greens
Favorite salad toppings
Favorite low-fat or nonfat dressing

GREEN SALAD

Place salad greens in serving bowls. Add toppings and drizzle with dressing.

Taco Beef Skillet Dinner

HOMINY CASSEROLE • CORN CHIPS

Prep Time: 30 minutes • Total Time: 1 hour 5 minutes

1 pound ground beef
¼ cup chopped onion
1 3-ounce can mushrooms, undrained
1 envelope taco seasoning mix
1¼ teaspoons seasoned salt
3 cups fine egg noodles, uncooked
2¼ cups tomato juice
⅛ teaspoon hot pepper sauce
1 cup sour cream
1 tablespoon parsley flakes

TACO BEEF SKILLET DINNER

In a large skillet brown the meat. Add the onion and cook until limp. Stir in the mushrooms and liquid, seasoning mix, and seasoned salt. Scatter the uncooked noodles over the meat. Pour the tomato juice and hot pepper sauce over the noodles, pressing the noodles down into the liquid. Cover and simmer about 30 minutes or until the noodles are tender. Combine the sour cream and parsley; spread over the top. Cover and let stand about 5 minutes.

Serves 5 generously.

2 16-ounce cans white or yellow hominy
Butter
1 medium onion, diced
3 cups grated Cheddar cheese
1 4-ounce can diced green chilies
1 medium tomato, cored, seeded, and diced
1 or 2 green onions, trimmed

HOMINY CASSEROLE

Rinse the hominy under cool water, drain. Pat dry on paper towel. Butter a 7 x 11-inch casserole. Place half of the hominy in the casserole. Sprinkle with half of the chopped onion and cheese. Top with the chilies. Add the remaining hominy, chopped onions, and cheese. Top with diced tomatoes and green onions. Cover with foil. Bake at 400° until bubbly.

1 bag corn chips

CORN CHIPS

Chop an additional onion for Day 4.

Quiche

GREEN SALAD • GARLIC BREAD

Prep Time: 30 minutes • Total Time: 1 hour 15 minutes

½ cup chopped onion
2 tablespoons butter or margarine
1 unbaked 9-inch deep-dish pie shell
½ cup chopped ham from Day 2
Chopped mushrooms, broccoli, or
    whatever is on hand
1 cup grated cheese (can be Swiss,
    Jack, Cheddar)
4 eggs
2 cups milk
¼ to ½ teaspoon salt
¼ teaspoon nutmeg
Dash cayenne pepper

QUICHE

In a skillet sauté the onion in butter or margarine until translucent. Sprinkle the onions in the bottom of the pie shell. Add the ham, mushrooms, and any other vegetable of your choice. Sprinkle with cheese. Beat the eggs, add the milk and seasonings and mix well. Pour the mixture into the pie shell. Bake at 400° for 15 minutes. Lower the oven to 300° and bake for 35 to 40 additional minutes.

Serves 6 to 8.

1 bag salad greens
Favorite salad toppings
Favorite low-fat or nonfat dressing

GREEN SALAD

Place salad greens in serving bowls. Add toppings and drizzle with dressing.

1 loaf ready-to-heat garlic bread

GARLIC BREAD

Warm the bread in the oven with the quiche during its last 15 minutes of baking time.

One Chicken Dish

GREEN SALAD

Prep Time: 10 minutes • Total Time: 30 minutes

2 tablespoons butter
1 pound skinless, boneless chicken breasts, cut into thin strips
1 10-ounce box frozen broccoli cuts
¾ cup thinly sliced carrots
1 10½-ounce can cream of broccoli soup
1 cup milk
¼ teaspoon pepper
1¼ cups instant rice

ONE CHICKEN DISH

In a skillet melt the butter and cook the chicken. Add the broccoli and carrots, and stir-fry until tender crisp. Stir in the soup, milk, and pepper, and heat to a boil. Reduce the heat to low, and simmer for 10 minutes. Stir in the rice. Cover, remove from the heat. Let stand 5 minutes.

1 bag salad greens
Favorite salad toppings
Favorite low-fat or nonfat dressing

GREEN SALAD

Place the salad greens in serving bowls. Add toppings and drizzle with dressing.

Sicilian Meat Roll

GREEN BEANS • GARLIC BREAD

Prep Time: 20 minutes • Total Time: 2 hours

2   eggs, beaten
¾   cup soft bread crumbs (1 slice)
½   cup tomato juice
2   tablespoons snipped parsley
½   teaspoon oregano
¼   teaspoon each salt and pepper
1   clove minced garlic
2   pounds ground beef
8   thin slices boiled ham
6   ounces mozzarella cheese, grated (1½ cups)
3   slices mozzarella cheese, halved diagonally (use large pre-sliced slices)

SICILIAN MEAT ROLL

Combine the eggs, crumbs, tomato juice, parsley, oregano, salt, pepper, and garlic. Add the beef; mix well. On waxed paper or foil, pat the meat into a 12 x 10-inch rectangle. Arrange the ham on top of the meat, leaving a small margin around the edges. Sprinkle shredded cheese over the ham. Starting from the short end, carefully roll up the meat using the paper to lift. Seal the edges and ends. Place the roll seam side down in a 13 x 9-inch pan. Bake at 350° until done, about 1½ hours. Place cheese wedges on top of the roll. Bake for 5 minutes until the cheese melts.

---

1   16-ounce can green beans

GREEN BEANS

Heat as directed on the can.

---

1   loaf ready-to-heat garlic French bread

GARLIC BREAD

Prepare as directed on the package.

Chicken Marsala

EGG NOODLES • DINNER ROLLS

Prep Time: 20 minutes • Total Time: 1 hour

3 tablespoons flour
½ teaspoon seasoned salt
Dash pepper
Dash paprika
4 boneless, skinned chicken breasts
Pinch oregano
3 tablespoons olive oil
2 tablespoons butter
1 cup sliced carrots
1 cup sliced fresh mushrooms
⅓ cup Marsala cooking wine
⅓ cup chicken broth

CHICKEN MARSALA

Combine the flour, seasoned salt, pepper, and paprika. Cut the chicken in bite-size pieces and dredge in the seasoned flour. Sprinkle with a pinch of oregano. In a heavy iron skillet heat the olive oil and butter over medium heat. Brown the chicken for about 5 minutes on each side. Add the carrots, mushrooms, Marsala, and chicken broth. Lower the heat, cover, and simmer for 30 minutes.

---

1 package egg noodles

EGG NOODLES

Prepare enough for your family, as directed.

---

1 package prepared dinner rolls
Butter

DINNER ROLLS

Warm the rolls and serve with butter.

Crock Pot
next day—read ahead!

Tangy Pork Chops

WHITE RICE • PEAS

Prep Time: 30 minutes • Total Time: All day

4   pork chops (½-inch thick)
½   teaspoon salt (optional)
⅛   teaspoon pepper
2   medium onions, chopped
2   ribs celery, chopped
1   large green bell pepper, sliced
1   14½-ounce can stewed tomatoes
½   cup catsup
2   tablespoons cider vinegar
2   tablespoons brown sugar
2   tablespoons Worcestershire sauce
1   tablespoon lemon juice
1   beef bouillon cube
2   tablespoons cornstarch
2   tablespoons water

TANGY PORK CHOPS

Place the chops in a slow cooker. Sprinkle with salt, if desired, and pepper. Add the onions, celery, green pepper, and tomatoes. Combine catsup, vinegar, brown sugar, Worcestershire sauce, lemon juice, and bouillon, and pour over the vegetables. Cover and cook on low for 5 to 6 hours. Mix the cornstarch and water until smooth; stir into the liquid in the slow cooker. Cover and cook on high for 30 minutes or until thickened.

Serves 4.

Instant or long grain rice

WHITE RICE

Cook as directed on the package for 8 to 10 servings. Save half for Day 4.

---

1   16-ounce can peas

PEAS

Heat as directed on the can.

 Chop an additional onion for Day 5. Chop 2 additional celery stalks for Day 5. Slice an additional green pepper for Day 4 and make extra rice for Day 4.

Stir-Fried Chicken and Vegetables

WHITE RICE • PEACHES

Prep Time: 15 minutes • Total Time: 25 minutes

2　teaspoons cornstarch
½　cup cold water
2　teaspoons soy sauce
2　teaspoons oil
1　medium onion, peeled, halved and sliced
1　teaspoon minced garlic
2　whole boneless skinless chicken breasts, cut in ¾-inch pieces
1　green bell pepper, cored, seeded and cut in thin strips
2　tomatoes, cored and cut in wedges

STIR-FRIED CHICKEN AND VEGETABLES

Mix the cornstarch, water, and soy sauce; set aside. In an uncovered wok or electric skillet heat the oil to 375°. Add the onion and garlic, and stir-fry for 1 minute. Add the chicken and bell pepper, and stir-fry for 3 minutes. Add the tomatoes and stir-fry for 1 minute. Stir the cornstarch mixture and add to the wok; cook until the sauce thickens. Serve over White Rice.

WHITE RICE

Heat the reserved rice from Day 3.

1　16-ounce can peaches

PEACHES

Serve the peaches chilled.

White Squash and Shrimp Casserole

CARROTS • DINNER ROLLS

Prep Time: 15 minutes • Total Time: 1 hour

2 pounds white squash
1 tablespoon oil
1 onion, chopped
2 pieces celery, chopped
Salt and pepper
Cracker crumbs
1 pound shrimp, uncooked, peeled and cleaned

WHITE SQUASH AND SHRIMP CASSEROLE

Peel and cut up the squash. Boil until tender. In a skillet heat the oil and sauté the onions and celery. Drain the squash and mash. Add the squash to the onions and celery; sauté. Add salt and pepper to taste, plus enough cracker crumbs to hold the mixture together. Stir in the shrimp and transfer to a shallow baking dish. Bake at 350° for 45 minutes or until lightly brown on top.

1 16-ounce can carrots

CARROTS

Open the canned carrots and heat as directed on the can.

1 package prepared dinner rolls
Butter

DINNER ROLLS

Warm the rolls and serve with butter.

Barbecue Tri-Tip Roast

GRILLED VEGETABLES • SLICED FRENCH BREAD

Prep Time: 15 minutes • Total Time: 55 minutes

---

1 6- to 8-pound tri-tip or chuck roast
Favorite barbecue sauce
Salt and pepper

BARBECUE TRI-TIP ROAST

Prepare a grill. Rub the outside of the beef with salt and pepper. Roast over a slow fire until as cooked or rare as desired. Baste with sauce toward the end of cooking. Allow about 15 minutes cooking time per pound.

---

3   crookneck squash
3   zucchini
2   onions
2   green or red peppers
Salt and pepper
¼   cup butter, melted

GRILLED VEGETABLES

Slice all vegetables. Place on a large doubled-foil square. Season with butter, salt, and pepper, and seal. Broil 10 to 15 minutes or until tender.

---

1   loaf French bread
Butter

SLICED FRENCH BREAD

Serve with butter.

Herbed Chicken in Casserole

RICE • BAKED ZUCCHINI • GREEN SALAD

Prep Time: 50 minutes • Total Time: 2 hours

4 chicken breasts, cut in half
Salt and pepper
¼ cup butter or margarine
1 10½-ounce can condensed cream of mushroom soup
¾ cup cooking wine
1 5-ounce can water chestnuts, drained and sliced
1 3-ounce can broiled button mushrooms
2 tablespoons chopped green bell pepper
¼ teaspoon crushed thyme

HERBED CHICKEN IN CASSEROLE

Lightly season the chicken with salt and pepper. In a skillet brown the chicken slowly in butter. Arrange the browned chicken skin side up in a 9 x 13-inch baking dish. Add soup to the drippings in the pan. Slowly add the wine, stirring until smooth. Add the remaining ingredients and heat to boiling. Pour over the chicken. Cover with foil. Bake at 350° for 1 hour or until the chicken is tender.

Note: Can be made ahead and refrigerated and baked later in the day.

Instant or long grain rice

RICE

Cook as directed on the package for 6 to 8 people.

3 zucchini, cut in bite-size pieces

SAUCE:
1 cup cottage cheese
1 cup grated Cheddar cheese
2 eggs, beaten
½ teaspoon each: salt and dill seed
¼ teaspoon pepper

BAKED ZUCCHINI

Parboil the zucchini for 5 minutes in boiling water. Drain and put in a shallow, buttered baking dish.

Mix all sauce ingredients except ¼ cup Cheddar cheese. Pour sauce over zucchini and top with reserved Cheddar. Bake 40 minutes at 350°.

Serves 4.

1 bag salad greens
Favorite salad toppings
Favorite low-fat or nonfat dressing

GREEN SALAD

Place salad greens in serving bowls. Add toppings and drizzle with dressing.

Time Saver *Bake an additional 4 chicken breasts without seasonings. Store in refrigerator for Day 4.* *Grate an additional 3½ cups cheese for Day 4 and Day 5.*

Spinach Meatballs

NOODLES • SLICED APPLES

Prep Time: 30 minutes • Total Time: 1 hour 5 minutes

1   10-ounce package frozen chopped spinach
1   medium onion, chopped
1   pound ground beef
1   egg
Garlic powder, salt, and pepper to taste
½   10½-ounce can cream of mushroom soup, undiluted
2   tablespoons Worcestershire sauce
1   10½-ounce can golden mushroom soup, undiluted
½   can water

SPINACH MEATBALLS

Cook the spinach and drain well. Mix the spinach, onion, meat, egg, and seasonings and roll into small balls. Brown in a 12-inch skillet. Drain. Combine the soups and water and pour over the meatballs. Simmer for 20 minutes or until done.

Serves 4 to 6.

1   package egg noodles

NOODLES

Cook as directed on the package for 4 to 6 servings. Cook an additional 2 cups for use on Day 5.

4 to 6 apples

SLICED APPLES

Slice the apples and remove core.

Time Saver *Chop an additional onion and store in the refrigerator for use on Day 4 and Day 5. If time permits, prepare tomorrow's recipe to the freezing point. Prepare tomorrow's strata while the meatballs are cooking, otherwise allow for an extra hour to prepare Day 4's meal.*

Baked Chicken Strata

CHEESE POTATOES • GREEN BEANS WITH BACON BITS

Prep Time: 30 minutes • Total Time: 1 hour

8   slices bread
2   cooked, chopped chicken breasts
½   10½-ounce can undiluted cream
    of mushroom soup
¼   cup chicken gravy
1   tablespoon minced onions
1   tablespoon minced pimento
1   5-ounce can water chestnuts,
    chopped
2   eggs, beaten
1   tablespoon milk
1   4-ounce package potato chips,
    crushed

BAKED CHICKEN STRATA

Trim the crust from bread. Combine the chicken, soup, gravy, onions, pimento, and chestnuts. Spoon the mixture on 4 slices of bread. Top with the remaining slices. Wrap for freezing. Freeze until 1½ hours before serving time.

To serve: Dip each sandwich in beaten eggs to which milk has been added. DO NOT DEFROST! Dip into potato chips. Place on a greased cookie sheet and bake at 300° for 1 hour.

Makes 4 sandwiches.

3   tablespoons butter or margarine
¼   teaspoon pepper
1   small bag hash brown potatoes
2   cups (8 ounces) grated Cheddar
    cheese
1   teaspoon salt
Chopped fresh parsley

CHEESE POTATOES

In a large non-stick skillet melt the butter. Cook the potatoes as directed. Sprinkle with salt and pepper. Sprinkle with cheese and allow to melt. Stir, sprinkle with parsley, and serve immediately.

Serves 6.

1   16-ounce can green beans
¼   cup bacon bits

GREEN BEANS WITH BACON BITS

Drain the green beans and place in a microwave-safe dish. Add the bacon bits. Heat in the microwave for 3 to 4 minutes.

Tuna-Sour Cream Casserole

POTATO CHIPS • SLICED STRAWBERRIES • GREEN SALAD

Prep Time: 20 minutes • Total Time: 50 minutes

---

2 cups cooked pasta 1 6½-ounce can tuna fish, drained ¼ cup sliced or chopped black olives 1 cup sour cream ½ teaspoon salt Pepper 1½ cups grated Cheddar cheese ¼ cup finely chopped onions	**TUNA–SOUR CREAM CASSEROLE** Combine all of the ingredients. Transfer to a buttered casserole. Sprinkle with extra grated cheese. Bake at 350° for 30 minutes. Serve with green salad.

---

1 bag potato chips	**POTATO CHIPS**

---

1 basket strawberries	**SLICED STRAWBERRIES**

---

1 bag salad greens Favorite salad toppings Favorite low-fat or nonfat dressing	**GREEN SALAD** Place salad greens in serving bowls. Add toppings and drizzle with dressing.

Baked Ham

MACARONI AND CHEESE • FRESH FRUIT SALAD

Prep Time: 15 minutes • Total Time: 1 hour 15 minutes

1 6-pound ham 1 can beer **HAM GLAZE** ½ cup packed brown sugar ½ teaspoon dry mustard 2 tablespoons orange juice	**BAKED HAM** Preheat the oven to 350°. Score the ham and pour the beer over it. Bake for 1 hour. In a small bowl combine all of the glaze ingredients. Glaze ham and cook 30 minutes more.

1 package macaroni and cheese	**MACARONI AND CHEESE** Follow the package directions.

Fresh fruit (grapes, melons, strawberries, etc.), sliced	**FRESH FRUIT SALAD** In a salad bowl toss all of the fruit together.

 Time Saver *Save 1 pound of ham for use on Day 3.*

Chicken and Rice

SPINACH • ORANGES

Prep Time: 5 minutes • Total Time: 40 minutes

---

6   boneless, skinless chicken breasts
2   tablespoons hot oil
Salt and pepper
1   10½-ounce can condensed cream
     of chicken soup
1⅓ cups water
2   cups uncooked instant rice

CHICKEN AND RICE

In a large non-stick skillet brown the chicken breasts in 2 tablespoons of hot oil for 5 minutes on each side or until done. Season with salt and pepper. Remove from the pan. Add the chicken soup and 1⅓ cups water to the skillet. Bring to a boil. Stir in the uncooked rice. Top with chicken; cover, cook on low heat for 5 minutes. Stir.

---

1   16-ounce can spinach
¼   cup minced onion
1   slice uncooked bacon, chopped

SPINACH

Make enough spinach for your family. Cook with minced onion and 1 bacon slice for flavor.

---

6 to 8 oranges

ORANGES

Peel and section the oranges.

Time Saver   *Chop a whole onion and save remainder for use on Day 3 and Day 5.*

Quick Ham Barbecue

HAMBURGER BUNS • GREEN SALAD • CORN CHIPS

Prep Time: 10 minutes • Total Time: 45 minutes

5 tablespoons vinegar
1/4 cup catsup
2 tablespoons Worcestershire sauce
3 bay leaves
3 stalks celery, chopped
1 clove garlic, minced
1 tablespoon chopped onion
1 cup canned tomatoes, chopped
1/2 lemon, thinly sliced
1/2 cup water
1/2 cup margarine
2 tablespoons dark brown sugar
3 tablespoons cornstarch mixed with 3 tablespoons water
1 pound cooked ham, shredded from Day 1

QUICK HAM BARBECUE

Combine the first 10 ingredients in a large saucepan; mix well. Simmer for 15 to 20 minutes; strain.

Add the margarine and brown sugar, stirring until the margarine is melted. Mix the cornstarch with water, stirring to blend; add to the mixture. Stir in the ham. Serve on buns or open face on bread.

Serves 6.

---

1 package hamburger buns

HAMBURGER BUNS

---

1 bag salad greens
Favorite salad toppings
Favorite low-fat or nonfat dressing

GREEN SALAD

Place salad greens in serving bowls. Add toppings and drizzle with dressing.

---

1 bag corn chips

CORN CHIPS

 Time Saver *Marinate turkey for Day 4.*

Grilled Turkey Breast

STUFFING · CORN IN THE COB

Prep Time: 15 minutes • Total Time: 30 minutes

¾ cup red cooking wine
¼ cup soy sauce
½ teaspoon garlic powder
½ teaspoon crushed basil
1 tablespoon olive oil
1 pound turkey scallops

GRILLED TURKEY BREAST

In a shallow bowl combine the wine, soy sauce, garlic, basil, and oil. Mix well. Rinse the turkey and pat dry. Marinate the turkey in sauce in the refrigerator for about 1 hour.

Drain, reserving the marinade. Grill the turkey over hot coals, or in a hot oven, for 10 minutes or until tender, basting occasionally with reserved marinade.

Serves 6.

---

1 box instant stuffing mix

STUFFING

Follow the package directions.

---

6 fresh or frozen cobs corn

CORN ON THE COB

In a large pot of boiling water cook the corn until tender.

Fettuccine with Tomato-Basil Sauce

GREEN BEANS WITH OREGANO • CRUSTY FRENCH BREAD

Prep Time: 20 minutes • Total Time: 35 minutes

1/4 cup chopped onion
1 clove garlic, minced
1/4 cup olive oil
1 28-ounce can peeled tomatoes, chopped
6 fresh basil leaves, chopped
1 teaspoon salt
1/2 teaspoon pepper
12 ounces fettuccine, cooked, drained
Freshly grated Parmesan cheese
Chopped fresh basil and chives

FETTUCCINE WITH TOMATO-BASIL SAUCE

In a skillet heat the oil and sauté the onion and garlic. Add the undrained tomatoes, 6 basil leaves, salt, and pepper. Simmer, covered, for 20 minutes.

Combine with the fettuccine in a bowl; toss to mix well. Top with Parmesan cheese and additional fresh basil and chives.

Serves 4.

---

3 cups chopped fresh green beans
4 slices bacon, crisp-fried, crumbled
1 10 1/2-ounce can cream of mushroom soup
4 ounces fresh mushrooms
1/2 envelope onion soup mix
1/4 teaspoon oregano

GREEN BEANS WITH OREGANO

In a saucepan cook the beans in water to cover just until crisp-tender; drain. In a bowl combine with half the bacon, mushroom soup, mushrooms, onion soup mix, and oregano; mix well.

Preheat the oven to 350°. Spoon the bean mixture into a baking dish. Bake for 35 minutes. Top with remaining bacon.

Serves 4.

---

1 loaf French bread
Butter
Basil

CRUSTY FRENCH BREAD

Slice the bread in half lengthwise, spread with butter, and sprinkle with basil. Wrap in foil and bake with the green beans for 20 minutes.

Cranberry Chicken

ASPARAGUS CASSEROLE • FRENCH BREAD

Prep Time: 15 minutes • Total Time: 1 hour 40 minutes

1   16-ounce can cranberry sauce
    (jellied or whole)
1   package dry onion soup mix
8   ounces French-style salad dressing
8 to 10 half chicken breasts

CRANBERRY CHICKEN

Mix all ingredients except the chicken breasts. Place the chicken in a 9 x 13-inch pan. Pour the cranberry mixture on top. Cover with foil. Bake at 350° for 1½ hours.

2   tablespoons onion juice
2   tablespoons pimento
2   teaspoons Worcestershire sauce
2   10½-ounce cans mushroom soup,
    undiluted
2   16-ounce cans white
    asparagus, drained
1   box cheese crackers, crushed
½   cup butter, melted and poured
    over crackers

ASPARAGUS CASSEROLE

In a medium bowl combine the onion juice, pimento, Worcestershire sauce, and mushroom soup. Pour the mixture on the bottom of a casserole, then layer the asparagus, and top with crushed crackers and melted butter. Bake at 350° until bubbly.

Serves 4 to 6.

1   loaf French bread
Butter

FRENCH BREAD

Lasagna

SPICY GARLIC BREAD • GREEN SALAD

Prep Time: 30 minutes • Total Time: 1 hour 30 minutes

1½ pounds ground beef
¾ teaspoon salt
¾ teaspoon oregano
3 8-ounce cans tomato sauce
1 8-ounce package lasagna noodles
1 8-ounce package grated mozzarella
   cheese
1½ cups cottage cheese
⅓ cup grated Parmesan cheese

LASAGNA

In a medium skillet cook and stir the ground beef until brown. Drain off the fat. Stir in the tomato sauce, salt, and oregano. Heat to boiling, stirring occasionally. Reduce the heat, cover, and simmer for 20 minutes.

Cook the noodles as directed on the package. Drain. In an ungreased 11½ x 7½ x 1½-inch baking dish alternate layers of ⅓ each; noodles, mozzarella cheese, cottage cheese, and meat sauce, ending with 1¼ cups meat sauce. Heat the oven to 350°. Bake the casserole, uncovered, for 40 minutes. Sprinkle with Parmesan cheese.

Serves 6 to 8 generously.

---

1 bulb garlic
1 tablespoon chopped fresh basil, or
1 teaspoon dried basil
½ cup mayonnaise
6 scallions, sliced
¼ teaspoon each, salt and pepper
1 tablespoon chopped parsley
¼ teaspoon ground red pepper
1 loaf Italian bread

SPICY GARLIC BREAD

Preheat the oven to 400°. Slice the top ⅓ off the garlic bulb and remove the papery outer skin. Wrap in foil and bake for 30 minutes. Let cool slightly.

Reduce the oven temperature to 350°. Squeeze the garlic into the bowl of a food processor. Add the mayonnaise, scallions, herbs, and spices and process until smooth.

Cut the bread into 16 slices, making sure not to cut all the way through loaf. Spread the garlic mixture in between the slices. Wrap in foil. Bake for 20 minutes or until heated through.

---

1 bag salad greens
Favorite salad toppings
Favorite low-fat or nonfat dressing

GREEN SALAD

Place salad greens in serving bowls. Add toppings and drizzle with dressing.

Blackened Fish

CHEESY POTATO CASSEROLE • STEAMED CAULIFLOWER

Prep Time: 30 minutes • Total Time: 1 hour 5 minutes

4 fresh or frozen catfish, cod, haddock or snapper fillets (about 1 pound)
¼ teaspoon ground white pepper
¼ teaspoon dried thyme, crushed
¼ teaspoon pepper
½ teaspoon onion powder
⅛ teaspoon ground sage
½ teaspoon garlic salt
½ teaspoon ground red pepper
½ teaspoon dried basil, crushed
¼ cup margarine or butter, melted

BLACKENED FISH

Thaw the fish, if frozen. In a small mixing bowl combine the remaining ingredients except margarine or butter. Brush both sides of the fish with melted margarine or butter; coat both sides with seasonings. Preheat the skillet until a drop of water sizzles. (Can prepare pan with Pam before heating for easier cleaning.) Pan-fry until blackened.

6 or 7 medium potatoes, boiled in jackets
¼ cup butter
1 10½-ounce can condensed cream of chicken soup
1 cup sour cream
1 tablespoon dried minced onion
1½ cups grated Cheddar cheese
Seasoned bread crumbs

CHEESY POTATO CASSEROLE

Cool, peel, and grate the potatoes on a coarse grater. (Fine grater causes potatoes to "mush.") Combine the butter and soup; heat, but do not boil. Add the sour cream, onion and cheese. Turn into a 7 x 11-inch or a 9 x 13-inch pan; top with bread crumbs. Bake uncovered at 350° for 45 to 60 minutes. Watch so the casserole does not brown too rapidly. (Cover loosely with foil if necessary.)

Serves 10 to 12.

1 head fresh cauliflower or 2 10-ounce packages frozen cauliflower

STEAMED CAULIFLOWER

Steam cauliflower for 6 to 8 servings or heat frozen cauliflower as directed on package.

Broccoli Soup

CRACKERS AND PEANUT BUTTER

Prep Time: 30 minutes • Total Time: 50 minutes

2   heads broccoli or 20 ounces frozen broccoli

4   teaspoons instant minced onion

1   cup boiling water

4   cups milk

2   10½-ounce cans condensed cream of potato soup

1   cup grated Swiss cheese

BROCCOLI SOUP

In a saucepan cook the broccoli and onion in boiling water until tender. Do not drain. Stir in the milk and soup, heat through. Add the cheese, and stir until melted. Cool slightly. Place half at a time in a blender, cover, and blend until smooth.

Return the soup to the pan and heat through if needed.

CRACKERS AND PEANUT BUTTER

Chicken Enchiladas

SPANISH RICE • REFRIED BEANS

Prep Time: 30 minutes • Total Time: 55 minutes

4 tablespoons butter
2 onions, thinly sliced
2 cups shredded, cooked chicken
   (reserved from Day 1)
4 tablespoons diced green chilies
6 ounces cream cheese
Oil
8 to 10 flour tortillas
⅔ cup heavy cream
2 cups grated Monterey Jack cheese
Favorite toppings for garnish

CHICKEN ENCHILADAS

In a skillet melt the butter and add the onion. Cook over low heat for 20 minutes or until limp, but not brown. Remove from the heat and add the chicken, chilies, and cream cheese. Salt to taste.

Preheat the oven to 375°. In a small skillet fry the tortillas in oil until limp, remove and drain on paper towels. Spoon ¼ of the filling down the center of each tortilla and roll up. Place the filled enchiladas seam side down in a baking dish and brush the tops with cream. Sprinkle with cheese and bake uncovered for 20 minutes.

Garnish with chopped green onion, sliced black olives, lime wedges, or salsa.

White or instant rice
1 cup salsa

SPANISH RICE

Prepare rice as directed on package for 4 to 6 servings. When cooked, stir in 1 cup salsa.

1 16-ounce can refried beans
¼ cup grated Cheddar or Monterey
   Jack cheese

REFRIED BEANS

Heat the beans as directed on the can. Stir in the grated cheese.

Crock Pot
next day—read ahead!

Hearty New England Dinner

DINNER ROLLS

Prep Time: 30 minutes • Total Time: 7 to 9 hours

2   medium carrots, sliced
1   stalk celery, sliced
1   boneless chuck roast (about 6 pounds)
1   teaspoon salt, divided
1/4 teaspoon pepper
1   envelope onion soup mix
1   tablespoon dried minced onion
1   tablespoon vinegar
2   cups water
1   bay leaf
1/2 small head cabbage, cut into wedges
3   tablespoons butter or margarine
2   tablespoons all-purpose flour
1   medium onion, sliced
2   tablespoons prepared horseradish

HEARTY NEW ENGLAND DINNER

Place the carrots and celery in a 5-quart slow cooker. Place the roast on top; sprinkle with 1/2 teaspoon of salt and the pepper. Add the soup mix, dried minced onion, water, vinegar, and bay leaf. Cover and cook on low for 7 to 9 hours or until the beef is tender.

Remove the beef and keep warm; discard the bay leaf. Add the cabbage. Cover and cook on high for 30 to 40 minutes or until the cabbage is tender.

Meanwhile, melt the butter in a small saucepan; stir in the flour and onion. Add 1 1/2 cups of cooking liquid from the slow cooker. Stir in the horseradish and remaining salt; bring to a boil. Cook and stir over low heat until thick and smooth, about 2 minutes. Serve with roast and vegetables.

Serves 6 to 8.

---

1   package prepared dinner rolls
Butter

DINNER ROLLS

Warm the rolls and serve with butter.

Time Saver *Leftover roast and juice will be used on Day 3.*

Parmesan Yogurt Chicken

ASPARAGUS • BAKED POTATOES

Prep Time: 15 minutes • Total Time: 1 hour 5 minutes

---

1   3-pound broiler chicken, cut up
2   tablespoons lemon juice
Salt and pepper
½   cup plain yogurt
¼   cup mayonnaise
1   tablespoon Dijon mustard
1   tablespoon Worcestershire sauce
½   teaspoon ground thyme
¼   teaspoon cayenne pepper
¼   cup thinly sliced green onion
½   cup grated Parmesan cheese

PARMESAN YOGURT CHICKEN

In rimmed baking dish arrange chicken pieces, skin side up, in a single layer. Drizzle with lemon juice, and season with salt and pepper.

Thoroughly blend the yogurt, mayonnaise, mustard, Worcestershire, thyme, and cayenne; stir in the green onion. Spread the mixture evenly over the chicken. Bake uncovered at 350° for 50 minutes or until the chicken is cooked.

Remove the chicken from the oven and drain off the pan juices. Sprinkle with cheese, then broil until the cheese is slightly brown, about 3 minutes.

---

1   bunch asparagus, sliced
2 to 3 tablespoons margarine
Garlic powder to taste
Parmesan cheese

ASPARAGUS

In a glass casserole place the asparagus and dot with margarine. Sprinkle with garlic powder and Parmesan cheese. Microwave on high for 5 minutes.

---

4   baking potatoes
Butter
Sour cream
Salt and pepper to taste

BAKED POTATOES

Bake the potatoes in the oven with chicken. Serve with butter, sour cream, salt, and pepper.

Crock Pot
next day—read ahead!

Barbecue Beef Sandwiches

CARROTS • POTATO CHIPS

Prep Time: 10 minutes • Total Time: 1 to 2 hours

Remaining roast from Day 1
Remaining gravy from roast
Barbecue sauce
Hamburger buns

BARBECUE BEEF SANDWICHES

Use leftover roast from Day 1. Shred and place in a crock pot. Add any leftover gravy or juice. Add equal amounts of barbecue sauce and cook on low for 1 to 2 hours. Serve over hamburger buns.

1   10-ounce package frozen sliced carrots

CARROTS

Prepared the carrots as directed on the package.

1   bag potato chips

POTATO CHIPS

 Time Saver *Marinate round steak for Day 4.*

Brandied Round Steak

GREEN BEANS • PILAF

Prep Time: 15 minutes • Total Time: 30 minutes

---

1 pound beef round steak, cut
½-inch thick, tenderized
¼ cup dry sherry
2 tablespoons water
1 tablespoon snipped chives
1 tablespoon steak sauce
½ teaspoon dry mustard
2 tablespoons cooking oil
1 3-ounce can mushrooms, drained
¼ cup brandy

BRANDIED ROUND STEAK

Cut the round steak into 4 serving-sized portions. Combine the sherry, water, chives, steak sauce, and dry mustard. Pour over the round steak in a shallow dish. Cover. Marinate in the refrigerator for several hours or overnight.

Drain the steak, reserving the marinade. Pat the meat dry with paper towels. In a skillet brown the steak pieces, 2 at a time, in hot cooking oil, about 2 minutes each side. Remove the cooked meat to a serving platter. Cover. Keep warm in the oven. Add the reserved marinade and mushrooms to the skillet. Bring the mixture to boiling. Pour over the meat to serve. Warm the brandy in a ladle, ignite, and slowly pour over the meat. Serve when flame subsides.

---

1 16-ounce can green beans

GREEN BEANS

Prepare the canned green beans as directed on the can.

---

1 box rice pilaf

PILAF

Prepare the rice as directed on the package.

Scampi Fettuccine

GREEN SALAD • GARLIC BREAD

Prep Time: 10 minutes • Total Time: 25 minutes

½	cup butter
1	medium onion, finely chopped
4	cloves garlic, minced
½	teaspoon Worcestershire sauce
2	tablespoons lemon juice
½	teaspoon dried tarragon
1½	teaspoons steak sauce
¼	teaspoon hot sauce
1	pound peeled shrimp
2	tablespoons parsley, chopped
1	package fettuccine, cooked

SCAMPI FETTUCCINE

In a large skillet melt the butter. Add the onion and garlic and cook over medium heat for 3 to 4 minutes, stirring constantly. Add the next 5 ingredients. Bring to a boil. Add the shrimp. Stir constantly for 5 to 6 minutes or until the shrimp turns pink. Sprinkle with parsley and serve over hot fettuccine.

1 bag salad greens
Favorite salad toppings
Favorite low-fat or nonfat dressing

GREEN SALAD

Place salad greens in serving bowls. Add toppings and drizzle with dressing.

1 loaf ready-to-heat garlic bread

GARLIC BREAD

Prepare as directed on the package.

Roast Beef

SQUASH CASSEROLE • DINNER ROLLS

Prep Time: 30 minutes • Total Time: 2 hours 15 minutes

1 3- to 4-pound roast beef
Favorite steak sauce (salsa,
   Worcestershire, etc.)

ROAST BEEF

Place the beef in roasting pan, uncovered. Roast at 375° for 1 hour.

Turn off the oven, but do not open the oven door. Forty minutes before serving, turn the oven to 300° and allow the beef to reheat.

Remove and slice. Serve with favorite steak sauce.

---

1   pound zucchini
Dash pepper
1/3 cup crumbled salted soda crackers
    (5 crackers)
1/2 cup finely diced celery
1/2 cup grated American or Cheddar
    cheese
1   medium onion, chopped
2   tablespoons melted butter or
    margarine
2   tablespoons finely diced green
    pepper
1/4 teaspoon salt
1 1/2 cups milk

SQUASH CASSEROLE

Wash and slice the squash. Cook in boiling salted water for 10 minutes. Drain and mash.

Mix the squash with the remaining ingredients in the order given. Pour into a 1½-quart baking dish. Bake at 300° for 40 minutes or until a knife inserted in the center comes out clean. Serve at once.

Serves 6.

---

1   package prepared dinner rolls
Butter

DINNER ROLLS

Warm the rolls and serve with butter.

Time Saver — Chop an additional 5 onions for use through the week. Chop an additional green pepper for Day 4. Chop an additional 3 cups celery for use through the week.

Baked Pork Chops and Rice

SPINACH AND ORANGE SALAD

Prep Time: 20 minutes • Total Time: 1 hour 35 minutes

1   teaspoon salt
1/4   teaspoon pepper
6   pork chops
Cooking oil
1   cup uncooked brown rice
1   8-ounce can tomato sauce
2   tablespoons olive oil
1 1/2   cups water
1   tablespoon chopped onion
1/2   cup grated Cheddar cheese
1   clove garlic, minced or mashed
1/2   teaspoon salt
1/8   teaspoon pepper

BAKED PORK CHOPS AND RICE

Salt and pepper the pork chops and brown slightly on both sides in fat or oil. In a medium bowl mix together all of the ingredients except the pork chops. Place in a greased baking dish or casserole. Arrange the browned pork chops on top and cover. Bake at 350° for 1 hour and 15 minutes, until the meat is tender.

Serves 6.

3   cups chopped spinach
2   oranges, peeled, halved, and sliced
1   head lettuce, torn into small pieces
1/2   cucumber, sliced
2   tablespoons chopped red onion

DRESSING:
1   cup mayonnaise
1 1/2   tablespoons caraway seeds
2   tablespoons lemon juice
1/4   cup honey

SPINACH AND ORANGE SALAD

In a salad bowl assemble the salad ingredients. In a separate bowl combine the dressing ingredients and blend well. Drizzle over the salad and toss to coat.

 Time Saver *Grate an additional 1 1/3 cups cheese for use throughout the week.*

Broccoli Chicken Roll-ups

GREEN SALAD

Prep Time: 30 minutes • Total Time: 1 hour 30 minutes

4 skinless, boneless chicken breasts
1 bunch fresh broccoli, cooked
2 10½-ounce cans condensed cream of mushroom soup
1 cup milk
1 cup grated Cheddar cheese
½ can dried onions
1 package flour tortillas

BROCCOLI CHICKEN ROLL-UPS

Boil the chicken and broccoli until done. Tear into bite-sized pieces. Combine the soup and milk; set aside. Combine the chicken, broccoli, ½ cup of cheese, and ¼ can of onions. Stir in three-fourths of the soup mixture. Pour onto the tortillas and roll up. Place in a lightly greased 9 x 13-inch baking dish. Pour the remaining soup over the top. Bake uncovered at 350° for 35 minutes. Top the center of the tortillas with the remaining cheese and onions. Bake 5 minutes longer.

1 bag salad greens
Favorite toppings
Favorite low-fat or nonfat dressing

GREEN SALAD

Place salad greens in serving bowls. Add toppings and drizzle with dressing.

Time Saver — *Cook Day 4 breast meat with the chicken. Salt the eggplant for Day 4 to save time. Wash after 30 minutes or so, dry, and store.*

Turkey Tetrazzini

BAKED STUFFED EGGPLANT • DINNER ROLLS

Prep Time: 30 minutes • Total Time: 1 hour 45 minutes

½ pound mushrooms, sliced
½ cup finely chopped onion
1 stalk celery, minced
¼ cup butter or margarine
2 cups chicken gravy
2 tablespoons dry sherry
½ pound linguini, cooked
3 cups cubed, cooked turkey breast meat
¾ cup soft fine bread crumbs
⅓ cup grated Cheddar cheese
1 cup whipping cream

TURKEY TETRAZZINI

In a skillet sauté the mushrooms, onion, and celery in ¼ cup butter until tender. Remove the vegetables and set aside. In a saucepan heat the chicken gravy. Stir in the sherry and vegetables. Fold in the linguini and turkey. Turn into a buttered 3-quart casserole. Sprinkle with crumbs and cheese. Bake at 350° uncovered for 30 minutes or until bubbly.

Serves 8 to 10.

2 large eggplants
½ cup olive oil
1 green pepper, chopped
2 medium yellow onions, chopped
½ teaspoon sweet basil
1 8-ounce can tomato sauce
¼ cup chopped parsley
Salt, pepper, garlic, to taste
1 tomato, diced
Lettuce

BAKED STUFFED EGGPLANT

Cut the eggplant lengthwise into quarters (8 pieces all together) and cover with salt. Let stand for 30 minutes to 1 hour.

Stuffing: In a skillet heat half of the olive oil and sauté the pepper and onions. When soft, add the parsley, tomato, garlic, and seasonings; cook for 4 to 5 minutes.

Wash the eggplant of salt, dry with a towel. Brush well with olive oil. Bake at 450° until light brown. Remove from the oven and slit the eggplants from end to end, but not all the way through, forming a pocket; fill with stuffing. Arrange in a baking pan, pour tomato sauce over, and bake at 350° for approximately 45 minutes. Chill.

Serve on lettuce leaves as a salad. Can also be served hot.

1 package prepared dinner rolls
Butter

DINNER ROLLS

Time Saver *Start today's meal with the eggplant dish.*

Tuna-Water Chestnut Casserole

STEAMED ASPARAGUS WITH SAUCE

Prep Time: 10 minutes • Total Time: 1 hour

2   6½-ounce cans tuna
1   5-ounce can water chestnuts, sliced
2   10½-ounce cans cream of
     mushroom soup
¾   cup mayonnaise
½   cup water
2   tablespoons lemon juice
2   cups chopped celery
½   cup minced onion
1   large package Chinese noodles

TUNA–WATER CHESTNUT CASSEROLE

Combine all of the ingredients except 3/4 cup of Chinese noodles. Place in a 9 x 13-inch casserole, and sprinkle the top with the remaining noodles. Bake at 425° for 40 minutes.

Serves 12 to 14. For fewer servings, divide in half.

3 to 4 pounds asparagus, trimmed and
     peeled
½   cup sour cream
¼   teaspoon salt
¼   cup mayonnaise
½   teaspoon paprika
1¼ teaspoons lemon juice

STEAMED ASPARAGUS WITH SAUCE

Stand the asparagus in a tall pot with an inch of salted water in the bottom. Cover and turn the heat to high. Cook just until the thick part of the stalk can be pierced with a knife.

In a small bowl combine the remaining ingredients and mix well. Pour over the asparagus and serve.

Serves 6 to 8.

Crock Pot
next day—read ahead!

Spaghetti

GREEN SALAD • GARLIC BREAD

Prep Time: 20 minutes • Total Time: 2 hours, plus slow cooker time

½ medium onion, chopped	**SPAGHETTI SAUCE**
1 clove garlic, minced	
1 tablespoon olive oil	In a large skillet heat the olive oil and sauté the onion
1 pound ground beef	and garlic until soft. Add the beef and brown, then stir
1 6-ounce can tomato paste	in the sauce, paste, wine, water, and seasonings. Mix
1 8-ounce can tomato sauce	well. Simmer on the stove 1½ hours or place in a slow
½ cup each: dry white wine and water	cooker on low all day.
1 teaspoon oregano	
1 teaspoon basil	
½ teaspoon each; salt, pepper, sugar	
1 teaspoon parsley	

1 package spaghetti

SPAGHETTI NOODLES

Cook as directed on package, enough for your family.

Salad greens
Favorite salad toppings
Favorite low-fat or nonfat dressing

GREEN SALAD

Place salad greens in serving bowls. Add toppings and drizzle with dressing.

1 loaf ready-to-heat garlic bread

GARLIC BREAD

Prepare as directed on the package.

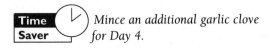 **Time Saver** *Mince an additional garlic clove for Day 4.*

Chicken Supreme

PEAS • FLAKY BISCUITS

Prep Time: 15 minutes • Total Time: 1 hour 45 minutes

4	skinless, boneless chicken breasts
1	cup grated Jack cheese
1	10½-ounce can cream of chicken soup
½	cup water
½	cup margarine
2	cups herb stuffing mix

CHICKEN SUPREME

Lay the chicken breasts in a shallow baking dish. Cover with cheese. Mix the soup and water. Pour over the chicken. Melt the margarine and add the stuffing. Pour over the top and bake at 375° for 1 hour.

---

1   10-ounce package frozen peas

PEAS

Cook the frozen peas as directed on the package.

---

2   large cans flaky biscuits

FLAKY BISCUITS

Bake as directed on the package.

 Time Saver *Prepare Jell-O for Day 3.*

Barbecue Burgers

BAKED BEANS • CHIPS • JELL-O

Prep Time: 10 minutes • Total Time: 30 minutes

8   pre-formed hamburger patties
Salt
Pepper
Barbecue sauce
8   hamburger buns

BARBECUE BURGERS

Season the hamburger patties with salt and pepper, and top with barbecue sauce. Barbecue on a grill or in the oven. Serve on buns with your favorite condiments. Serves 8.

1   17-ounce can baked beans

BAKED BEANS

Heat the beans according to the directions on the can.

1   bag chips

CHIPS

2   packages gelatin, any flavor

JELL-O

Prepare as directed on the package. Serves 8.

Smothered Pork Chops

APPLESAUCE • STEAMED RICE • STEAMED BROCCOLI, CARROTS, CAULIFLOWER

Prep Time: 25 minutes • Total Time: 50 minutes

6   pork chops, boned
2   tablespoons catsup
½   cup chicken broth
¼   cup soy sauce
¼   teaspoon ground ginger
⅓   cup honey
1   clove garlic, minced

SMOTHERED PORK CHOPS

Preheat an electric skillet to 350°. Sear the pork chops on both sides. Reduce the temperature to 225° to 250°. Combine the remaining ingredients and mix well. Pour over the pork chops. Simmer, covered, for 20 minutes until the sauce thickens, stirring frequently.

Serves 4 to 6.

1   jar old-fashioned–style applesauce
     with cinnamon

APPLESAUCE

Serve warm or cold, according to taste.

3   cups water
3   cups instant rice

STEAMED RICE

Bring the water to a boil. Stir in the rice; cover and remove from the heat. Let stand 5 minutes or until the water is absorbed. Fluff with fork.

Serves 6.

1   large bag frozen mixed broccoli,
     carrots, and cauliflower

STEAMED BROCCOLI, CARROTS, CAULIFLOWER

Cook the vegetables according to the package directions.

Fish Sticks and Fries

CANNED SLICED FRUIT SALAD

Prep Time: 10 minutes • Total Time: 25 minutes

Frozen fish sticks
Frozen French fries

FISH STICKS AND FRIES

Choose your favorite frozen fish sticks and fries. Place on a cookie sheet and bake as directed. To save time, combine temperatures and cooking times for an average.

Lettuce leaves
2   cups cottage cheese
1   16-ounce can fruit salad

CANNED SLICED FRUIT SALAD

Make salad cups with a leaf of lettuce and scoop of cottage cheese with some canned fruit (peaches, pears, etc.) on top.

Chicken Casserole

GARLIC SPINACH • POTATO CHIPS

Prep Time: 15 minutes • Total Time: 40 minutes

1	7-ounce can white chicken meat
1	can cream of mushroom soup
1/2	cup milk
1/2	onion, chopped
1	can drained peas
1/4	teaspoon salt
1/2	cup crushed potato chips

CHICKEN CASSEROLE

Place the chicken in a greased 1½-quart casserole. Blend the soup and milk, and add the onions, peas, and salt. Pour over the chicken. Sprinkle potato chips on top. Bake uncovered at 375° for 25 minutes.

Serves 4.

1	10-ounce box frozen chopped spinach
1	teaspoon minced garlic
1	teaspoon butter, melted

GARLIC SPINACH

Cook the spinach in a little water until thawed, then add the pressed garlic and butter. Heat just until done.

1	bag potato chips

POTATO CHIPS

Time Saver *Chop an additional 2 onions for use on Day 3 and Day 5.*

Baked Ham

BROCCOLI-CORN BAKE • BREADSTICKS

Prep Time: 15 minutes • Total Time: 1 hour 15 minutes

1 4- to 5-pound boneless cooked ham ½ cup orange marmalade	**BAKED HAM** Bake the ham at 325° for approximately 30 minutes. Remove from the oven. Score and spread with marmalade. Bake an additional 30 minutes.

1   16-ounce can cream-style corn
1   10-ounce package frozen chopped broccoli, cooked and drained
1   egg, beaten
½   cup coarse salted cracker crumbs (12 crackers)
1   tablespoon instant minced onion
2   tablespoons butter or margarine, melted
½   teaspoon salt
Dash pepper
¼   cup coarse salted cracker crumbs
2   tablespoons butter or margarine, melted

BROCCOLI-CORN BAKE

    Combine the first 8 ingredients and transfer to a 1-quart casserole. Combine ¼ cup of crumbs and the remaining butter. Sprinkle over the top. Bake uncovered at 325° for 50 minutes.

    Serves 6.

1   package prepared breadsticks

BREADSTICKS

Leftover ham will be used on Day 4. If night is easy, brown Day 3 pork chops.

Mexican Chili Con Carne

FLOUR TORTILLAS • CORN ON THE COB

Prep Time: 15 minutes • Total Time: 2 hour 15 minutes, plus all day in slow cooker

6   pork steaks
1   onion, chopped
1   teaspoon cumin
1/4   teaspoon crushed red pepper
1   tablespoon Worcestershire sauce
Sprinkle of salt
2   16-ounce cans stewed tomatoes

MEXICAN CHILI CON CARNE

Cut the meat in small pieces. Brown with the onion in a small amount of oil. Add the spices and Worcestershire sauce; brown. Drain the fat, add the tomatoes, and simmer about 2 hours or cook in a crock pot all day. Can roll the meat inside tortillas like a burrito.

Flour tortillas

FLOUR TORTILLAS

Warm tortillas in the microwave or low oven.

6   ears corn
1/2   cup mayonnaise
1/2   cup grated Parmesan cheese

CORN ON THE COB

Boil the corn until tender. Brush with mayonnaise and roll in cheese.

Ham and Cheese Crepes

STEAMED CARROTS • GREEN SALAD

Prep Time: 20 minutes • Total Time: 1 hour 5 minutes

12 flour tortillas
12 slices ham
2   cups grated Monterey Jack cheese
1   6-ounce can Ortega chilies, washed and cut into strips
¼   cup butter
½   cup flour
1   quart milk
3   cups grated sharp Cheddar cheese
1   teaspoon dry mustard
1   teaspoon salt
Dash Accent

HAM AND CHEESE CREPES

Cover each tortilla with thinly sliced ham, grated Jack cheese, and strips of green chilies. Roll and place in a buttered 9 x 13-inch pan. Place the remaining ingredients in a blender and blend until smooth. Pour over the tortillas and bake uncovered at 350° for 45 minutes.

1½ to 2 pounds carrots, peeled and cut into slices or chunks
Lemon juice
Salt and pepper to taste

STEAMED CARROTS

Place the carrots in a steamer over an inch or two of salted boiling water. Cover and cook for about 20 to 30 minutes until tender.

Drizzle with lemon juice and season with salt and pepper.

1   bag salad greens
Favorite salad toppings
Favorite low-fat or nonfat dressing

GREEN SALAD

Place salad greens in serving bowls. Add toppings and drizzle with dressing.

Shrimp Curry

RICE • PEAS

Prep Time: 15 minutes • Total Time: 1 hour 5 minutes

---

2 tablespoons butter or margarine
½ cup finely chopped onion
½ cup finely chopped apple
1 teaspoon curry powder
1 10½-ounce can condensed cream of shrimp soup
1 cup sour cream
2 7-ounce cans cooked shrimp

SHRIMP CURRY

In a saucepan melt the butter; add the onion, apple, and curry powder, and simmer until the apple and onion are thoroughly cooked. Stir in the soup and bring just to a boil. Add the sour cream and shrimp. Heat to boiling, but do not boil.

Serves 4 to 6.

Instant rice

RICE

Prepare rice as directed on the package for 4 to 6 servings.

---

1 16-ounce can peas

PEAS

Prepare frozen or canned peas as directed.

Crock Pot
next day—read ahead!

Glazed Corned Beef

DINNER ROLLS

Prep Time: 15 minutes • Total Time: 10 hours

3¹/₂ to 4 pounds corned beef
Water
2   tablespoons prepared mustard
1¹/₂ teaspoons horseradish
2   tablespoons red wine vinegar
¹/₄ cup molasses
1   head cabbage, quartered
12 carrots, sliced
20 boiling onions

In a slow-cooking pot, cover the corned beef with water. Cover and cook on low for 10 hours.

Drain the cooked corned beef; place on a broiler pan or oven-proof platter. Reserve the water. Combine the mustard, horseradish, wine vinegar, and molasses. Brush on all sides of the meat. Brown at 400° for about 20 minutes or until it begins to brown. Brush with sauce several times while browning.

Add the cabbage, carrot, and onions to the reserved water. Bring the water to boil and cook until the vegetables are soft.

Serves 6 to 8.

---

1   package prepared dinner rolls
Butter

DINNER ROLLS

Warm the rolls and serve with butter.

Crock Pot
next day—read ahead!

Chicken and Herb Dumplings

GREEN BEANS • GREEN SALAD

Prep Time: 20 minutes • Total Time: 7 hours

1	2½- to 3-pound chicken, cut up plus 2 chicken breasts
1	teaspoon salt
¼	teaspoon pepper
2	whole cloves
8 to 10	small white onions
1	clove garlic, minced
¼	teaspoon powdered marjoram
¼	teaspoon powdered thyme
1	bay leaf
½	cup dry white wine
1	cup sour cream
1	cup packaged biscuit mix
1	tablespoon chopped parsley
6	tablespoons milk

CHICKEN AND HERB DUMPLINGS

Sprinkle the chicken with salt and pepper; place in a slow-cooking pot.

Insert the cloves in 1 onion. Put all onions in a pot. Add the garlic, marjoram, thyme, bay leaf, and wine. Cover and cook on low 5 to 6 hours.

Remove the bay leaf and cloves. Stir in the sour cream. Turn the heat to high. Combine the biscuit mix with the parsley; stir the milk into the biscuit mix with a fork until well moistened. Drop the dumplings from a teaspoon around the edge of the pot. Cover and cook on high for 30 minutes.

Serves 5.

---

1   16-ounce can green beans

GREEN BEANS

Heat the green beans as directed on the can.

---

1   bag salad greens
Favorite salad toppings
Favorite low-fat or nonfat dressings

GREEN SALAD

Place salad greens in serving bowls. Add toppings and drizzle with dressing.

 Time Saver *Reserve chicken breasts for Day 4.*

Layered Supper

FRUIT SALAD • DINNER ROLLS

Prep Time: 30 minutes • Total Time: 1 hour 10 minutes

3	pounds ground beef
2	cups chopped onion (2 large)
2	pounds hash browns
Salt and pepper to taste	
2	17-ounce cans whole kernel corn, drained ·
1	cup chopped green bell pepper
2	cans sliced carrots
2	15-ounce cans tomato sauce
2	cups grated sharp American cheese

LAYERED SUPPER

In a skillet brown the ground beef. Add the onion and cook until soft. Divide the potatoes between 2 12 x 7½-inch baking dishes. Season with salt and pepper. Arrange the corn and green pepper over the potatoes in each casserole. Layer the carrots in each. Crumble the beef evenly over the vegetables, and sprinkle with more salt and pepper. Pat gently to smooth. Top each casserole with tomato sauce. Bake covered at 350° for 35 minutes.

Uncover; sprinkle with cheese. Let stand 10 to 15 minutes before serving.

Makes 2 casseroles, 8 or 9 servings each. Make half the recipe for 1 casserole or freeze second casserole for a non-cook day.

Sliced strawberries
Sliced bananas
Sliced kiwi

FRUIT SALAD

In a salad bowl combine all together.

---

1 package prepared dinner rolls
Butter

DINNER ROLLS

Warm the rolls and serve with butter.

Time	*Shred an additional 1 cup of cheese for use*
Saver	*on Day 5. Hard-boil 3 eggs for Day 4.*

Chicken Puff Casserole

ASPARAGUS • DINNER ROLLS

Prep Time: 30 minutes • Total Time: 55 minutes

¼ cup butter or margarine
¼ cup all-purpose flour
½ teaspoon salt
Dash pepper
1½ cups milk
1 cup chicken broth
2 cups cubed cooked chicken
1 cup frozen peas, cooked and drained
2 tablespoons chopped pimento
3 egg whites
3 egg yolks
½ cup all-purpose flour
1 teaspoon baking powder
½ teaspoon salt
½ teaspoon paprika
½ cup milk
1 tablespoon cooking oil

CHICKEN PUFF CASSEROLE

In a saucepan melt the butter or margarine; blend in ¼ cup of flour, ½ teaspoon of salt, and the pepper. Add 1½ cups of milk and the chicken broth all at once. Cook and stir until thickened and bubbly. Stir in the chicken, peas, and pimento; heat through. Cover and keep hot.

Beat the egg whites until stiff peaks form, about 1½ minutes on medium speed of an electric mixer; set aside. In a small bowl beat the egg yolks until thick and lemon-colored, about 5 minutes on high speed of an electric mixer. Stir together ½ cup of flour, the baking powder, ½ teaspoon of salt, and paprika. Combine ½ cup of milk and the cooking oil. Stir the flour mixture into the beaten yolks alternately with the milk mixture. Fold in the beaten egg whites. Turn the hot chicken mixture into an 11 x 7½ x 1½-inch baking pan. Spread the batter over all. Bake uncovered at 425° for 20 to 25 minutes.

Serves 4 to 5.

3 pounds fresh asparagus, trimmed and peeled

ASPARAGUS

Steam the asparagus in a tall pot with an inch of salted water in the bottom. Cover and turn the heat to high. Cook just until the thick part of the stalk can be pierced with a knife.

Serves 6.

1 package prepared dinner rolls
Butter

DINNER ROLLS

Warm the rolls and serve with butter.

Cheesy Hash-Spinach Pie

SLICED ORANGES • GREEN SALAD

Prep Time: 20 minutes • Total Time: 1 hour 5 minutes

2   9-inch deep-dish pie crusts
2   10-ounce packages frozen chopped
    spinach
2   beaten eggs
1   10¾-ounce can condensed cream
    of mushroom soup
1   tablespoon prepared horseradish
1   teaspoon prepared mustard
¼   cup all-purpose flour
1   15-ounce can corned beef hash
1   cup shredded American cheese
2   tablespoons chopped pimento

Prick the bottom and sides of the pie crusts well with a fork. Bake at 450° for 10 to 12 minutes. Remove from the oven; reduce the oven temperature to 350°.

Cook the spinach according to the package directions, except omit the salt. Drain well, pressing out excess water. Combine the eggs, mushroom soup, flour, horseradish, and mustard; stir in the drained spinach. Spread half of the hash in each baked pastry shell; spoon half of the spinach mixture in each over the top. Bake uncovered at 350° for 45 minutes.

Combine the cheese and pimento; sprinkle over each pie. Bake 2 to 3 minutes longer. Let stand 5 minutes.

Freeze the second pie for later.

Serves 6.

Oranges

SLICED ORANGES

1   bag salad greens
Favorite salad toppings
Favorite low-fat and nonfat dressing

GREEN SALAD

Place salad greens in serving bowls. Add toppings and drizzle with dressing.

Crock Pot
next day—read ahead!

· SUMMER TUNA SALAD · SPINACH SANTA CRUZ ·

· STRING BEANS ORIENTAL · SEAFOOD AND RICE CASSEROLE ·

· SLOW-COOKER ENCHILADAS · SUNNY FRUIT FIESTA · SALAD ·

· FIRE AND ICE TOMATOES · CAESAR SALAD · CORN ON THE COB ·

· CHEESE TUNA AND ZHOU MASHED POTATOES ·

Summer

· ZUCCHINI BEEF CASSEROLE · RICE PILAF · CHICKEN KEBABS ·

· FRANKFURTER CASSEROLE · STEAMED VEGETABLES ·

· BEEF TERIYAKI · SESAME SHRIMP ·

· SKILLET ITALIANO · CHINESE CHICKEN SALAD · MOCK PIZZA ·

· BLUE CHEESE BURGERS · ROSEMARY WALNUT BEEF

SQUARES · PEACHES AND PEARS · MASHED POTATOES · RANCH BEANS ·

· STUFFED MUSHROOMS · SALAD · LEMON-GLAZED

CARROTS · ASIAN CHICKEN · SLICED PLUMS ·

· CORN ON THE COB · WATERMELON · GRILLED VEGETABLES ·

· TOSTADAS · ZESTY ZUCCHINI SAUTÉ · FRUIT SALAD · GREEN SALAD ·

· PASTA WITH CHICKEN & SQUASH · SESAME SHRIMP ·

· ORIENTAL SEAFOOD SALAD ·

· BALLPARK BAKED BEANS · DUGOUT HOT DOGS ·

· BAKED TOMATO HALVES ·

	Day	Main Dish	Side	Side	Side
WEEK 5	Day 1	Chicken Breasts Divine	Herb Rice	Green Beans	
	Day 2	Taco Salad	Warm Tortillas		
	Day 3	Quick-to-Fix Chops & Apples	Veggie Brew	Dinner Rolls	
	Day 4	Frankfurter Casserole	Mixed Vegetables	Applesauce	
	Day 5	Summer Tuna Salad	Garlic French Bread		
WEEK 6	Day 1	Swiss Steak	Summer Squash Casserole	Green Salad	
	Day 2	Chicken Salad	Breadsticks		
	Day 3	Mexican Prawns & Pineapple	Rice	Steamed Broccoli & Cauliflower	
	Day 4	Blue Cheese Burgers	Santa Maria Beans	Green Salad	
	Day 5	Chicken with Rice	Spinach Santa Cruz	Sliced Peaches	
WEEK 7	Day 1	Lemon Chicken	Rice	Sliced Apples & Pears	
	Day 2	Lasagna Belmonte	Green Salad	French Bread	
	Day 3	Mom's Meat Loaf	Mom's Mac 'n' Cheese	Applesauce	
	Day 4	Smothered Steak	Mashed Potatoes	Green Beans	
	Day 5	Chicken Kebabs	Rice Pilaf	Corn on the Cob	French Bread
WEEK 8	Day 1	Easy-Mix Casserole	Oven-Fried Eggplant	Sliced Plums	
	Day 2	Quick & Easy Frypan Chicken	Zesty Zucchini Sauté	French Bread	
	Day 3	Oriental Seafood Salad	French Bread		
	Day 4	Chicken & Wild Rice	Baked Tomato Halves	Sliced Peaches	
	Day 5	Tostadas	Chips & Salsa		

Summer Menus at a Glance

WEEK 1
Day	Main	Side	Side
Day 1	Spareribs "Cooked Easy"	Scalloped Potatoes	Oriental Asparagus Salad
Day 2	Onion Halibut Bake	Broccoli & Cauliflower	French Fries
Day 3	Italian Flank Steak	Seven-Vegetable Salad	Herbed Potatoes & Onions
Day 4	Chicken Casserole	Sliced Apples	Dinner Rolls
Day 5	Slow-Cooker Enchiladas	Green Salad	Chips & Salad

WEEK 2
Day	Main	Side	Side
Day 1	Meat Loaf	Mashed Potatoes	Sliced Peaches
Day 2	Saucy Pork Chops	Noodles	Green Beans Deluxe
Day 3	Steak Fromage	Corn on the Cob	French Bread
Day 4	Chicken Oriental	Rice	Spinach Salad
Day 5	Zucchini Beef Casserole	Tossed Green Salad	Garlic Bread

WEEK 3
Day	Main	Side	Side
Day 1	Honey-Garlic Chicken Wings	Rice	Steamed Vegetables
Day 2	Ground Beef Roll-up	Mushroom Stroganoff	Fresh Fruit Salad
Day 3	Bombay Chicken Salad	French Bread	
Day 4	Steak Kebabs	Sunny Fruit Fiesta	French Bread
Day 5	Seafood & Rice Salad	Sliced Melon	Dinner Rolls

WEEK 4
Day	Main	Side	Side
Day 1	Gourmet Casserole	Caesar Salad	French Bread
Day 2	Armenian Shish Kebabs	Wild Rice Casserole	
Day 3	Cheese Tuna Chop Chop	Fire & Ice Tomatoes	Apples
Day 4	Honey Soy Chicken	String Beans Oriental	Rice
Day 5	Drunk Turkey	Artichokes	Oven-Roasted Potatoes

WEEK 13

Day 1	Barbecue Burgers	French Fries	Ranch Beans	Fruit Salad
Day 2	Lasagna Belmonte	Green Salad	French Bread	
Day 3	Smothered Steak	Mashed Potatoes	Green Beans	
Day 4	Barbecue Chicken	Rice Pilaf	Green Salad	Garlic Bread
Day 5	Rosemary Walnut Beef Skewers	Zesty Potato Salad	Company Brussels Sprouts	

Summer Menus at a Glance

WEEK 9

Day	Main	Side	Side
Day 1	Pasta with Chicken & Squash	Green Salad	
Day 2	Pork Chops O'Brien	Green Beans	Dinner Rolls
Day 3	Garlic Swiss Steak	Lemon-Glazed Carrots	Dinner Rolls
Day 4	Turkey Minestrone	Dinner Rolls	
Day 5	Dugout Hot Dogs	Ballpark Baked Beans	Corn Chips

WEEK 10

Day	Main	Side	Side
Day 1	Fantastic Chicken	Stuffed Mushrooms	French Bread
Day 2	Beef Teriyaki	Rice	Garlic Tomatoes
Day 3	Sesame Shrimp	Fruit Salad	French Bread
Day 4	Chicken Salad	Won Tons	
Day 5	Tuna Salad Submarines	Potato Chips	Watermelon

WEEK 11

Day	Main	Side	Side
Day 1	Skillet Italiano	Green Salad	Garlic Bread
Day 2	Chili Dogs	Sliced Plums	Potato Chips
Day 3	Chicken Salad	Croissants	
Day 4	Barbecue Steaks	Confetti Pasta Salad	Garlic Bread
Day 5	Linguine-Tuna Salad	Sliced Peaches	Dinner Rolls

WEEK 12

Day	Main	Side	Side
Day 1	Asian Chicken	Chinese Crispy Noodles	Fruit
Day 2	Mock Pizza	Green Salad	
Day 3	Vegetable-Beef Burgers	Baked French Fries	
Day 4	Stuffed Pasta Shells	Spinach	Dinner Rolls
Day 5	Chinese Chicken Salad	Sliced Peaches & Pears	

Spareribs "Cooked Easy"

SCALLOPED POTATOES • ORIENTAL ASPARAGUS SALAD

Prep Time: 20 minutes • Total Time: 50 minutes, plus all day in crock pot

3 pounds spareribs (boneless, country-style)	

SPARERIBS "COOKED EASY"

3   pounds spareribs (boneless, country-style)
½   cup vinegar
½   cup brown sugar
4   cloves garlic, chopped
½   cup soy sauce
2   tablespoons cornstarch
1   6-ounce can pineapple juice

Bring the spareribs, vinegar, brown sugar, garlic, and soy sauce to a boil. Simmer and stir occasionally. Cook in a crock pot all day on low.

Make a cornstarch paste with 2 tablespoons cornstarch and the can of pineapple juice. Pour over the meat and cook for 15 minutes.

---

1   box scalloped potatoes

SCALLOPED POTATOES

Prepare favorite boxed potatoes as directed.

---

1   pound asparagus, cut into 2-inch pieces
2   tablespoons soy sauce
1   tablespoon vegetable oil
1   tablespoon vinegar
1½   teaspoons sugar
1   teaspoon sesame seeds, toasted
¼ to ½   teaspoon ground ginger
¼   teaspoon ground cumin

ORIENTAL ASPARAGUS SALAD

In a saucepan cook the asparagus in a small amount of water until crisp-tender, about 3 to 4 minutes. Drain well and place in a large bowl. Combine the soy sauce, oil, vinegar, sugar, sesame seeds, ginger, and cumin; pour over the asparagus and toss to coat. Cover and chill for 1 hour.

Drain before serving.

Serves 4.

Time Saver *Prepare the asparagus salad as you prepare the crock pot.*

Crock Pot *today!*

Onion Halibut Bake

STEAMED BROCCOLI AND CAULIFLOWER · FRENCH FRIES

Prep Time: 20 minutes • Total Time: 50 minutes

2 cups thinly sliced onions
1 tablespoon melted butter
1 tablespoon olive oil
1 teaspoon crushed dill
Salt and pepper, to taste
4 4- to 6-ounce North American
   halibut steaks, thawed (if necessary)

ONION HALIBUT BAKE

In a 9-inch square baking dish combine the onions, butter, olive oil, dill, salt, and pepper. Bake at 400° for about 10 to 15 minutes, or until the onions begin to brown.

Season the halibut, if desired; place on the onion mixture and top with a few of the onion slices. Bake for 10 to 15 minutes, or until the fish flakes when tested with a fork.

Serves 4.

1 pound broccoli
1 pound cauliflower

STEAMED BROCCOLI AND CAULIFLOWER

Place the broccoli and cauliflower in a steamer above an inch or two of salted water. Cover and steam for 6 to 8 minutes or until crisp-tender.

Serves 6.

1 bag frozen fries (home-style)

FRENCH FRIES

Cook as directed on the package.

Time Saver *Slice an additional onion for use on Day 3.*
Marinate the flake steak, as directed, for Day 3.

Italian Flank Steak

SEVEN-VEGETABLE SALAD · HERBED POTATOES AND ONIONS

Prep Time: 25 minutes • Total Time: 45 minutes

2 .7-ounce envelopes fat-free Italian salad dressing mix
2 tablespoons vegetable oil
1 tablespoon fresh lemon juice
1 flank steak (2 pounds)

ITALIAN FLANK STEAK

Combine the salad dressing mix, oil, and lemon juice. Brush onto both sides of the steak; place in a shallow dish. Cover and refrigerate several hours or overnight.

Grill over hot coals for 4 minutes per side for medium, 5 minutes per side for medium-well, or until desired doneness is reached.

Serves 4.

1¾ cups cauliflowerets
1¼ cups chopped cucumbers
1 cup sliced celery
½ cup quartered cherry tomatoes
¼ cup julienne green pepper
¼ cup julienne sweet red pepper
2 tablespoons sliced green onions
¼ cup fat-free salad dressing

SEVEN-VEGETABLE SALAD

In a large bowl combine all vegetables. Pour the salad dressing over; toss to coat.

Serves 5.

3 medium red potatoes, thinly sliced
1 medium onion, thinly sliced
½ teaspoon Italian seasoning
⅛ teaspoon pepper
2 tablespoons reduced-fat margarine, melted

HERBED POTATOES AND ONIONS

In an ungreased 2-quart microwave-safe baking dish, layer half the potato and onion slices. Combine the Italian seasoning and pepper; sprinkle half over the onion and potato layer. Drizzle with 1 tablespoon of margarine. Repeat the layers. Cover with vented plastic wrap. Microwave on high for 12 minutes or until the potatoes are tender, turning the dish after 6 minutes.

Serves 4.

 Time Saver *Boil Day 4's chicken.*

Cheesy Chicken Casserole

SLICED APPLES · DINNER ROLLS

Prep Time: 15 minutes • Total Time: 1 hour 40 minutes or 40 minutes if chicken boiled ahead

---

4   boneless chicken breasts
1 to 2 celery stalks
1½ small onions (1 chopped and ½ chunked)
Dash salt
1   16-ounce can bean sprouts, drained
2   10-ounce packages frozen French-cut green beans, cooked for 5 minutes
1   8-ounce can mushroom soup, diluted with ½ cup milk
2   cups grated sharp Cheddar cheese
1 to 2 2.8-ounce cans French fried onions

CHEESY CHICKEN CASSEROLE

Boil the chicken with the celery, chunked onion, and salt for 1 hour. Drain and cube.

In a large bowl mix the chicken with the chopped onion, sprouts, beans, and mushroom soup. Arrange in a casserole dish. Top with cheese and cover with foil. Bake at 350° for 20 minutes. The cheese will melt and flow through the casserole.

Uncover and sprinkle with French fried onions. Return to the oven, uncovered, and brown for 15 minutes.

Serves 4.

Apples

SLICED APPLES

---

1   package prepared dinner rolls
Butter

DINNER ROLLS

Warm the rolls and serve with butter.

Time Saver   *Chop an additional onion for use on Day 5. Grate an additional cup of Cheddar cheese for use on Day 5. See Day 5's Time Saver.*

Crock Pot
next day—read ahead!

Slow-Cooker Enchiladas

GREEN SALAD · TORTILLA CHIPS AND SALSA

Prep Time: 20 minutes • Total Time: 5 to 7 hours

1   pound ground beef
1   cup chopped onion
½   cup chopped green pepper
1   16-ounce can pinto beans, rinsed and drained
1   15-ounce can black beans, rinsed and drained
1   10-ounce can diced tomatoes and green chilies, undrained
⅓   cup water
1   teaspoon chili powder
½   teaspoon ground cumin
¼   teaspoon pepper
½   teaspoon salt
1   cup shredded sharp Cheddar cheese
1   cup shredded Monterey Jack cheese
6   flour tortillas (6- or 7-inch)

SLOW-COOKER ENCHILADAS

In a skillet cook the beef, onion, and green pepper until the beef is browned and the vegetables are tender; drain. Add the next 8 ingredients; bring to a boil. Reduce the heat, cover, and simmer for 10 minutes.

Combine the cheeses. In a 5-quart slow cooker, layer about ¾ cup of beef mixture, 1 tortilla, and ⅓ cup cheese. Repeat the layers. Cover and cook on low for 5 to 7 hours or until heated through.

Serves 4.

---

1   bag salad greens
Favorite salad toppings
Favorite low-fat or nonfat dressing

GREEN SALAD

Place salad greens in serving bowls. Add toppings and drizzle with dressing.

---

1   bag tortilla chips
1   jar salsa

TORTILLA CHIPS AND SALSA

Time Saver *If time is short, prepare enchiladas on Day 4 and put on to cook in slow cooker on morning of Day 5.*

Prize-Winning Meat Loaf

MASHED POTATOES · SLICED PEACHES

Prep Time: 20 minutes • Total Time: 1 hour 50 minutes

1½ pounds ground beef
1 cup tomato juice
½ cup uncooked oatmeal (quick)
1 large egg, well beaten
¼ cup chopped onion
1 teaspoon salt
¼ teaspoon pepper
1 tablespoon catsup

PRIZE-WINNING MEAT LOAF

Preheat the oven to 350°. Combine all ingredients except the catsup and mix well. Press firmly into a loaf and spread catsup over the top. Bake at 350° for 1 to 1½ hours. Allow to cool for 5 minutes before slicing.

Serves 6 to 8.

1 package instant mashed potatoes

MASHED POTATOES

Prepare the mashed potatoes as directed on the package.

5 to 6 peaches, sliced, or 1 large can of sliced peaches, drained

SLICED PEACHES

Divide the peaches among serving bowls.

Time Saver *Chop entire onion plus 1 for use on Day 3 and Day 5. Day 2 pork chops can be put in the crock pot, depending on your schedule.*

Saucy Pork Chops

NOODLES · GREEN BEANS DELUXE

Prep Time: 30 minutes • Total Time: 1 hour 30 minutes or all day in crock pot

2 tablespoons oil
6 pork chops, ³/₄-inch thick
Salt and pepper
1 medium onion, thinly sliced
1 10½-ounce can condensed cream
   of chicken soup
¼ cup catsup
2 to 3 teaspoons Worcestershire sauce

SAUCY PORK CHOPS

In a skillet heat the oil and brown the chops on both sides. Drain and season with salt and pepper. Top with onion slices. Combine the remaining ingredients; pour over the chops. Cover and simmer for 45 to 60 minutes or until done. Remove the chops to a platter; spoon the sauce.

If using crock pot, layer pork chops and onions in pot, cover with sauce, and cook on low all day.

Serves 6.

---

3 cups egg noodles

NOODLES

Cook the noodles as directed on the package.

---

2 10-ounce packages frozen French-
   cut green beans
1 10½-ounce can cream of mushroom soup, undiluted
1 6-ounce can water chestnuts,
   drained and sliced
1 package sliced almonds
3 green onions, sliced
1 2.8-ounce can French fried onions
Salt and pepper, to taste

GREEN BEANS DELUXE

Cook the string beans according to the package instructions; drain.

Stir together the soup, water chestnuts, almonds, sliced onions, salt, and pepper, and add the green beans. Turn into a 2-quart greased casserole. Bake at 350° for at least 30 minutes. During the last 5 minutes of baking time, top the casserole with the French fried onions.

Serves 8.

Steak Fromage

CORN ON THE COB · FRENCH BREAD

Prep Time: 15 minutes • Total Time: 1 hour 30 minutes

1 to 2 pounds beef round steak, cut
    ½-inch thick
¼ cup flour
½ teaspoon salt
⅛ teaspoon pepper
¼ teaspoon garlic salt
3 tablespoons shortening
¾ cup water
¼ cup chopped onion
⅓ cup grated Cheddar cheese
2 tablespoons chopped parsley

STEAK FROMAGE

Cut the steak into 8 to 10 pieces. Pound to ¼-inch thickness. Mix together the flour, salt, pepper, and garlic salt. Dredge the steak in the seasoned flour. Sprinkle any remaining flour over the steak. In a skillet heat the shortening and brown the steak. Add the water and onion. Cover tightly and simmer for 1 hour or until tender. (Do not allow the liquid to boil.)

Sprinkle cheese and parsley on the meat. Cover and simmer 2 to 3 additional minutes or until the cheese is melted.

Serves 4 to 6.

4 to 6 ears of corn

CORN ON THE COB

Boil in water until soft, approximately 15 minutes.

6 to 8 slices French bread
Butter

FRENCH BREAD

Spread with butter and toast in the oven on a cookie sheet.

Time Saver *Grate an additional cup of cheese for Day 5.*

Chicken Oriental

RICE · SPINACH SALAD

Prep Time: 30 minutes • Total Time: 1 hour 20 minutes

2½ pounds chicken pieces, fat trimmed, skinned, if desired
1 6-ounce package frozen pea pods
1 medium red or green bell pepper, cut into strips
½ cup thinly sliced celery
1 6-ounce can sliced water chestnuts, drained
1 2-ounce jar sliced mushrooms, drained
½ 2.8-ounce can French fried onions
½ cup water
¼ cup catsup
3 tablespoons soy sauce
½ teaspoon ground ginger
¼ teaspoon garlic powder

CHICKEN ORIENTAL

Preheat the oven to 400°. Arrange the chicken in a 9 x 13-inch baking dish. Bake uncovered at 400° for 30 minutes; drain.

Place the pea pods, red pepper, celery, water chestnuts, mushrooms and ½ can of fried onions around and under the chicken. In a small bowl combine the water, catsup, soy sauce, ginger, and garlic powder; pour over the chicken and vegetables. Bake, covered, for 10 minutes or until the chicken is done. Top the chicken with the remaining onions and bake, uncovered, for 1 to 3 minutes or until the onions are golden brown. Serve over rice.

Serves 4 to 6.

3 cups instant rice
3 cups water

RICE

Bring the water to a boil. Stir in the rice; cover and remove from the heat. Let stand 5 minutes or until the water is absorbed. Fluff with a fork.

Serves 6.

1 package ready-to-serve spinach salad
2 hard-boiled eggs, sliced
Favorite low-fat or nonfat dressing

SPINACH SALAD

Place spinach in serving bowls. Top with sliced eggs and drizzle with dressing.

Zucchini Beef Casserole

GREEN SALAD · GARLIC BREAD

Prep Time: 30 minutes • Total Time: 1 hour 30 minutes

3   cups sliced zucchini
1½ cups water
1½ teaspoons salt
1   medium onion, chopped
½   green bell pepper, chopped
1   pound ground beef
1   cup grated cheese
½   cup uncooked rice
1   can condensed tomato soup
¾   cup water
⅛   teaspoon pepper
½   teaspoon paprika

ZUCCHINI BEEF CASSEROLE

Cook the zucchini in salted water until tender; drain. Sauté the onion and green pepper; add the ground beef and cook until done. Drain. Combine all ingredients and turn into a buttered 2-quart baking dish. Bake at 325° for 45 to 60 minutes.

If your family does not like zucchini, spinach can be substituted.

Serves 6.

---

1   bag salad greens
Favorite salad toppings
Favorite low-fat or nonfat salad dressing

GREEN SALAD

Place salad greens in serving bowls. Add toppings and drizzle with dressing.

---

1   loaf ready-to-heat garlic bread

GARLIC BREAD

Heat as directed on the package.

Honey-Garlic Chicken Wings

RICE · STEAMED VEGETABLES

Prep Time: 25 minutes • Total Time: 1 hour

2	pounds chicken wings
1/3	cup honey
2	tablespoons instant chicken bouillon
2	tablespoons soy sauce
1	tablespoon lemon juice
1/2	teaspoon garlic powder
1/4	teaspoon ground ginger

HONEY-GARLIC CHICKEN WINGS

Preheat the oven to 425°. Cut the chicken wings into 3 pieces, discarding the tips. Rinse the chicken; pat dry. Place the chicken in a large baking pan. Bake for 10 minutes. Combine the remaining ingredients and mix well. Pour over the chicken. Increase the oven temperature to 475°. Bake for 25 minutes.

Serves 4.

3	cups water
3	cups instant rice

RICE

Bring the water to a boil. Stir in the rice; cover and remove from the heat. Let stand 5 minutes or until the water is absorbed. Fluff with a fork.

Serves 6.

Favorite vegetables

STEAMED VEGETABLES

Steam your favorite summer vegetables in bite-sized chunks.

Time Saver *Cook an additional 1 1/2 cups of rice to equal 3 cups for use on Day 4.*

Ground Beef Roll-up

MUSHROOM STROGANOFF · FRESH FRUIT SALAD

Prep Time: 30 minutes • Total Time: 1 hour 30 minutes

1 pound ground beef
½ cup finely chopped celery
¼ cup chopped onion
1 tablespoon Worcestershire sauce
¼ cup catsup
1 egg, beaten
¼ cup oats
½ teaspoon salt
1 package refrigerated bread loaf

GROUND BEEF ROLL-UP

Preheat the oven to 375°. In a skillet brown the ground beef, stirring until crumbly; drain. Add the celery, onion, Worcestershire sauce, catsup, egg, oats, and salt; mix well.

Roll the bread loaf to a 10 x 12-inch rectangle. Spread the ground beef mixture to within ½-inch of the edges. Roll up as for a jellyroll. Seal the edge; turn under the ends. Place on a greased baking sheet. Bake for 20 to 25 minutes or until golden brown.

Serves 6 to 8.

---

1 tablespoon vegetable oil
1 tablespoon butter
1 onion, sliced
1 8-ounce can sliced mushrooms
1 clove garlic, minced
2 tablespoons catsup
1 teaspoon Worcestershire sauce
1 14-ounce can beef broth
3 tablespoons all-purpose flour
1 cup sour cream
4 cups cooked egg noodles

MUSHROOM STROGANOFF

In a skillet heat the oil and butter and sauté the onion, mushrooms, and garlic for 5 minutes or until crisp-tender. Stir in the catsup, Worcestershire sauce, and 2/3 of the beef broth. Simmer until heated through.

Blend the flour with the remaining broth; add to the mushroom mixture. Bring to a boil. Cook for 1 minute, stirring constantly; reduce the heat. Add the sour cream. Cook until heated through. Serve over noodles.

Serves 4.

---

4 to 6 pieces of fruit, any combination

FRESH FRUIT SALAD

Cut up favorite fruit, mix, and serve.

 Chop ½ onion for use on Day 4.

Bombay Chicken Salad

FRENCH BREAD

Prep Time: 10 minutes • Total Time: 1 hour 10 minutes

---

2 5-ounce cans chunk white chicken
1 11-ounce can mandarin oranges,
   drained
1 banana, sliced
Lemon juice
1/4 cup mayonnaise
2 tablespoons orange juice
1/2 teaspoon curry powder
Salad greens

BOMBAY CHICKEN SALAD

In a bowl combine the chicken and oranges. Sprinkle the banana with lemon juice. Add the bananas, mix together the mayonnaise, orange juice, and curry powder, and add to the salad; mix gently. Chill until serving time. Serve on crisp salad greens.

Serves 6 to 8.

---

1 loaf crusty French bread or rolls
Butter

FRENCH BREAD

Serve some crusty French bread or rolls—your choice.

Time Saver | *Marinate beef for Day 4.*

Steak Kebabs

SUNNY FRUIT FIESTA · FRENCH BREAD

Prep Time: 30 minutes • Total Time: 1 hour

2 tablespoons reduced-sodium soy sauce
2 tablespoons honey
1 tablespoon grated fresh ginger or 1 teaspoon ground ginger
1 clove garlic, crushed
1 teaspoon grated lemon peel
¼ teaspoon crushed hot red pepper flakes
2 pounds boneless sirloin steak, trimmed, cut into 1-inch cubes
8 cherry tomatoes
4 large mushrooms, cut in half
1 green bell pepper, cored, seeded and cut into 8 squares

STEAK KEBABS

In a shallow glass dish combine the soy sauce, honey, ginger, garlic, lemon peel, and red pepper flakes. Mix well. Add the beef; stir to coat. Cover with plastic wrap; refrigerate for 1 to 2 hours or overnight, stirring occasionally.

Preheat the broiler. Remove the beef from the marinade. Discard the marinade. On 4 10-inch metal skewers alternately thread the beef, tomatoes, mushrooms, and bell pepper. Place on a broiler pan. Broil 2 inches from the heat, turning 2 or 3 times, until the meat is medium-rare and the vegetables are lightly browned, about 10 minutes, or broil over hot coals for 10 to 12 minutes. Place on serving plates and serve immediately. Serves 4.

---

1 cantaloupe melon, halved and seeded
½ honeydew melon, seeded
¼ cup superfine or granulated sugar
¼ cup fresh lime juice
2 tablespoons fresh lemon juice
1 tablespoon orange-flavored liqueur (optional)
1½ teaspoons grated lime peel
1 cup sliced fresh strawberries
1 cup black or red seedless grapes

SUNNY FRUIT FIESTA

Using a melon baller, scoop the flesh from the cantaloupe and honeydew into balls; set aside. In a large glass or ceramic bowl combine the sugar, lime juice, lemon juice, orange liqueur, and lime peel. Stir well to dissolve sugar. Add the cantaloupe and honeydew balls, strawberries, and grapes. Toss gently to combine. Cover the bowl with plastic wrap and refrigerate for at least 1 hour to blend flavors, stirring once or twice.

Spoon the fruit mixture into serving bowls or hollowed-out melon halves, dividing evenly. Serve at once. Serves 4 to 6.

---

1 loaf French bread and butter

FRENCH BREAD

Seafood and Rice Salad

DINNER ROLLS · SLICED MELON

Prep Time: 20 minutes • Total Time: 1 hour

---

1 pound cooked shrimp, tuna or crabmeat
3 cups cooked instant rice
1 10-ounce package green peas, thawed
¼ teaspoon lemon pepper
½ cup chopped red bell pepper
2 tablespoons chopped onion
1 cup mayonnaise

SEAFOOD AND RICE SALAD

Combine all ingredients in a bowl; mix well. Serve warm or cold.

Serves 6 to 8.

---

1 package prepared dinner rolls
Butter

DINNER ROLLS

Warm the rolls and serve with butter.

Melon of your choice

SLICED MELON

Slice cantaloupe, watermelon, or other melon fruit and serve on the side.

Gourmet Casserole

CAESAR SALAD · FRENCH BREAD

Prep Time: 30 minutes • Total Time: 1 hour 30 minutes

1 12-ounce package wide egg noodles
1½ pounds ground beef
2 8-ounce cans tomato sauce
1 8-ounce package cream cheese
½ pound cottage cheese
¼ cup sour cream
⅓ cup minced green onion
1 tablespoon chopped green bell pepper
2 tablespoons melted butter

GOURMET CASSEROLE

Cook the noodles, drain, and set aside. Brown the meat, drain, and stir in the tomato sauce. Remove from the heat. Combine all cheese, sour cream, green onion, and green pepper together. In a buttered 9 x 13-inch glass pan place a layer of noodles, cover with cheese combination; add the remaining noodles. Spread the melted butter over the last layer of noodles and cover with the meat mixture. Bake uncovered at 325° for 45 to 60 minutes.

Serves 10.

1 clove garlic
½ cup salad oil
1 head romaine lettuce
Croutons
1 beaten egg
1 teaspoon Worcestershire sauce
¼ cup lemon juice
½ teaspoon pepper
½ teaspoon salt
Anchovies (optional)
½ cup grated Parmesan cheese

CAESAR SALAD

Mash the garlic and add to the salad oil; let stand. Wash and dry the romaine. Just before serving, break the lettuce into a bowl. Add the croutons. Strain the oil and pour over the lettuce. Combine the remaining ingredients and beat well. Pour over the salad and toss lightly. Serve immediately.

Serves 6.

1 loaf crusty French bread, sliced
Butter

FRENCH BREAD

Brush the slices of bread with butter and warm in the oven.

 Time Saver *Marinate meat tonight for Day 2.*

Armenian Shish Kebabs

WILD RICE CASSEROLE

Prep Time: 30 minutes • Total Time: 1 hour 30 minutes

½ cup salad oil
¼ cup lemon juice
1 teaspoon salt
1 teaspoon dried marjoram, crushed
1 teaspoon dried thyme, crushed
½ teaspoon pepper
1 clove garlic, minced
½ cup chopped onion
¼ cup snipped parsley
2 pounds boneless lamb, cut into
  1½-inch cubes
Green bell peppers, quartered
Sweet red bell peppers, quartered
Onions
Cherry tomatoes
Mushrooms

ARMENIAN SHISH KEBABS

Combine the salad oil, lemon juice, salt, marjoram, thyme, pepper, garlic, onion and parsley; add the meat and stir to coat. Refrigerate several hours or overnight.

Fill skewers with meat cubes and vegetables. Broil over hot coals for 10 to 12 minutes, turning and brushing often with marinade.

Serves 6.

---

1 cup wild rice
2¼ cups chicken broth
2 cups chopped celery
¾ cup chopped onion
¼ cup butter or margarine
1 8-ounce can sliced mushrooms, drained
1 tablespoon dried parsley flakes
½ teaspoon salt
¼ teaspoon dried thyme, crushed

WILD RICE CASSEROLE

Rinse the rice according to the package directions. In a 2-quart saucepan combine the rice and chicken broth; bring to boiling. Cover, reduce the heat, and simmer 40 minutes. Do not drain. Meanwhile, cook the celery and onion in butter until tender, but not brown. Stir in the mushrooms, parsley flakes, salt, and thyme; stir into the rice. Turn into a 1½-quart casserole. Bake covered at 375° for 35 to 40 minutes. Stir.

Serves 4 to 6.

 Time Saver *Chop an additional onion for Day 5.*

Cheese Tuna Chop Chop

FIRE AND ICE TOMATOES · SLICED APPLES

Prep Time: 25 minutes • Total Time: 1 hour 10 minutes

2   cups diced celery
1   7-ounce can tuna
1   10½-ounce can cream of mush-
     room soup
½   cup milk
1   10-ounce package frozen peas,
     defrosted
1   cup grated cheese
Chow mein noodles

CHEESE TUNA CHOP CHOP

Combine the celery, tuna, mushroom soup, milk, peas, and cheese. Turn into a 2-quart casserole. Sprinkle chow mein noodles around the edge of the casserole. Cover and bake at 350° for 30 minutes. Uncover and bake 10 to 15 minutes longer, until the mixture is bubbly and the noodles are crisp.

Serves 4 to 6.

¾   cup vinegar
1½   teaspoons celery salt
1½   teaspoons mustard seed
½   teaspoon salt
4½   teaspoons sugar
⅛   teaspoon cayenne pepper
⅛   teaspoon black pepper
¼   cup water
6   large tomatoes, sliced
1   large green bell pepper, cut in strips
1   large red onion, peeled, cut into
     rings
1   peeled cucumber, sliced

FIRE AND ICE TOMATOES

Boil the first 8 ingredients furiously for 1 minute. Pour over the vegetables except the cucumber. When cooled, add the cucumber.

Serves 4 to 6.

Apples or other fresh summer fruit

SLICED APPLES

Time Saver *Grate an additional ¾ cup of cheese for Day 4. Marinate chicken tonight for tomorrow's dinner.*

Honey Soy Chicken

STRING BEANS ORIENTAL · RICE

Prep Time: 20 minutes • Total Time: 1 hour

Salt and fresh ground pepper
1/4 cup vegetable oil
2   teaspoons sesame oil
1   cup soy sauce
1/2 cup honey
1/2 cup dry sherry
4   cloves garlic, minced
2   teaspoons finely grated ginger
7   chicken breasts

HONEY SOY CHICKEN

Combine all of the ingredients except the chicken in a jar and shake until blended. Marinate the chicken pieces overnight in the mixture.

Prepare a barbecue grill. Place the chicken pieces on the hot grill. Brush with marinade and turn occasionally. Grill the chicken about 20 minutes each side.

Serves 6.

3   10-ounce packages frozen green beans, or fresh green beans
1   medium onion, chopped
1/2 cup butter
1/3 cup flour
2   cups milk
3/4 cup grated Cheddar cheese
1   5-ounce can water chestnuts
2   teaspoons soy sauce
1   teaspoon salt
1/2 teaspoon pepper
1   4-ounce can sliced mushrooms
1/3 cup sliced almonds

STRING BEANS ORIENTAL

Cook the beans until barely tender, drain. In a saucepan melt the butter and sauté the onion. Add the flour and blend. Slowly add the milk and cheese. Cook until thick. Add the seasonings and beans, water chestnuts, and mushrooms. Pour into a 2-quart buttered casserole. Top with sliced almonds. Bake uncovered at 375° for 30 minutes.

Serves 6.

3   cups water
3   cups instant rice

RICE

Bring the water to a boil. Stir in the rice; cover and remove from the heat. Let stand 5 minutes or until the water is absorbed. Fluff with a fork.

Serves 6.

Time Saver *Prepare Drunk Turkey for Day 5.*

Drunk Turkey

ARTICHOKES · OVEN-ROASTED POTATOES

Prep Time: 20 minutes • Total Time: 1 hour 20 minutes

2	pounds cold sliced white turkey meat
½	cup butter
1	tablespoon crushed oregano
½	cup grated orange rind
½	cup finely chopped onion
Salt to taste	
1	pint pale dry sherry

DRUNK TURKEY

In a baking dish with a cover place a layer of turkey, dot with butter, sprinkle with oregano, orange rind, and onion (salt if desired). Add sherry to moisten. Continue layering. Cover and let stand in the refrigerator overnight. Bake covered at 350° for 30 minutes.

Serves 4 to 6.

⅛	cup garlic, minced
¼	cup butter, melted
4	artichokes

ARTICHOKES

Mix the garlic and butter together. Cut the artichokes into quarters and steam, boil or microwave until tender or the leaves are easy to pull from the flower. Serve with melted butter and garlic.

Serves 4.

1	envelope dry onion soup mix
2	pounds potatoes, cut into large chunks
⅓	cup olive or vegetable oil

OVEN-ROASTED POTATOES

Preheat the oven to 350°. In a large plastic bag, combine all ingredients. Close the bag and shake until the potatoes are evenly coated. Empty the potatoes into a shallow baking pan; discard the bag. Bake for 60 minutes, stirring occasionally.

Serves 6 to 8.

Chicken Breasts Divine

HERB RICE · GREEN BEANS

Prep Time: 25 minutes • Total Time: 45 minutes

4	large or 8 small boneless chicken breasts
1/2	teaspoon salt
1/4	teaspoon pepper
2	tablespoons melted margarine
2	tablespoons vegetable oil
Juice of 1/2 lemon	
3	tablespoons chopped green onions
3	tablespoons chopped parsley
2	teaspoons Dijon mustard
1/4	cup chicken broth

CHICKEN BREASTS DIVINE

Rinse the chicken; pat dry. Place between sheets of plastic wrap; pound slightly. Sprinkle with salt and pepper. In a glass dish combine the margarine and oil. Place the chicken in the dish, coating each piece with oil mixture. Microwave on high for 3 minutes. Let stand for 1 minute. Turn the chicken over. Microwave for 3 minutes longer or until done; do not overcook. In a glass bowl combine the lemon juice, green onions, parsley, and mustard. Microwave on high for 1 minute. Stir in the broth and any chicken pan juices. Pour over the chicken. Serve immediately.

Serves 4.

1	cup uncooked rice
3	tablespoons margarine
1/4	teaspoon salt
3	cups chicken broth
1/2	teaspoon each: savory, thyme, rosemary and marjoram

HERB RICE

In a heavy skillet brown the rice in the margarine, stirring frequently. Stir in the remaining ingredients. Simmer on low for 25 minutes or until liquid is absorbed.

Serves 4 to 6.

2	pounds green beans, washed and trimmed

GREEN BEANS

Place the beans in a steamer above an inch or two of salted water. Cover and cook for 4 to 6 minutes, until bright green and tender.

Serves 6.

Time Saver *Chop 2 additional green onions for Day 2.*
Cook 1 cup green beans for Day 5.

Taco Salad

WARM TORTILLAS

Prep Time: 20 minutes • Total Time: 40 minutes

2   pounds ground beef
1   envelope taco seasoning mix
1/2 head lettuce, torn
2   tomatoes, chopped
2   green onions, chopped
1   stalk celery, chopped
2   16-ounce cans dark red kidney beans, drained and rinsed
2   6-ounce cans black olives, chopped
2   6-ounce canned chili peppers, chopped
1/2 to 1 cup grated Cheddar cheese
2   avocados, chopped
1/4 package tortilla chips, crushed
Catalina salad dressing

TACO SALAD

In a skillet brown the ground beef, stirring until crumbly; drain. Stir in the taco seasoning mix according to the package directions. In a glass bowl combine with the remaining ingredients; toss lightly.

Serves 6 to 10.

---

1 package flour tortillas

WARM TORTILLAS

Warm the tortillas and serve with butter.

Hint: A Styrofoam tortilla holder keeps tortillas warm throughout your meal.

 Time Saver *Chop 5 celery stalks for Day 5.*

Quick-to-Fix Chops and Apples

VEGETABLE BREW · DINNER ROLLS

Prep Time: 30 minutes • Total Time: 1 hour

4   pork chops
2   tablespoons butter or margarine
1   cup chopped apple
1/4 cup packed light brown sugar
1/4 teaspoon cinnamon
4   slices lemon

QUICK-TO-FIX CHOPS AND APPLES

In a skillet cook the pork chops in butter over medium heat for 2 minutes on each side. Spoon 1/4 of the chopped apple onto each pork chop. Cook, covered, over low heat for 20 minutes or until the apple is tender. Sprinkle with a mixture of brown sugar and cinnamon; top with a slice of lemon. Cook, covered, for 5 minutes longer or until the sugar is melted.

Serves 4.

6   tomatoes, chopped
1   cucumber, chopped
3   green onions, chopped
Olive oil and vinegar
Catalina salad dressing
Salt and pepper to taste

VEGETABLE BREW

In a salad bowl combine the tomatoes, cucumbers, scallions, salad dressing, and seasonings; toss well to coat.

Serves 5.

1   package prepared dinner rolls
Butter

DINNER ROLLS

Warm the rolls and serve with butter.

Frankfurter Casserole

MIXED VEGETABLES · APPLESAUCE

Prep Time: 10 minutes • Total Time: 30 minutes

1 small onion, chopped
1 pound frankfurters, sliced lengthwise
½ cup margarine
1 10½-ounce can cream of tomato soup
1 soup can milk
½ soup can water
2 cups uncooked egg noodles
Sliced American cheese

FRANKFURTER CASSEROLE

In a skillet brown the onion and frankfurters in margarine over medium heat. Add the soup, milk, and water; mix well. Reduce the heat; stir in the noodles. Simmer until the noodles are cooked, stirring occasionally. Place cheese slices over the top just before serving. Let stand until melted.

Serves 8.

---

1 16-ounce package frozen mixed vegetables

MIXED VEGETABLES

Prepare as directed on the package.

---

1 large jar homestyle applesauce

APPLESAUCE

Serve warm or cold.

Summer Tuna Salad

GARLIC FRENCH BREAD

Prep Time: 20 minutes • Total Time: 40 minutes

1 large crown summer squash
1 head lettuce, torn
1 cup flaked tuna, chilled
1 cup cooked peas, chilled
1 cup chopped celery
1 green bell pepper, minced
French salad dressing
2 tomatoes, sliced
2 boiled eggs, sliced
Mayonnaise
Parsley

SUMMER TUNA SALAD

In a saucepan boil or steam the squash until tender. Scoop out the seed and center pulp. Drizzle with French salad dressing. Chill in the refrigerator.

Place the squash on a bed of lettuce on a serving plate. In a bowl combine the tuna, peas, celery, and green pepper. Add enough French salad dressing to make of desired consistency; mix well. Spoon into the squash. Alternate tomato slices and egg slices in an overlapping layer around edge. Garnish with mayonnaise and parsley.

Serves 4.

1 loaf ready-to-heat garlic bread

GARLIC FRENCH BREAD

Heat as directed on the package.

Swiss Steak

SUMMER SQUASH CASSEROLE · GREEN SALAD

Prep Time: 30 minutes • Total Time: 1 hour 20 minutes

2	tablespoons flour
1	teaspoon garlic salt
1/8	teaspoon pepper
1/2	teaspoon oregano
1 1/2	pounds round steak
2	tablespoons oil
1	onion, sliced
1/2	cup Burgundy wine
1	16-ounce can stewed tomatoes
1	4-ounce can sliced or button mushrooms
2	tablespoons chopped parsley

SWISS STEAK

Mix the flour, garlic salt, pepper, and oregano. Put the meat on a board and sprinkle half of the flour mixture on one side and pound into the meat. Turn the meat and top with the remaining mixture and pound in. Cut in 4 serving pieces and brown slowly and well on both sides in heated oil. Add the onions for the last 5 minutes of browning and cook until soft. Add the wine and tomatoes and cover; boil slowly until the meat is almost fork tender or bake in a 350° oven. Add the undrained mushrooms and parsley. Cook 10 to 15 minutes longer.

Serves 4.

2	pounds yellow summer squash, sliced (6 cups)
1/4	cup chopped onion
1	10 1/2-ounce can cream of chicken soup
1	cup sour cream
1	cup grated carrots
1	8-ounce package herb-seasoned stuffing mix
1/2	cup melted butter

SUMMER SQUASH CASSEROLE

Cook the squash and onion in boiling salted water for 5 minutes; drain. Combine the soup and sour cream. Stir in the grated carrot. Fold in the squash and onion. Combine the stuffing mix and butter. Spread half of the stuffing mixture in the bottom of a 9 x 13-inch baking dish. Spoon the vegetable mixture on top. Top with the remaining stuffing. Bake at 350° for 25 to 30 minutes.

Serves 6.

1	bag salad greens
Favorite salad toppings	
Favorite salad dressing	

GREEN SALAD

Place salad greens in serving bowls. Add toppings and drizzle with dressing.

 Time Saver *Chop an additional 3 onions to use through the week. Start cooking squash first.*

Best Chicken Salad

BREADSTICKS

Prep Time: 30 minutes • Total Time: 30 minutes

3 boneless chicken breasts
1 tablespoon minced onion
1 teaspoon salt
2 tablespoons lemon juice
1 cup thinly sliced celery
1 cup seedless grapes
1/3 to 1/2 cup mayonnaise
1 can drained mandarin oranges
1/2 cup slivered almonds
2 eggs, hard-boiled
1 can sliced olives

BEST CHICKEN SALAD

Boil the chicken; let cool, dice. Mix all ingredients. Chill and serve. Garnish with ripe olives and/or hard-boiled eggs.

Serves 4.

1 package prepared breadsticks

BREADSTICKS

Mexican Prawns and Pineapple

RICE · STEAMED BROCCOLI AND CAULIFLOWER

Prep Time: 15 minutes • Total Time: 1 hour

3　tablespoons butter
1　pound uncooked large prawns or shrimp, shelled and deveined
1　small green bell pepper, seeded and cut into 1/4-inch rings
4　slices fresh pineapple or 1 14-ounce can pineapple slices, drained
Salt
Freshly ground black pepper
2　teaspoons chili powder, or to taste

MEXICAN PRAWNS AND PINEAPPLE

In a skillet melt the butter over medium heat. Add the prawns, green pepper, and pineapple. Season generously with salt, pepper, and chili powder. Sauté, turning just until the shrimp turn pink and are tender and the green pepper is crisp-tender, about 8 to 10 minutes.

Serves 4.

2　cups water
2　cups instant rice

RICE

Bring the water to a boil. Stir in the rice, cover, and remove from heat. Let stand for 5 minutes or until the water is absorbed. Fluff with a fork.

Serves 4.

1　pound broccoli
1　pound cauliflower

STEAMED BROCCOLI AND CAULIFLOWER

Place the broccoli and cauliflower in a steamer above an inch or two of salted water. Cover and steam for 6 to 8 minutes or until crisp-tender.

Serves 6.

Blue Cheese Burgers

SANTA MARIA BEANS · GREEN SALAD

Prep Time: 15 minutes • Total Time: 30 minutes

1   pound ground beef
1/4 cup chopped onion
1/4 cup crumbled blue cheese
1   teaspoon salt
1/2 tablespoon Worcestershire sauce
1/2 loaf French bread
1/4 cup butter, softened
1/8 cup Dijon mustard

BLUE CHEESE BURGERS

Combine the first 5 ingredients. Shape the mixture into 5 oval patties slightly larger than the diameter of French loaf.

Cut the French loaf in 10 ½-inch slices (freeze any extra bread). Blend the butter and mustard; spread generously on 1 side of each bread slice. Reassemble the loaf, buttered sides together. Wrap in heavy foil; place on grill over medium coals 15 minutes. Broil the burgers 5 to 6 minutes; turn and broil about 5 minutes. Serve between slices of bread.

Serves 5.

---

2   15-ounce cans pinquitos beans
1/4 pound bacon, diced
1   clove garlic, minced

SANTA MARIA BEANS

Place the beans in a pot. In a skillet sauté the bacon and garlic. Add to the beans when the bacon is cooked. Simmer 20 minutes.

Serves 5 to 6.

---

1   bag salad greens
Favorite salad toppings
Favorite low-fat or nonfat dressing

GREEN SALAD

Place salad greens in serving bowls. Add toppings and drizzle with the dressing.

Chicken with Rice

SPINACH SANTA CRUZ · SLICED PEACHES

Prep Time: 30 minutes • Total Time: 1 hour 30 minutes

1	4-pound frying chicken, cut into serving pieces
1¼	teaspoon salt
½	teaspoon pepper
⅛	teaspoon paprika
¼	cup olive oil
1	clove garlic, minced
1	medium onion, chopped
2	cups water
3½	cups canned whole tomatoes
2	chicken bouillon cubes
¼	teaspoon powdered saffron
1	bay leaf
2	cups raw rice
1	package frozen peas
3	pimentos, cut in pieces

CHICKEN WITH RICE

Season the chicken with salt, pepper, and paprika. In a skillet heat the oil, add the chicken and brown all sides. Remove the chicken. Add the garlic and onion to the skillet and sauté until the onion is tender. Add the water and heat. Add the tomatoes, bouillon cubes, and seasonings. Bring to a boil. Add the chicken. Add the rice and stir. Cover tightly and cook for 30 minutes or until the rice is cooked.

Uncover and add the peas and pimentos. Cook 10 minutes longer.

Serves 4 to 6.

3	10-ounce packages frozen chopped spinach
1	pint sour cream
1	envelope onion soup (dry mix)
1	2.8-ounce can French fried onions

SPINACH SANTA CRUZ

Cook the spinach according to the package directions; drain well. Stir in the sour cream and soup mix. Pour into a greased 7½ x 11½-inch baking dish. Bake at 350° for 20 minutes. Remove the pan from the oven; sprinkle canned onions over the top. Bake for an additional 10 minutes.

Serves 6 to 8.

4 to 6 fresh peaches

SLICED PEACHES

Slice the peaches and place in a serving bowl.

 Time Saver *Mince an additional 2 cloves garlic for Day 4.*

Lemon Chicken

RICE · SLICED APPLES AND PEARS

Prep Time: 5 minutes • Total Time: 20 minutes

4	boneless chicken breast halves
1/4	cup flour
1	tablespoon oil
1	cup chicken broth
1 1/3	cups fried onions
1	tablespoon lemon juice
4	thin slices lemon

LEMON CHICKEN

Coat the chicken in flour. In a skillet heat the oil and cook the chicken for 10 minutes, until well browned on both sides. Stir in the chicken broth, 2/3 cup of onions, lemon juice, and lemon slices. Heat to boiling. Simmer, covered, for 5 minutes until the chicken is no longer pink and sauce thickens slightly, stirring. Top with the remaining onions.

Serves 4.

2	cups water
2	cups instant rice

RICE

Bring the water to a boil. Stir in the rice, cover, and remove from the heat. Let stand for 5 minutes or until the water is absorbed. Fluff with a fork.

Serves 4.

3	apples
3	pears

SLICED APPLES AND PEARS

Slice the fruit and place in a serving bowl.

Time Saver *Prepare Day 2's lasagna sauce tonight.*

Lasagna Belmonte

GREEN SALAD · FRENCH BREAD

Prep Time: 30 minutes · Total Time: 30 minutes, plus all day in crock pot

1	medium onion, chopped
3	tablespoons olive or salad oil
1½	pounds ground beef
2	8-ounce cans tomato sauce
1	6-ounce can tomato paste
½	cup each: dry red wine and water
½	teaspoon each: salt, pepper, sugar
1½	teaspoons each: oregano, basil, and parsley
1	package spaghetti sauce mix
12	ounces lasagna noodles
1½	to 2 pounds mozzarella cheese, grated
2	cups ricotta cheese
1	egg (mix with ricotta; sometimes I add a little cottage cheese to the ricotta-egg mix)
½	cup Parmesan cheese

LASAGNA BELMONTE

In a large skillet or Dutch oven with cover, cook the onion in oil until soft. Add the beef and cook until brown, then stir in the tomato sauce, paste, wine, and water. Add the seasonings and spaghetti sauce mix, stirring until mixed. Cover. Simmer in a crock pot all day on low or 1½ hours on stovetop.

Meanwhile cook the noodles as directed on the package (15 minutes), drain. Rinse with cold water, pat dry. Arrange ⅓ of the noodles in the bottom of a lasagna pan. Spread ⅓ of the sauce over the noodles, then ⅓ of the ricotta and ⅓ of the mozzarella. Repeat layering 2 more times. Top with Parmesan. Bake at 350° uncovered for 30 minutes until the cheese melts and sauce bubbles.

Serves 6.

---

1 bag salad greens
Favorite salad toppings
Favorite low-fat or nonfat dressing

GREEN SALAD

Place salad greens in serving bowls. Add toppings and drizzle with dressing.

---

1 loaf French bread
Butter
Garlic or garlic powder
Parmesan cheese

FRENCH BREAD

Slice the French bread. Brush with butter and sprinkle with Parmesan and garlic. Place on a baking sheet and toast in the oven.

Time Saver *Chop ½ onion for use on Day 3. Cook sauce in crock pot all day on low for quick assembly at dinner time.*

Mom's Meat Loaf

MOM'S MACARONI AND CHEESE · APPLESAUCE

Prep Time: 30 minutes • Total Time: 1 hour 30 minutes

1½ pounds ground beef
½ cup chopped onion
½ cup chopped bell pepper
¾ cup oats
1 egg
2 teaspoons Worcestershire sauce
1 teaspoon salt
¼ teaspoon pepper
½ cup milk
1 teaspoon mustard
¼ cup tomato sauce

SAUCE:
1 cup tomato sauce
1 tablespoon mustard
1 teaspoon Worcestershire sauce
¼ cup catsup
¼ cup packed brown sugar

MOM'S MEAT LOAF

In a large bowl combine all of the meat loaf ingredients. Shape into a loaf and place in an oblong pan.

Combine the sauce ingredients and pour over the loaf. Bake at 350° for 1 hour.

Serves 4 to 6.

1½ cups uncooked elbow macaroni
5 tablespoons butter or margarine, divided
3 tablespoons all-purpose flour
1½ cups milk
1 cup shredded Cheddar cheese
2 ounces process American cheese, cubed
½ teaspoon salt
¼ teaspoon pepper
2 tablespoons dry bread crumbs

MOM'S MACARONI AND CHEESE

Cook the macaroni according to package directions; drain. Place in a greased 1½-quart baking dish; set aside. In a saucepan melt 4 tablespoons of butter over medium heat. Stir in the flour until smooth. Gradually add the milk, and bring to a boil. Cook and stir for 2 minutes; reduce the heat. Stir in the cheeses, salt, and pepper until cheese is melted. Pour over the macaroni; mix well. Melt the remaining butter; add the bread crumbs. Sprinkle over the casserole. Bake uncovered at 350° for 30 minutes.

Serves 6.

---

1 jar old-fashioned chunky cinnamon applesauce

APPLESAUCE

Serve hot or cold.

Smothered Steak

MASHED POTATOES · GREEN BEANS

Prep Time: 15 minutes • Total Time: 1 hour 15 minutes

2	pounds round or cubed steak
1	tablespoon oil
1/4	onion, chopped
1	clove garlic, pressed
1	10½-ounce can cream of mushroom soup
1	4-ounce can sliced mushrooms, undrained
2	tablespoons Worcestershire sauce
1	teaspoon catsup, or to taste

Steak sauce, to taste
Seasoned salt

SMOTHERED STEAK

Tenderize the meat with a tenderizer or the back of a butcher knife. Flour and brown the round steak in oil. Add the onion and garlic. Add the mushrooms, soup, water, Worcestershire, catsup, and steak sauce. Season with seasoned salt and cover the meat with liquid. Add enough water to do so. Cook until tender on simmer, about 1 hour.

1	box instant mashed potatoes

MASHED POTATOES

Prepare instant potatoes as directed for 6 servings.

2	16-ounce cans cut green beans
2	slices bacon, chopped

Fresh diced onion, if desired

GREEN BEANS

In a large saucepan place the green beans, bacon, and onion. Cook according to the directions on the can.

Time Saver *Marinate tomorrow's chicken.*

Chicken Kebabs

RICE PILAF · CORN ON THE COB · FRENCH BREAD

Prep Time: 30 minutes • Total Time: 35 minutes

1/4 cup butter, melted
1 cup catsup
2 tablespoons chili powder
1/4 cup lemon juice
1/2 cup water
1 tablespoon Worcestershire sauce
1 1/2 tablespoons dry mustard
1 clove garlic, minced
1/4 cup white vinegar
1 tablespoon sugar
3 to 4 boneless, skinless chicken breasts, cut in kabob-size chunks
1 onion, cut in chunks
1 can pineapple chunks
1 red and green bell pepper
12 mushrooms

CHICKEN KEBABS

In a medium bowl combine the butter, catsup, chili powder, lemon juice, water, Worcestershire sauce, dry mustard, garlic, vinegar, and sugar.

Place the chicken, onion, pineapple, bell pepper, and mushrooms on skewers.

Marinate the chicken and vegetables in the barbecue sauce for about 1 hour.

Barbecue on the grill for 15 to 20 minutes, turning frequently.

Serves 4 to 6.

---

1 package rice pilaf

RICE PILAF

Cook as directed on the package.

---

6 ears fresh or frozen corn

CORN ON THE COB

Fresh or frozen—your choice. If frozen, follow the package directions. For fresh, boil water, add the corn, and cook for 5 to 8 minutes, until tender. Do not overcook.

---

1 loaf ready-to-heat French bread

FRENCH BREAD

Easy-Mix Casserole

OVEN-FRIED EGGPLANT · SLICED PLUMS

Prep Time: 30 minutes • Total Time: 1 hour 15 minutes

3 pounds ground beef, browned (1 pound for Day 5)

8 ounces spaghetti, broken, or elbow macaroni

1 package onion soup mix

1 tablespoon soy sauce

4 dashes hot sauce

1 package cream of mushroom soup mix

1 tablespoon Worcestershire sauce

½ pound mushrooms, chopped and sautéed (optional)

2 10¾-ounce cans cream of tomato soup, undiluted

½ soup can water

EASY-MIX CASSEROLE

Reserve 1 pound of beef for Day 5. Cook the spaghetti or elbow macaroni according to the package directions. Add the remaining ingredients to the browned ground chuck. Mix with the cooked pasta. Transfer to a lightly greased casserole. Bake uncovered at 350° for approximately 30 minutes or until hot.

Serves 6 to 8.

1 cup crushed salted soda crackers

½ cup Parmesan cheese

2 medium eggplants (about 20 ounces), peeled and cut in ½-inch slices

Lemon wedges (optional)

Buttermilk dressing (optional)

OVEN-FRIED EGGPLANT

Mix together the soda crackers and Parmesan cheese. Press the eggplant slices into the cracker mixture, then arrange in a single layer on an ungreased baking sheet. Bake at 350°, turning after 20 minutes, and continue cooking until light brown, about 25 minutes total. Serve with lemon wedges or a dollop of buttermilk dressing.

Serves 6.

Plums

SLICED PLUMS

Time Saver *Start with the eggplant for today's meal. Refrigerate 1 pound ground beef for Day 5.*

Quick and Easy Frypan Chicken

ZESTY ZUCCHINI SAUTÉ · FRENCH BREAD

Prep Time: 30 minutes • Total Time: 1 hour 35 minutes

1 clove garlic
3½- to 4-pound frying chicken, cut up
2 tablespoons olive oil
1 tablespoon flour
1 tablespoon tomato paste
2 tablespoons white wine
1 cup chicken bouillon or broth
¼ pound mushrooms, sliced
10 pimento-stuffed olives
1 green bell pepper, cut in thin strips
1 sweet red bell pepper, cut in thin strips or 1 small jar pimento, cut in thin strips
Salt and pepper to taste

QUICK AND EASY FRYPAN CHICKEN

Cut the clove of garlic into 3 or 4 slices. Rub the chicken with the garlic. In an electric skillet brown the chicken pieces in olive oil at 360°. Reduce the temperature to 220°. Combine the flour, tomato paste, wine, and bouillon; add to the chicken in the skillet. Add the mushrooms, olives, green and red pepper. Season to taste. Continue to cook at 220° for about 45 minutes.

Serves 4.

4 medium-sized zucchini
2 teaspoons seasoned salt
2 teaspoons parsley flakes
1 teaspoon instant minced onion
½ teaspoon ground oregano
¼ teaspoon garlic powder
¼ teaspoon pepper
¼ cup olive oil

ZESTY ZUCCHINI SAUTÉ

Wash the zucchini, but do not peel. Slice in rounds about ¼-inch thick. Mix together the remaining ingredients except the olive oil. Sprinkle over the zucchini and toss until the seasoning is well distributed. In a skillet heat the oil; add the zucchini and sauté until browned on both sides, about 10 minutes. Drain on absorbent paper.

Serves 4.

1 loaf ready-to-heat French bread

FRENCH BREAD

Heat as directed on the package.

 Prepare tomorrow's salad if time permits or prepare first thing in the morning.

Oriental Seafood Salad

FRENCH BREAD

Prep Time: 15 minutes • Total Time: 8 hours 15 minutes if not prepared ahead

1   9-ounce package frozen peas and pearl onions
½   cup small water chestnuts, sliced, drained
½   pound bay shrimp, cooked
½   cup sliced celery
¼   pound crab, cooked
½   cup bean sprouts
1   tablespoon fresh lemon juice
¼ to ⅓ cup mayonnaise
½   teaspoon soy sauce
⅛   teaspoon curry powder
1   tablespoon lemon juice
½   teaspoon salt

ORIENTAL SEAFOOD SALAD

In a large bowl combine the peas, water chestnuts, shrimp, celery, crab, and bean sprouts. Squeeze the lemon juice over all. In a separate bowl combine the remaining ingredients and mix well. Pour over the salad. Toss when finished. Refrigerate overnight. Toss again.

Serves 4.

Note: Best when done a day ahead.

1   loaf French bread
Butter

FRENCH BREAD

Chicken and Wild Rice

BAKED TOMATO HALVES · SLICED PEACHES

Prep Time: 20 minutes • Total Time: 1 hour 10 minutes

1 6-ounce package seasoned long grain and wild rice mix
2⅓ cups water
1 2.8-ounce can French fried onions
4 chicken breast halves or 2 pounds chicken pieces, fat trimmed, skinned, if desired
½ teaspoon seasoned salt
1 10-ounce package frozen peas

CHICKEN AND WILD RICE

Preheat the oven to 375°. In a 9 x 13-inch baking dish combine the uncooked rice and contents of the rice seasoning packet; stir in ½ can of fried onions. Arrange the chicken on the rice; pour the water over all. Sprinkle the chicken with seasoned salt. Bake, covered, at 375° for 40 minutes.

Stir the peas into rice. Bake, uncovered, 10 minutes or until the chicken and peas are done. Top the chicken with the remaining onions; bake, uncovered, 3 minutes or until the onions are golden brown.

Serves 4.

2 large tomatoes
4 tablespoons butter
¼ cup onion, finely chopped
1 teaspoon prepared mustard
½ teaspoon Worcestershire sauce
2 tablespoons herbed stuffing mix
2 teaspoons parsley, chopped

BAKED TOMATO HALVES

Cut the tomatoes in half crosswise. Place cut side up in a shallow baking dish. In 2 tablespoons of butter, sauté the onion until tender. Stir in the mustard and Worcestershire sauce. Spread on the tomatoes. Melt the remaining 2 tablespoons of butter and stir in the stuffing mix and parsley. Top each tomato half with a bit of the stuffing and parsley mixture. Bake uncovered at 375° for 15 minutes or until crumbs are crisp.

Serves 4.

1 can sliced peaches

SLICED PEACHES

Tostadas

CHIPS AND SALSA

Prep Time: 20 minutes • Total Time: 40 minutes

1 pound ground beef
1 package flour tortillas
1 tomato, chopped
1 16-ounce can refried beans
1 4-ounce can sliced olives
1 cup grated Cheddar cheese
1 to 3 tablespoons oil
¼ head lettuce, shredded

TOSTADAS

Brown the ground beef; drain. Fry the tortillas until crisp. Heat the refried beans. Top the tortillas with each ingredient in the listed order.

Serves 4 to 6.

1 bag tortilla chips
1 jar salsa

CHIPS AND SALSA

Pasta with Chicken and Squash

GREEN SALAD

Prep Time: 30 minutes • Total Time: 50 minutes

1	16-ounce package spiral pasta
2	cups whipping cream
1	tablespoon butter or margarine
2	cups grated Cheddar cheese
1	small onion, chopped
1	garlic clove, minced
5	tablespoons olive or vegetable oil, divided
2	medium yellow summer squash, julienned
2	medium zucchini, julienned
1¼	teaspoons salt, divided
⅛	teaspoon pepper
1	pound boneless skinless chicken breasts, julienned
¼	teaspoon each: dried basil, marjoram, and savory
¼	teaspoon dried rosemary, crushed
⅛	teaspoon rubbed sage

PASTA WITH CHICKEN AND SQUASH

Cook the pasta according to the package directions. Meanwhile, heat the cream and butter in a large saucepan until the butter melts. Add the cheese; cook and stir until melted. Rinse and drain the pasta; add to the cheese mixture. Cover and keep warm. In a skillet over medium heat sauté the onion and garlic in 3 tablespoons of oil until the onion is tender. Add the squash and zucchini; cook until tender. Add 1 teaspoon of salt and pepper; remove and keep warm. Add the remaining oil to the skillet; cook the chicken with the herbs and remaining salt until the juices run clear. Place the pasta on a serving platter; top with chicken and squash.

Serves 8.

1	bag salad greens
	Favorite salad toppings
	Favorite low-fat or nonfat dressing

GREEN SALAD

Place salad greens in serving bowls. Add toppings and drizzle with dressing.

Time Saver *Grate 1 cup Cheddar cheese for use on Day 2. Chop 3 onions for use throughout the week. Mince 4 garlic cloves for use on Days 3 and 4. Thaw hash browns for Day 2.*

Pork Chops O'Brien

GREEN BEANS · DINNER ROLLS

Prep Time: 15 minutes • Total Time: 1 hour

6	pork loin chops, ½-inch thick
1	tablespoon cooking oil
1	10¾-ounce can condensed cream of celery soup, undiluted
½	cup milk
½	cup sour cream
¼	teaspoon pepper
1	cup grated Cheddar cheese, divided
1	2.8-ounce can French fried onions, divided
1	24-ounce package frozen hash brown potatoes, thawed
½	teaspoon seasoned salt

PORK CHOPS O'BRIEN

In a skillet over medium-high heat brown the pork chops in oil; set aside. Combine the soup, milk, sour cream, pepper, ½ cup of cheese and ½ cup of onions. Fold in the potatoes. Spread in a greased 13 x 9-inch baking dish. Arrange the chops on top, sprinkle with seasoned salt. Cover and bake at 350° for 40 to 45 minutes or until the pork is tender.

Uncover, sprinkle with the remaining cheese and onions. Return to the oven for 5 to 10 minutes or until the cheese melts.

Serves 6.

---

1   bag frozen green beans

GREEN BEANS

Prepare as directed on the package.

---

1   package prepared dinner rolls
Butter

DINNER ROLLS

Warm the rolls and serve with butter.

Garlic Swiss Steak

LEMON-GLAZED CARROTS · DINNER ROLLS

Prep Time: 20 minutes • Total Time: 1 hour 50 minutes

1½ pounds bone-in round steak
⅓ cup all-purpose flour
1 teaspoon salt
½ teaspoon pepper
2 tablespoons vegetable oil
1 14½-ounce can stewed tomatoes
1 small onion, chopped
½ medium green bell pepper, chopped
2 garlic cloves, minced

GARLIC SWISS STEAK

Cut the steak into serving-size pieces; discard the bone. Combine the flour, salt, and pepper; sprinkle over the steak and pound into both sides. In a large skillet over medium heat brown steak on both sides in oil. Transfer to a greased 13 x 9-inch baking dish. Combine the tomatoes, onion, green pepper, and garlic; pour over the steak. Cover and bake at 350° for 1½ hours or until tender.

Serves 6.

1½ pounds medium carrots, cut into
    ½-inch diagonal slices
3 tablespoons butter or margarine
3 tablespoons brown sugar
3 tablespoons lemon juice
¼ teaspoon salt
Grated lemon peel (optional)

LEMON-GLAZED CARROTS

Place the carrots in a saucepan, cover with water, and bring to a boil. Reduce the heat, cover, and simmer for 10 to 12 minutes or until crisp-tender.

Meanwhile, in a small saucepan melt the butter. Add the brown sugar, lemon juice, and salt; bring to a boil, stirring constantly. Drain the carrots; add the butter mixture and toss gently. Garnish with lemon peel, if desired.

Serves 6.

1 package prepared dinner rolls
Butter

DINNER ROLLS

Warm the rolls and serve with butter.

Turkey Minestrone

DINNER ROLLS

Prep Time: 30 minutes • Total Time: 30 minutes

1½ cups elbow macaroni
⅔ cup chopped onion
2 tablespoons vegetable oil
½ pound ground turkey
½ pound hot Italian turkey links, casings removed
½ cup minced fresh parsley
2 garlic cloves, minced
1 teaspoon dried oregano
1 teaspoon dried basil
2 14½-ounce cans Italian stewed tomatoes
6 cups chicken broth
1 medium zucchini, sliced
1 10-ounce package frozen mixed vegetables
1 16-ounce can kidney beans, rinsed and drained
2 tablespoons cider vinegar
½ teaspoon salt (optional)
Pinch pepper

TURKEY MINESTRONE

Cook the noodles according to the package directions. Meanwhile, in a large kettle over medium heat sauté the onion in oil until tender, about 4 minutes. Add the next 6 ingredients; cook until the meat is no longer pink. Add the tomatoes, broth, zucchini, and mixed vegetables; cover and cook on low heat for 5 minutes. Add the beans, macaroni, vinegar, salt if desired, and pepper; simmer for 3 to 4 minutes or until heated through.

Serves 16.

1 package prepared dinner rolls
Butter

DINNER ROLLS

Warm the rolls and serve with butter.

Dugout Hot Dogs

BALLPARK BAKED BEANS · CORN CHIPS

Prep Time: 20 minutes • Total Time: 40 minutes

¾ cup catsup
2 to 4 tablespoons chopped onion
2 tablespoons brown sugar
2 tablespoons cider vinegar
10 hot dogs
10 hot dog buns, split
Relish
Mustard

DUGOUT HOT DOGS

In a saucepan combine the catsup, onion, sugar, and vinegar. Simmer 2 to 3 minutes. Add the hot dogs; simmer 5 to 10 minutes longer or until heated through. Serve on buns topped with the relish and mustard.

Serves 10.

---

2 16-ounce cans baked beans
¼ cup brown sugar, packed
2 tablespoons catsup
2 teaspoons prepared mustard
1 20-ounce can pineapple tidbits, drained

BALLPARK BAKED BEANS

In a 2-quart baking dish combine the beans, brown sugar, catsup, and mustard. Bake uncovered at 350° for 30 minutes.

Stir in the pineapple; bake 30 minutes longer. Serves 10.

---

1 bag corn chips

CORN CHIPS

Or other chips of your choice.

Fantastic Chicken

STUFFED MUSHROOMS · FRENCH BREAD

Prep Time: 30 minutes • Total Time: 2 hours

1	8-ounce jar apricot preserves
1	bottle Russian salad dressing
1	package dry onion soup mix
3	broiler chickens, quartered

FANTASTIC CHICKEN

Mix together the preserves, salad dressing, and onion soup mix. Spread the chicken pieces in 9 x 13-inch baking pan. Spoon the sauce over the chicken. Bake at 350° for 1½ hours.

Serves 6.

24	medium mushrooms
4	tablespoons butter, divided
2	teaspoons vermouth
1	clove garlic, minced
2	tablespoons parsley, chopped
½	teaspoon salt
1	cup crushed pecans

STUFFED MUSHROOMS

Wipe the mushrooms. Remove the stems and chop. In a saucepan melt 2 tablespoons of butter in saucepan and sauté all ingredients except the pecans for 10 minutes. Add the pecans, mix, and stuff the caps. Melt 2 tablespoons of butter in a 9 x 13-inch baking dish, add the mushrooms. Bake at 350° for 12 to 15 minutes.

1	loaf French bread
Butter	

FRENCH BREAD

Time Saver *Save remaining chicken for Day 4. Cut and marinate beef for Day 2. Mince an additional 3 cloves of garlic for Day 2. Reserve one broiler chicken for Day 4.*

Beef Teriyaki

WHITE RICE · GARLIC TOMATOES

Prep Time: 20 minutes • Total Time: 50 minutes

1	pound sirloin beef, cut 1-inch thick
2	tablespoons lemon juice
¾	cup soy sauce
1	teaspoon ground ginger
¼	cup dark brown sugar, packed
½	teaspoon garlic powder
½	teaspoon onion salt
1	8-ounce can pineapple chunks

BEEF TERIYAKI

Cut the meat into bite-sized cubes. Combine the remaining ingredients; pour over the beef cubes and let stand at room temperature for 1 hour or in the refrigerator for several hours. Thread cubes of meat onto a skewer (pineapple chunks alternated with the beef cubes). Broil about 3 inches from the heat for 10 to 12 minutes, turning once, or cook over a grill.

Serves 4 to 6.

3	cups water
3	cups instant rice

WHITE RICE

Bring the water to a boil. Sir in the rice; cover and remove from the heat. Let stand 5 minutes or until the water is absorbed. Fluff with fork.

Serves 6.

4	fresh tomatoes
½	cup seasoned herb stuffing mix, crushed into crumbs
4	tablespoons melted butter
3	large cloves fresh garlic, minced
½	teaspoon basil
	Salt and pepper, to taste
	Fresh minced parsley

GARLIC TOMATOES

Cut the tomatoes into halves. Moisten the stuffing crumbs with a mixture of butter, garlic, basil, and seasonings. Place the crumb mixture on the tomato halves and broil under a preheated broiler 10 inches from the heat, until browned and heated.

Garnish with minced parsley and serve.

Serves 4.

 Prepare tomorrow's salad or prepare it first thing.

Sesame Shrimp

FRUIT SALAD · FRENCH BREAD

Prep Time: 20 minutes • Total Time: 30 minutes

½	teaspoon ground ginger root
1	cup barbecue sauce
⅛	teaspoon sesame oil
⅛	cup soy sauce
2	pounds jumbo shrimp

SESAME SHRIMP

Mix all ingredients. Grill or broil the shrimp, brushing frequently with sauce, for 10 to 15 minutes, until no longer pink.

Serves 4 to 6.

1	16-ounce can whole berry cranberry sauce
¾	cup sugar
½	package miniature marshmallows
1	14-ounce can crushed pineapple
1	cup chopped walnuts
½	pint whipping cream

FRUIT SALAD

In a large bowl mix the first 5 ingredients. Whip the cream and fold in with the rest of the ingredients. Chill in the refrigerator for several hours or overnight.

Serves 4 to 6.

1	loaf French bread
Butter	

FRENCH BREAD

Chicken Salad

WON TONS

Prep Time: 20 minutes • Total Time: 20 minutes

Lettuce leaves
1   cooked chicken, boned and cubed
1   11-ounce can mandarin oranges,
    drained
1   green bell pepper, thinly sliced
2 to 3 stalks celery, thinly sliced
1   8-ounce can pineapple chunks,
    drained
1   8-ounce can water chestnuts,
    drained and sliced
Salt and pepper to taste
Sliced almonds for garnish

CHICKEN SALAD

Line a shallow bowl with lettuce leaves. In a separate bowl combine the remaining ingredients except the almonds. Transfer to the lettuce-lined bowl.

Garnish with almonds.

Serves 4 to 6.

DRESSING:

Mayonnaise, thinned with lemon juice and seasoned with curry.

---

1   can won tons

WON TONS

Time Saver *Chop an additional 1/2 cup of celery for Day 5. Hard-boil eggs for Day 5.*

Tuna Salad Submarines

POTATO CHIPS • WATERMELON

Prep Time: 30 minutes • Total Time: 40 minutes

---

1   6- to 7-ounce can tuna
2   hard-boiled eggs, chopped
1/2 cup chopped celery
1/4 cup chopped sweet pickle relish
1/2 cup salad dressing or mayonnaise
1/2 teaspoon prepared mustard
6 to 8 French rolls
Soft butter or margarine

TUNA SALAD SUBMARINE

Place the tuna in a mixing bowl. Break up any chunks with a fork. Add the chopped eggs, celery, pickle relish, salad dressing, and mustard. If using pickle relish, drain well before adding or the filling will be soupy. Toss with a fork to mix well. If the rolls are not already split, cut them in half lengthwise.

Spread the buns with softened butter or margarine. Stuff with filling.

Tuna salad submarines are also good warmed. You may even like them better this way! Wrap in foil and heat for 15 minutes in a 350° oven.

Makes 6 to 8 sandwiches.

---

1   bag potato chips

POTATO CHIPS

Watermelon

WATERMELON

Slice into wedges.

Skillet Italiano

GREEN SALAD · GARLIC BREAD

Prep Time: 15 minutes • Total Time: 35 minutes

1   pound lean ground beef
2   cloves garlic, minced
1   onion, chopped
$^1/_2$ green bell pepper, chopped
Salt and pepper, to taste
$1^1/_2$ to 2 teaspoons each: thyme and
    Italian seasoning
2   16-ounce cans tomatoes, crushed
1   8-ounce can tomato sauce
2   cups red wine
$3^1/_2$ to 4 cups uncooked rigatoni
2   cups water

SKILLET ITALIANO

In an electric skillet brown the ground beef and garlic, stirring until crumbly; drain. Add the onion and green pepper, and sauté until tender. Stir in the seasonings, tomatoes, tomato sauce, wine, and rigatoni. Cook over medium heat for 10 minutes, stirring occasionally. Add water. Cook for 15 to 20 minutes longer.

Serves 6.

1   bag salad greens
Favorite salad toppings
Favorite low-fat or nonfat dressing

GREEN SALAD

Place salad greens in serving bowls. Add toppings and drizzle with dressing.

1   loaf ready-to-heat garlic bread

GARLIC BREAD

Heat the bread according to the package directions.

Time Saver *Mince 1 garlic clove for use on Day 4. Chop $^1/_2$ onion for use on Day 3. Chop an additional green pepper for use on Day 3 and 4.*

Chili Dogs

SLICED PLUMS · POTATO CHIPS

Prep Time: 15 minutes • Total Time: 35 minutes

---

2   15-ounce cans chili beans
1   8-ounce can tomato sauce
¼   teaspoon chili powder
¼   teaspoon cumin
⅛   teaspoon cayenne pepper
12 frankfurters
6   slices American cheese, cut into 36 strips

CHILI DOGS

Preheat the oven to 400°. In a bowl combine the beans, tomato sauce, and seasonings; mix well. Pour into a 7 x 11-inch baking pan. Make 3 diagonal ½-inch-deep slits in each frankfurter. Insert cheese strips into the slits. Arrange over the bean mixture. Bake for 20 minutes.

Serves 4 to 5.

Plums

SLICED PLUMS

---

1   bag potato chips

POTATO CHIPS

Gourmet Chicken Salad

CROISSANTS

Prep Time: 30 minutes • Total Time: 1 hour 30 minutes

½ cup mayonnaise
2 teaspoons mustard
2 cooked chicken breasts, chopped
½ cup thinly sliced celery
¼ cup chopped green bell pepper
1 tablespoon finely chopped onion
½ cup sliced mushrooms
1 4-ounce can chopped black olives
1 cup green or red grape halves
1 20-ounce can pineapple chunks, drained
1 11-ounce can mandarin oranges, drained
Lettuce cups
Croutons

GOURMET CHICKEN SALAD

In a salad bowl mix the mayonnaise and mustard. Add the chicken, vegetables, and olives; mix well. Chill in the refrigerator for 1 hour.

Add the fruits; mix gently; serve in lettuce cups; top with croutons. Serve with croissants.

Serves 6.

6 croissants

CROISSANTS

Barbecue Steaks

CONFETTI PASTA SALAD · GARLIC BREAD

Prep Time: 20 minutes • Total Time: 1 hour

6   steaks
Salt and pepper to taste
Marinade or barbecue sauce, your
    favorite (optional)

BARBECUE STEAKS

Choose your favorite cut of steak and season accordingly to barbecue. Marinate if desired. Grill over hot coals.

---

12   ounces uncooked tiny shell pasta
1½   cups chopped radishes
1½   cups drained canned corn
1   cup chopped green bell pepper
1   clove garlic, minced
1   cup mayonnaise
⅓   cup sour cream
1   tablespoon Dijon mustard
⅓   cup chopped fresh dill
Salt, cayenne pepper, and paprika to
    taste

CONFETTI PASTA SALAD

Cook pasta according to package directions; rinse and drain. Combine vegetables, garlic, mayonnaise, sour cream, and mustard in salad bowl; mix well. Add pasta, dill, salt, and cayenne pepper; mix well. Garnish with paprika. Chill until serving time, if desired.

Serves 8.

---

1   loaf ready-to-heat garlic bread

GARLIC BREAD

Heat according to the package directions.

Linguine-Tuna Salad

SLICED PEACHES · DINNER ROLLS

Prep Time: 25 minutes • Total Time: 1 hour

¼ cup lemon juice
¼ cup vegetable oil
¼ cup sliced green onions
2 teaspoons sugar
½ teaspoon hot sauce
1 teaspoon seasoned salt
1 teaspoon Italian seasoning
1 7-ounce package linguine, broken, cooked, drained
1 12-ounce can white tuna, drained
1 10-ounce package frozen green peas, thawed
2 medium tomatoes, chopped

LINGUINE-TUNA SALAD

In a large bowl mix the lemon juice, oil, green onions, sugar, hot sauce, and seasonings; mix well. Add the hot linguine; toss to mix well. Add the tuna, peas, and tomatoes; mix lightly. Chill until serving time, 30 minutes.

Serves 6.

Peaches

SLICED PEACHES

---

1 package prepared dinner rolls
Butter

DINNER ROLLS

Warm the rolls and serve with butter.

Asian Chicken

CHINESE CRISPY NOODLES · FRUIT

Prep Time: 30 minutes • Total Time: 40 minutes

3	tablespoons peanut oil
1	5-pound frying chicken, cut into serving pieces, or the equivalent in chicken parts of your choice
2	small dried hot red peppers (optional)
¾	cup distilled white vinegar
¼	cup soy sauce
1	bulb (not clove) fresh garlic, peeled and coarsely chopped
3	tablespoons honey

ASIAN CHICKEN

In a large, heavy skillet heat the oil and brown the chicken well on all sides, adding the garlic and peppers toward the end. Add the remaining ingredients and cook over medium high heat until the chicken is done and the sauce has been reduced somewhat. This will not take long, less than 10 minutes. If you are cooking both white and dark meat, remove the white meat first, so it does not dry out. Watch very carefully so that the sauce does not burn or boil away. There should be a quantity of sauce left to serve with the chicken, and the chicken should appear slightly glazed.

Serves 4 to 6.

Chinese crispy noodles

CHINESE CRISPY NOODLES

Your favorite fruit, sliced and mixed

FRUIT

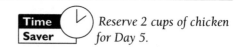

Time Saver *Reserve 2 cups of chicken for Day 5.*

Mock Pizza

GREEN SALAD

Prep Time: 20 minutes • Total Time: 20 minutes

½ pound Cheddar cheese, grated
1 4-ounce can chilies
½ pound Jack cheese, grated
1 4-ounce can sliced mushrooms, drained
1 10½-ounce can pizza sauce
1 small can sliced olives
¼ cup salad oil
1 package English muffins

MOCK PIZZA

Mix all of the above ingredients except the muffins thoroughly. Pile on split English muffin and broil until hot and bubbling.

Serves 6.

1 bag salad greens
Favorite salad toppings
Favorite low-fat or nonfat dressing

GREEN SALAD

Place salad greens in serving bowls. Add toppings and drizzle with dressing.

Vegetable-Beef Burgers

BAKED FRENCH FRIES

Prep Time: 30 minutes • Total Time: 1 hour

3	tablespoons vegetable oil
2	cups carrots, chopped
1	cup chopped onion
1	clove garlic, minced
2	cups chopped zucchini
2	cups chopped yellow squash
$1/4$	teaspoon salt, divided
$1/4$	teaspoon pepper, divided
1	pound ground beef
$2/3$	cup seasoned dry bread crumbs
1	egg, lightly beaten
2	tablespoons catsup
1	tablespoon red wine vinegar
$1/2$	teaspoon basil, crushed
$1/8$	teaspoon oregano, crushed

VEGETABLE-BEEF BURGERS

In a 10-inch skillet heat 2 tablespoons of oil over medium heat. Add the carrots, onion, and garlic. Cook, stirring often, for 5 minutes. Add the zucchini and squash. Cook, stirring often, 8 minutes or until soft. Stir in $1/8$ teaspoon of the salt and $1/8$ teaspoon of the pepper (yields 3 cups). Remove 1 cup of cooked vegetables into a large bowl; cool slightly. Transfer the remaining vegetables to an ovenproof dish and keep warm in the oven. To the 1 cup of vegetables add the beef, bread crumbs, egg, catsup, vinegar, basil, oregano and remaining $1/8$ teaspoon salt and $1/8$ teaspoon pepper. Stir until just blended. Form into 8 $3\frac{1}{2}$-inch patties. Rinse the skillet, wipe dry, and heat the remaining 1 tablespoon oil over medium-high heat. Cook 4 patties at a time, about 2 minutes on each side or until patties reach desired degree of doneness, adding additional oil if necessary. Keep warm in oven with remaining cooked vegetables. Serve with vegetables.

Serves 4.

continued on next page

4 medium potatoes

2 tablespoons unsalted butter or margarine, melted

BAKED FRENCH FRIES

Cut the potatoes lengthwise into strips about ½-inch thick. Soak in cold water 10 to 15 minutes, pat dry. Preheat the oven to 475°. Spread the potatoes in a shallow baking pan. Brush with half of the butter. Bake for 20 minutes.

Turn the potatoes; brush with the remaining butter. Bake 20 minutes or until tender.

Serves 4.

Time Saver *Chop an additional onion for Day 4. Shred an additional zucchini for Day 4.*

Stuffed Pasta Shells

SPINACH · DINNER ROLLS

Prep Time: 30 minutes • Total Time: 1 hour 25 minutes

½ 12-ounce package jumbo pasta shells
Vegetable cooking spray
1 medium onion, chopped
1 16-ounce container part-skim ricotta cheese
2 eggs, beaten
½ cup plain yogurt
1 large zucchini, grated and divided
½ teaspoon garlic powder
1 teaspoon salt
⅓ cup chopped parsley
6 tablespoons Parmesan cheese, divided
1 scallion, chopped

STUFFED PASTA SHELLS

Cook the shells in boiling salted water as directed on package; drain well. Spray a skillet with vegetable cooking spray, and sauté the onion until soft. Set aside. In a medium bowl mix the ricotta with the eggs until smooth. Add the sautéed onion. Reserve 2 tablespoons of the zucchini for the sauce and stir the rest into the ricotta mixture. Stir in the garlic powder, salt, parsley, and 3 tablespoons of the Parmesan cheese.

Preheat the oven to 350°. Spoon the filling into the shells and arrange the shells on the bottom of a 9 x 13-inch baking pan.

Next, make the sauce. Place the remaining filling in a blender. Add the yogurt and chopped scallion. Purée until smooth. Stir in the reserved zucchini; spoon over the filled shells. Top with the remaining Parmesan cheese. Bake for 30 minutes.

Serves 6.

---

1 16-ounce can spinach

SPINACH

Heat as directed on the can.

---

1 package prepared dinner rolls
Butter

DINNER ROLLS

Warm the rolls and serve with butter.

Chinese Chicken Salad

SLICED PEACHES AND PEARS

Prep Time: 20 minutes • Total Time: 20 minutes

2   cups chicken, from Day 1
Salt and freshly ground pepper
1   head iceberg lettuce, shredded
2   cups shredded spinach
1   onion, sliced
2   cups crisp rice noodles
1   cup sliced celery
1   tablespoon pickled ginger
1   tablespoon chopped cilantro
½   cup sliced toasted almonds
2   tablespoons chopped tomato
1   tablespoon toasted sesame seeds

VINAIGRETTE:
1½ cups rice vinegar
⅔   cup sesame oil
4   tablespoons soy sauce
½   tablespoon ground ginger
1   clove garlic, chopped
1   tablespoon sugar

CHINESE CHICKEN SALAD

Shred the chicken or slice thin. In a salad bowl combine the chicken with the shredded lettuce, spinach, onion, rice noodles, celery, pickled ginger, cilantro, and almonds. Prepare the vinaigrette by mixing all ingredients. Toss the chicken salad with the vinaigrette and divide among 4 serving plates. Garnish with chopped tomato and sesame seeds.

Serves 4.

Peaches
Pears

SLICED PEACHES AND PEARS

Barbecue Burgers

FRENCH FRIES · RANCH BEANS · FRESH FRUIT SALAD

Prep Time: 20 minutes • Total Time: 40 minutes

6 hamburger patties Salt, pepper, garlic powder Barbecue sauce Sliced cheese 6 hamburger buns	**BARBECUE BURGERS** Season the burgers and grill over hot coals. Baste with barbecue sauce. Melt the cheese over the burgers and toast the buns. Serve with lettuce, tomato, onion.

1 bag French fries	**FRENCH FRIES** Bake as directed on the package.

2 16-ounce cans ranch beans	**RANCH BEANS** Heat as directed on the can.

Grapes Honeydew Watermelon Apples Cantaloupe	**FRESH FRUIT SALAD** Dice and mix into a large salad bowl.

 Prepare tomorrow's sauce for crock pot tonight or in morning.

Lasagna Belmonte

GREEN SALAD · FRENCH BREAD

Prep Time: 30 minutes • Total Time: 1 hour

3 tablespoons olive or salad oil

1 medium onion, chopped

1½ pounds ground beef

1 clove garlic, minced

2 8-ounce cans tomato sauce

1 6-ounce can tomato paste

½ cup each: dry red wine and water

1½ teaspoons each: oregano, basil and parsley

½ teaspoon each: salt, pepper, sugar

1 package spaghetti sauce mix

1 12-ounce package lasagna noodles

1 pound or 2 cups ricotta cheese or cottage cheese

1 egg (mix with ricotta; sometimes I add a little cottage cheese to ricotta-egg mixture)

1½ to 2 pounds mozzarella cheese

½ cup Parmesan cheese

LASAGNA BELMONTE

In a large skillet or Dutch oven with cover heat the oil and cook the onion until soft. Add the beef and garlic. Cook until the meat is brown, then stir in the tomato sauce, paste, wine, and water. Add the seasonings and spaghetti sauce mix, stirring until mixed. Cover. Simmer in a crock pot all day on low or on stovetop for 1½ hours.

Meanwhile cook the noodles as directed on package for 15 minutes; drain. Rinse with cold water. Pat dry.

Arrange ⅓ of the noodles in the bottom of a lasagna pan. Spread ⅓ of the sauce over the noodles, then ⅓ of the ricotta and ⅓ of the mozzarella. Repeat layering 2 more times. Top with Parmesan. Bake at 350° uncovered for 30 minutes until the cheese melts and the sauce bubbles.

Serves 6.

---

1 bag salad greens

Favorite salad toppings

Favorite low-fat or nonfat dressing

GREEN SALAD

Place salad greens in serving bowls. Add toppings and drizzle with dressing.

---

1 loaf French bread, sliced open down the middle

½ cup melted margarine

Garlic or garlic powder

Parmesan cheese

FRENCH BREAD

Spread butter on the bread. Top with garlic and Parmesan. Bake until lightly toasted.

Time Saver *Chop 1¼ onions for use throughout the week.*

Smothered Steak

GREEN BEANS · MASHED POTATOES

Prep Time: 20 minutes • Total Time: 1 hour 15 minutes

---

1   tablespoon oil
Flour
2   pounds round or cubed steak
1/4   onion, chopped
1   clove garlic, pressed
1   4-ounce can sliced mushrooms, undrained
1   10½-ounce can cream of mushroom soup
½   soup can water
2   tablespoons Worcestershire sauce
1   teaspoon catsup, to taste
Steak sauce, to taste
Seasoning salt

SMOTHERED STEAK

In a large skillet heat the oil. Flour and brown the round steak. Add the onion and garlic. Add the mushrooms, soup, water, Worcestershire sauce, catsup, and steak sauce. Season with season salt and cover the meat with liquid, add enough water to do so. Cook until tender on simmer , about 1 hour.

Serves 6 to 8.

2½ to 3 pounds small green beans, washed and trimmed

GREEN BEANS

Bring a large pot of salted water to a boil. Place the beans in the water and cook for about 4 to 5 minutes or until bright green and tender.

Serves 6 to 8.

---

8   potatoes

MASHED POTATOES

Peel and cook the potatoes in salted water until tender. Mash with butter, salt, pepper and milk.

Serves 6 to 8.

Barbecue Chicken

RICE PILAF · GREEN SALAD · GARLIC BREAD

Prep Time: 15 minutes • Total Time: 45 minutes

1/4 cup reduced-sodium catsup
3 tablespoons cider vinegar
1 tablespoon ready-made white horseradish
2 teaspoons firmly packed dark brown sugar
1 clove garlic, minced
1/8 teaspoon dried thyme
1/4 teaspoon black pepper
6 skinless, boneless chicken breast halves (4 ounces each)

BARBECUE CHICKEN

Preheat the broiler, or heat the grill.

In a small saucepan combine the catsup, vinegar, horseradish, brown sugar, garlic, and thyme. Mix well. Bring to a boil over medium-low heat. Cook for about 5 minutes. Remove from the heat, stir in the pepper. Brush the tops of the chicken pieces lightly with sauce. Place the chicken sauce side down on a foil-lined broiler pan or grill rack. Brush the other sides lightly with sauce. Broil or grill 3 inches from heat, basting with the remaining sauce and turning until no longer pink in the center, about 5 to 7 minutes per side. Let the chicken stand for 5 minutes before serving.

Short Cut: When time is short, omit the sauce. Instead use 1/2 cup of ready-made reduced-sodium barbecue sauce mixed with a little cider vinegar, or red-wine vinegar and white horseradish. Proceed as directed.

Serves 6.

1 bag salad greens
Favorite salad toppings
Favorite low-fat or nonfat dressing

GREEN SALAD

Place salad greens in serving bowls. Add toppings and drizzle with dressing.

1 package rice pilaf

RICE PILAF

Cook as directed on the package.

1 loaf ready-to-heat garlic bread

GARLIC BREAD

Bake the bread according to the package directions.

Time Saver

Hard-boil 4 eggs for Day 5.
Prepare potato salad for Day 5.

Rosemary Walnut Beef Skewers

ZESTY POTATO SALAD • COMPANY BRUSSELS SPROUTS

Prep Time: 30 minutes • Total Time: 50 minutes

1½ pounds beef tenderloin or boneless
beef top sirloin steak
Salt and freshly ground pepper to taste
3 red bell peppers

SAUCE:
¼ cup finely chopped walnuts
½ cup butter, melted
¼ cup fresh lemon juice
4 cloves garlic, finely chopped
1 tablespoon finely chopped fresh
rosemary
2 teaspoons coarse-grained mustard
6 sprigs fresh rosemary (optional)
6 lemon wedges (optional)

ROSEMARY WALNUT BEEF SKEWERS

Trim the fat from the beef. Cut beef into 1-inch cubes. On 6 long metal skewers thread the beef cubes, leaving a small space between each piece. Season the beef with salt and freshly ground pepper, to taste. Remove the stem, ribs, and seeds from each pepper. Cut each pepper into 6 strips. In a skillet over medium heat toast the walnuts, stirring frequently, about 3 minutes or until well browned and fragrant. In a small bowl mix the remaining sauce ingredients; add the toasted walnuts. Brush the sauce generously over the beef and pepper. Place the skewers and peppers on a grid over medium coals. Grill for 10 to 14 minutes for medium-rare to medium doneness for beef; peppers should be tender. Baste and turn the skewers frequently using the remaining sauce, if any. Do not overcook. If desired, garnish with fresh rosemary sprigs and lemon wedges.

Serves 6 (serving size 1 skewer).

2 pounds red potatoes
½ cup mayonnaise
½ cup sour cream
2 tablespoons prepared horseradish
1 tablespoon chopped fresh parsley
½ teaspoon salt
½ teaspoon pepper
3 bacon strips, cooked and crumbled
4 hard-boiled eggs, chopped
2 green onions, sliced

ZESTY POTATO SALAD

Peel the potatoes; cook in boiling salted water for 20 minutes or until done. Drain and cool. Cut the potatoes into cubes. In a large bowl combine the mayonnaise, sour cream, horseradish, parsley, salt and pepper; mix until smooth. Stir in the potatoes, bacon, eggs and onions. Cover and chill up to 24 hours.

Serves 6.

continued on next page

4   bacon strips, diced
1   dozen Brussels sprouts, trimmed
    and halved
1   medium onion, chopped
2   tablespoons snipped fresh chives
1   carrot, thinly sliced
10 stuffed green olives, sliced
½   teaspoon dried basil
⅓   cup chicken broth or dry white wine
1   teaspoon olive oil
½   teaspoon pepper
Pinch salt

COMPANY BRUSSELS SPROUTS

In a skillet fry the bacon just until cooked. Drain, reserving 2 tablespoons of drippings. Add the remaining ingredients; cook and stir over medium-high heat for 10 to 15 minutes or until the Brussels sprouts are crisp-tender.

Serves 4.

• MUSHROOM CASSEROLE • GREEK BEANS • POTATO POCKETS •

• STEAMED BROCCOLI • PORK CHOPS WITH APRICOT RICE •

• BEEF TERIYAKI • WHITE RICE • CORN • NOODLES • CORN BREAD •

• MUSTARD-APRICOT PORK CHOPS • SPINACH CASSEROLE •

• GREEN CHILI CHICKEN CASSEROLE • TARRAGON POTATO TOSS •

Fall

• BOARDWALK SHRIMP • ASPARAGUS WITH ALMONDS •

• BAVARIAN BEEF • CHILI BEANS •

• CHICKEN TACOS • MEXICAN RICE •

• EXCELLENT CLAM CHOWDER • OYSTER CRACKERS •

• EASY POT ROAST • GREEN SALAD • GREEN BEANS •

• BAKED HALIBUT • SPINACH SALAD • CARROTS AND ZUCCHINI •

• CAVATELLI • GARLIC BREAD •

• HOT CRAB • STUFFED TOMATOES • APPLESAUCE •

• MASHED POTATOES • CHICKEN ROLL-UP • GREEN SALAD •

• LEMON BAKED CHICKEN • CHEDDAR

SQUASH BAKE • SPINACH TOMATOES •

• BEEF STROGANOFF • SPINACH CHEESE CASSEROLE •

• MINESTRONE SOUP •

	WEEK 8	WEEK 7	WEEK 6	WEEK 5

WEEK 5

	Entrée	Side	Side	Side
Day 1	Mustard-Apricot Pork Chops	Asparagus with Almonds		
Day 2	Easy Pot Roast	Green Salad	Dinner Rolls	
Day 3	Italian Grilled Cheese	Sausage Bean Soup		
Day 4	Oriental Beef	White Rice		
Day 5	Stuffed Chicken Rolls	Stuffing Mix	Green Beans	

WEEK 6

	Entrée	Side	Side	Side
Day 1	Bavarian Beef	Noodles	Vegetables	
Day 2	Garlic Turkey Breast	Potato Casserole	Greek Beans	
Day 3	Boardwalk Shrimp	Corn-Zucchini Bake	Sliced Tomatoes	
Day 4	Crab Louis	Crackers		
Day 5	French Pork Chops	Company Carrots	French Bread	

WEEK 7

	Entrée	Side	Side	Side	Side
Day 1	Chili Beans	Corn Bread			
Day 2	Tuna Casserole	French Bread			
Day 3	Beef Burgundy	Noodles	Sliced Peaches	Peas	Rolls
Day 4	Excellent Clam Chowder	Oyster Crackers			
Day 5	Chicken Tacos	Mexican Rice	Refried Beans	Green Salad/Chips	

WEEK 8

	Entrée	Side	Side	Side
Day 1	Roast Turkey	Broccoli-Stuffing Bake	Baked Yams	
Day 2	Sausage Au Gratin	String Bean Casserole	Dinner Rolls	
Day 3	Hot Crab-Stuffed Tomatoes	French Bread		
Day 4	Turkey Broccoli Casserole	Sliced Pears	Baked Garlic Potatoes	
Day 5	Fresh Tomato Soup	Josefinas	Green Salad	

FALL MENUS AT A GLANCE

WEEK 1

Day	Main	Side	Side
Day 1	Stuffed-up Chicken	Rice	Mixed Vegetables
Day 2	Sausage Popover Bake	Sweet Potato–Cranberry Bake	Garlic Bread
Day 3	Pork Chops with Apricot Rice	Steamed Broccoli	
Day 4	Grilled Turkey Tenderloin	Potato Pockets	Spinach Salad
Day 5	Easy Taco Salad	Flour Tortillas	

WEEK 2

Day	Main	Side	Side
Day 1	Taglarini	Green Salad	
Day 2	Short Ribs & Limas	Mixed Vegetables	Corn Bread
Day 3	Chili-Rubbed Chicken	Rice	Mushroom Casserole
Day 4	10-Minute Taco Salad		
Day 5	Shrimp Casserole	Peas	French Bread

WEEK 3

Day 1	Student Supper	Dinner Rolls		
Day 2	Sherried Chicken	White Rice	Zucchini and Carrots	
Day 3	Tri-Tip/Chuck Roast	Beans	Green Salad	Rice Pilaf
Day 4	White Enchiladas	Refried Beans	Green Salad	Tortilla Chips
Day 5	Beef Teriyaki Marinade	White Rice	Corn on the Cob	

WEEK 4

Day	Main	Side	Side
Day 1	Chicken and Broccoli	Mushroom Casserole	Dinner Rolls
Day 2	Swiss Steak	Noodles	Spinach Casserole
Day 3	Broiled Salmon with Caper Sauce	Tarragon Potato Toss	Carrot Sticks and Zucchini
Day 4	Sausage Supper	Dinner Rolls	
Day 5	Green Chili Chicken Casserole	Mexican Rice	Refried Beans

WEEK 13

Day 1	Baked Ham	Boiled Potatoes and Carrots	Crescent Rolls
Day 2	Rolled Stuffed Meat Loaf	Mixed Vegetables	Dinner Rolls
Day 3	Beef Stroganoff	Green Beans	Creamed Corn
Day 4	Student Supper	Dinner Rolls	
Day 5	Crispy Chicken Strips	Mashed Potatoes	Corn on the Cob

FALL MENUS AT A GLANCE

WEEK 9

Day 1	Cavatelli	Green Salad	Garlic Bread	
Day 2	Beefed-up Skillet Dinner	Potatoes	Dinner Rolls	
Day 3	Spicy & Sweet Pork Chops	Green Bean Casserole	Applesauce	
Day 4	Chicken Vegetable Casserole	Savory Rice		
Day 5	Baked Halibut	Spinach Salad	Carrots & Zucchini	Garlic Bread

WEEK 10

Day 1	Baked Ham	Spinach-Cheese Casserole	
Day 2	Cutlets with Jack	Italian Skillet Zucchini	Sliced French Bread
Day 3	Mandarin Ham Rolls	Company Carrots	Sliced French Bread
Day 4	Crab Florentine	Green Salad	French Bread
Day 5	Microwave Minestrone Soup	Garlic Bread	

WEEK 11

Day 1	Chicken Roll-ups	Green Bean Casserole	Noodles	
Day 2	Spaghetti	Salad	French Bread	
Day 3	Fish Sticks & Fries	Sliced Fruit		
Day 4	Hawaiian Kebabs	Corn on the Cob	Rice Pilaf	French Bread
Day 5	Family Tacos	Refried Beans	Tortilla Chips	

WEEK 12

Day 1	Lemon Baked Chicken	Cheddar-Squash Bake	Fruit Salad
Day 2	Meat Loaf	Baked Potatoes	Baked Carrots
Day 3	Crab Gratin	Spinach Tomatoes	French Bread
Day 4	Chicken Breasts and White Wine	Noodles	Zucchini
Day 5	Chili	French Bread	Sliced Peaches

Stuffed-up Chicken

RICE · MIXED VEGETABLES

Prep Time: 10 minutes • Total Time: 1 hour 40 minutes

1	whole frying chicken

Salt

2	tablespoons margarine
2	packages rondele cheese spread (1 garlic, 1 herb)
1/4	teaspoon parsley
1/4	teaspoon basil

Seedless grapes, sliced

1/4	cup white wine

Black pepper to taste

STUFFED-UP CHICKEN

Rinse the chicken cavity and rub the inside lightly with salt. Rub the chicken all over with margarine. Insert the cheese in the cavity and close. Sprinkle with parsley and basil. Bake at 350° for 1½ hours. The chicken is done when the legs move easily.

Remove the chicken from the oven and scoop out the cheese. Transfer the cheese to a frypan, add the grapes, and thin with wine for a delicious sauce. Season with pepper.

Serves 4 to 6.

3	cups water
3	cups instant rice

RICE

Bring the water to a boil. Stir in the rice; cover and remove from the heat. Let stand for 5 minutes or until the water is absorbed. Fluff with a fork.

Serves 6.

1	bag frozen mixed vegetables

MIXED VEGETABLES

Prepare mixed vegetables as directed on the package.

Sausage Popover Bake

SWEET POTATO–CRANBERRY BAKE · GARLIC BREAD

Prep Time: 30 minutes · Total Time: 1 hour

1 12-ounce can whole kernel corn with sweet peppers
1 4-ounce can mushrooms, stems and pieces
½ pound bulk Italian sausage
1 2.8-ounce can French fried onions, divided
2 eggs, slightly beaten
1 cup all-purpose flour
1 cup milk
1 tablespoon vegetable oil
½ teaspoon chili powder
1 cup (4 ounces) grated Monterey Jack cheese, divided

SAUSAGE POPOVER BAKE

Preheat the oven to 400°. Drain the corn and mushrooms. Crumble the sausage into a large skillet. Cook over medium-high heat until browned. Drain well. Stir in the corn, mushrooms, ½ cup cheese, and half of the onions. Spoon the sausage mixture into a well-greased 9-inch square baking dish (do not use cooking spray). In a small bowl combine the eggs, flour, milk, oil, and chili powder, beating until smooth and well blended. Pour over the sausage mixture. Bake uncovered for 30 minutes or until the top is golden brown. Top with the remaining cheese and onions and bake uncovered for 1 to 3 minutes.

1 40-ounce can whole sweet potatoes, drained
1 2.8-ounce can French fried onions, divided
2 cups fresh cranberries, divided
2 tablespoons packed brown sugar
⅓ cup honey, divided

SWEET POTATO–CRANBERRY BAKE

Preheat the oven to 400°. In a 1½-quart casserole layer the sweet potatoes, half of the onions and 1 cup of cranberries. Sprinkle with brown sugar; drizzle with half of the honey. Top with the remaining cranberries and honey. Bake covered for 35 minutes or until heated through. Gently stir.

Top with the remaining onions. Bake uncovered for 1 to 3 minutes.

Serves 4 to 6.

½ cup butter, melted
3 cloves garlic, pressed
1 loaf French bread, cut lengthwise

GARLIC BREAD

Spread the melted butter and garlic on the bread. Toast in the oven.

Pork Chops with Apricot Rice

STEAMED BROCCOLI

Prep Time: 15 minutes • Total Time: 40 minutes

1 15¼-ounce can apricot halves, undrained
3 tablespoons butter or margarine
6 pork chops (½-inch thick)
¼ cup chopped celery
2½ cups uncooked instant rice
¾ cup hot water
¼ cup golden raisins
½ teaspoon ground ginger
½ teaspoon salt
¼ teaspoon pepper
¼ cup slivered almonds

PORK CHOPS WITH APRICOT RICE

In a blender or food processor purée the apricots until smooth; set aside. In a skillet over medium heat melt the butter and brown the pork chops for 2 to 3 minutes on each side; remove and keep warm. In the same skillet sauté the celery until tender. Add the rice, water, raisins, ginger, salt, pepper, and apricot purée. Bring to a boil. Remove from the heat and stir in the almonds. Pour into an ungreased 13 x 9-inch baking dish. Place the chops on top. Cover and bake at 350° for 15 to 20 minutes or until the pork is no longer pink and the rice is tender.

Serves 6.

2 heads broccoli
Salt

STEAMED BROCCOLI

Place the broccoli in a steamer over an inch or two of boiling salted water. Cover and steam for 6 to 8 minutes or until bright green and tender.

Time Saver *Marinate Day 4's turkey.*

Grilled Turkey Tenderloin

POTATO POCKETS · SPINACH SALAD

Prep Time: 30 minutes · Total Time: 45 minutes

¹⁄₄ cup soy sauce
¹⁄₄ cup vegetable oil
¹⁄₄ cup apple juice
2 tablespoons lemon juice
2 tablespoons dried minced onion
1 teaspoon vanilla extract
¹⁄₄ teaspoon ground ginger
Dash each: garlic powder and pepper
2 turkey breast tenderloins, ¹⁄₂ pound each

GRILLED TURKEY TENDERLOIN

In a large resealable plastic bag or shallow glass dish combine the soy sauce, oil, apple juice, lemon juice, onion, vanilla, ginger, garlic powder, and pepper. Add the turkey. Seal or cover and refrigerate for at least 2 hours. Discard the marinade. Grill the turkey, covered, over medium coals for 8 to 10 minutes per side or until the juices run clear.

Serves 4.

4 medium potatoes, julienne
3 carrots, julienne
¹⁄₃ cup chopped red onion
2 tablespoons butter or margarine
¹⁄₂ teaspoon salt (optional)
¹⁄₈ teaspoon pepper
¹⁄₂ cup grated Cheddar cheese

POTATO POCKETS

Divide the potatoes, carrots, and onion equally between 4 pieces of heavy-duty aluminum foil (about 18 x 12 inches). Top with butter, sprinkle with salt, if desired, and pepper. Bring opposite short ends of the foil together over the vegetables and fold down several times. Fold the unsealed ends toward the vegetables and crimp tightly. Grill, covered, over medium coals for 20 to 30 minutes or until the potatoes are tender. Remove from the grill. Open the foil and sprinkle with cheese; reseal for 5 minutes or until the cheese melts.

Serves 4.

1 bunch spinach, cleaned
¹⁄₂ cup chopped walnuts
¹⁄₄ cup oil
¹⁄₂ cup lemon juice
Salt and pepper

SPINACH SALAD

Tear the spinach leaves and toss with the walnuts. Mix the oil and lemon juice, and drizzle over the spinach. Salt and pepper to taste.

 Time Saver *Grate an additional cup Cheddar cheese for Day 5.*

Easy Taco Salad

FLOUR TORTILLAS

Prep Time: 10 minutes • Total Time: 20 minutes

1   pound ground beef
1   15-ounce can kidney beans, drained
1   head lettuce, chopped
4   tomatoes, chopped
1   bunch green onions, chopped
1   medium package tortilla chips, crushed
1   cup grated Cheddar cheese
1   8-ounce bottle Catalina salad dressing

EASY TACO SALAD

In a skillet brown the ground beef, stirring until crumbly. Drain. Add the beans. Simmer for 5 minutes; cool. In a salad bowl combine the beef and beans, lettuce, green onions, and tomatoes; mix well. Add the chips, cheese, and salad dressing; toss lightly. Serve immediately. Serve with warm flour tortillas.

Serves 6 to 8.

Taglarini

GREEN SALAD

Prep Time: 30 minutes • Total Time: 1 hour 30 minutes

6	ounces narrow noodles
2	pounds ground beef
2	onions, chopped
2	cloves garlic, chopped
1	green bell pepper, chopped
1	28-ounce can (3½ cups) tomatoes, drained

Salt and pepper

1	12-ounce can whole kernel corn, drained
1	cup ripe olives, drained
1	4-ounce can mushrooms, drained
2	cups grated cheese

TAGLARINI

Cook the noodles according to the package directions. Drain. Sauté the meat, onions, garlic, and green pepper until brown. Add the tomatoes, salt and pepper. Simmer for 10 minutes. Combine the noodles and the meat mixture. Add the remaining ingredients, saving a little cheese to sprinkle over the top. Turn into a greased 13 x 9-inch baking dish. Sprinkle with cheese. Bake at 350° for 1 hour.

Serves 8 to 10.

---

1 bag salad greens
Favorite salad toppings
Favorite low-fat or nonfat salad dressing

GREEN SALAD

Place salad greens in serving bowls. Add toppings and drizzle with dressing.

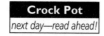

Crock Pot
next day—read ahead!

Time Saver 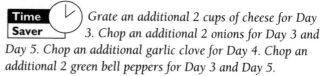 *Grate an additional 2 cups of cheese for Day 3. Chop an additional 2 onions for Day 3 and Day 5. Chop an additional garlic clove for Day 4. Chop an additional 2 green bell peppers for Day 3 and Day 5.*

Short Ribs and Limas

VEGETABLES · CORN BREAD

Prep Time: 20 minutes • Total Time: 10 hours

3½ pounds beef short ribs
2 10-ounce packages frozen lima beans
1 can condensed beef soup with vegetables and barley
1 soup can water
1 envelope dry onion soup mix
1 4-ounce can sliced mushrooms, undrained
¼ cup cold water
1 to 2 tablespoons all-purpose flour

SHORT RIBS AND LIMAS

Place the ribs in the bottom of a crock pot. Add the frozen limas. In a bowl stir together the soup, the can of water, dry soup mix, and undrained mushrooms. Pour into the crock pot. Cover and cook on low heat for 10 hours or until the meat is tender (or cook on high for 5 hours). Turn to the high setting. Remove the meat, beans, and mushrooms; keep warm. If necessary, spoon off the excess fat from the liquid in the cooker. Combine the cold water and flour, and add to the boiling juices in the crock pot. Cook and stir until thickened.

Serves 6.

1 bag frozen mixed vegetables

VEGETABLES

Prepare the vegetables as directed on the package.

1 package corn bread mix

CORN BREAD

Prepare as directed on the package.

Crock Pot
today!

Chili-Rubbed Chicken

RICE · MUSHROOM CASSEROLE

Prep Time: 30 minutes • Total Time: 2 hours 10 minutes

2 cloves garlic, minced
1 teaspoon salt
2 tablespoons minced fresh parsley
1 teaspoon ground cumin
1 tablespoon vegetable oil
1 teaspoon dried oregano
1 tablespoon chili powder
6 chicken breasts

CHILI-RUBBED CHICKEN

Heat the oven to 350°. In a small bowl combine the first 7 ingredients. Rub over the chicken. Roast on a rack set in a roasting pan for $1\frac{1}{2}$ hours or until a meat thermometer registers 180°; or at 350° for 1 hour if using boneless, skinless breasts.

3 cups water
3 cups instant rice

RICE

Bring the water to a boil. Stir in the rice; cover and remove from the heat. Let stand for 5 minutes or until the water is absorbed. Fluff with a fork.

continued next page

Crock Pot
next day—read ahead!

1	pound mushrooms
4	tablespoons butter or margarine
8	slices fresh white bread (large)
½	cup chopped onions
½	cup chopped celery
½	cup chopped green bell pepper
½	cup mayonnaise
¾	teaspoon salt
¼	teaspoon ground pepper
2	eggs, slightly beaten
1½	cups milk
1	can mushroom soup, undiluted
½	cup grated Cheddar cheese

MUSHROOM CASSEROLE

Slice the mushrooms and sauté in 4 tablespoons of butter until most of the liquid is absorbed. Butter 3 of the bread slices; cut into 1-inch squares; place in a greased 9 x 13-inch baking pan. Combine the mushrooms with the onions, celery, green pepper, mayonnaise, salt and pepper. Turn half of the mixture into a baking pan over cut-up bread. Cut 3 more of the bread slices into squares and place on the mushroom mixture. Top with the remaining mushroom mixture. Combine the eggs and milk; pour over all. Refrigerate 1 hour or longer.

Pour the can of soup over the casserole; top with the remaining 2 buttered cut-up bread slices. Bake at 350° for 50 to 60 minutes. Remove from oven; sprinkle with cheese; bake 10 minutes more. Freezes well.

Serves 12 to 15.

Time Saver *Freeze half of the Mushroom Casserole for Week 4's Day 1 meal.*
Chop an additional 2 cups of celery for Day 5.

10-Minute Taco Salad

Prep Time: 20 minutes • Total Time: 20 minutes

2   16-ounce cans chili beans, undrained
1   10½-ounce package corn chips
2   cups (8 oz.) shredded Cheddar cheese
4   cups chopped lettuce
2   small tomatoes, chopped
1   small onion, chopped
1   2¼-ounce can sliced ripe olives, drained
1¼ cups salsa
½   cup sour cream

10-MINUTE TACO SALAD

In a saucepan or microwave-safe bowl, heat the beans. Place the corn chips on a large platter. Top with beans, cheese, lettuce, tomatoes, onion, olives, salsa, and sour cream. Serve immediately.

Serves 8.

Shrimp Casserole

PEAS · FRENCH BREAD

Prep Time: 10 minutes • Total Time: 50 minutes

1   pint mayonnaise
1   medium onion, chopped
1   6-ounce can crabmeat
1   6-ounce can water chestnuts, diced
1½ pounds cooked shrimp
½   pound sliced mushrooms
2   cups diced celery
Buttered bread crumbs
1   green bell pepper, chopped

SHRIMP CASSEROLE

Mix all ingredients except bread crumbs in order given. Pour into a greased large casserole and top with the bread crumbs. Bake uncovered in a 350° oven for 40 minutes.

Serves 8.

1   package frozen peas, or 1 can peas, drained

PEAS

Prepare the peas as directed on the package.

1   loaf French bread
Butter

FRENCH BREAD

Student Supper

DINNER ROLLS

Prep Time: 20 minutes • Total Time: 40 minutes

1   pound ground beef
1   egg, beaten
1   cup seasoned bread crumbs
2   tablespoons butter
1   medium onion, chopped
1   4-ounce can sliced mushrooms
½   cup chopped green bell pepper
1   16-ounce can sliced potatoes
½   cup chopped celery
1   10½-ounce can golden mushroom
    soup
1   cup grated Cheddar cheese
⅓   cup milk
1   bay leaf
1   4-ounce can sliced olives
¼   teaspoon garlic salt
¼   teaspoon black pepper
¼   teaspoon paprika

STUDENT SUPPER

In a large bowl mix together the beef, egg, and bread crumbs. In a large skillet melt the butter and sauté the beef mixture until browned.

Add the onion, mushrooms, bell pepper, potatoes, celery, soup, and Cheddar.

Add the remaining ingredients and mix well. Simmer for about 15 minutes.

1   package prepared dinner rolls
Butter

DINNER ROLLS

Warm the rolls and serve with butter.

 Chop an additional onion for Day 4.

Sherried Chicken

WHITE RICE · ZUCCHINI AND CARROTS

Prep Time: 25 minutes • Total Time: 1 hour 35 minutes

3 whole chicken breasts, halved
Seasoned salt, as needed
3 to 4 tablespoons butter
⅔ cup sherry
1 4-ounce can button mushrooms
1 package gravy mix for chicken
1 cup sour cream

SHERRIED CHICKEN

Lightly sprinkle the chicken with the seasoned salt. Brown in butter in a Dutch oven. Add the sherry and liquid from mushrooms. Cover and bake at 350° for 45 minutes to 1 hour.

Remove the chicken to a serving dish. Measure the pan juices and add water, if necessary, to make 2 cups of liquid. Carefully blend the liquid and chicken gravy mix in a pan. Bring to a boil, reduce the heat, and simmer for 5 minutes, stirring continuously. Blend in the sour cream. Add the mushrooms. When the sauce is smooth and hot arrange the breasts over rice and pour the sauce over.

Serves 4.

2 cups water
2 cups instant rice

WHITE RICE

Bring the water to a boil. Stir in the rice; cover and remove from the heat. Let stand for 5 minutes or until the water is absorbed. Fluff with a fork.

Serves 4.

4 zucchini
1 white onion
4 large carrots

ZUCCHINI AND CARROTS

Slice the zucchini and carrots lengthwise and chunk the onion. Place in a steamer over an inch of boiling water and steam the vegetables for 10 minutes.

Serves 4.

Time Saver *Cook an additional 6 servings of rice for Day 5.*

Tri-tip or Chuck Roast

BEANS · RICE PILAF · GREEN SALAD

Prep Time: 25 minutes • Total Time: 45 minutes

1 large tri-tip or chuck roast (enough for 2 meals)	**TRI-TIP OR CHUCK ROAST** Buy pre-seasoned or season with salt, pepper, garlic, and cumin. Barbecue on the grill for approximately 15 minutes on each side. Slice and serve.
2 16-ounce cans ranch beans	**BEANS** Heat the beans according to the directions on the can.
1 tablespoon margarine 1/4 cup vermicelli Salt, pepper, parsley Garlic 1 can button mushrooms 1 cup white rice (long grain) 1 cup water Butter flavored sprinkles	**RICE PILAF** In a saucepan melt the margarine and brown the vermicelli. Season with the salt, pepper, garlic, and parsley. Add the rice and stir for 1 minute. Add the water and bring to a boil. Reduce the heat. Simmer for 20 minutes. Add the butter flavored sprinkles to taste.
1 bag salad greens Favorite salad toppings Favorite low-fat or nonfat dressing	**GREEN SALAD** Place the salad greens in serving bowls. Add toppings and drizzle with dressing.

 Leftover tri-tip will be used on Day 5.

White Enchiladas

REFRIED BEANS · GREEN SALAD · TORTILLA CHIPS

Prep Time: 20 minutes • Total Time: 45 minutes

1	pound ground beef
¾	cup chopped onions
1	4-ounce can green chilies, chopped
1	10½-ounce can cream of chicken soup
¾	cup milk
1	tablespoon chili powder
1	dozen flour tortillas
2	cups grated Jack cheese
1	4-ounce can sliced olives

WHITE ENCHILADAS

Brown the ground beef and the onion. Add the chilies, soup, milk, and chili powder. Roll inside the tortillas and cover with the cheese and olives. Place in a 9 x 13-inch pan. Bake at 425° for 20 minutes covered with foil. Use as many tortillas as you can fit.

Serves 6.

1 to 2 17-ounce cans refried beans

REFRIED BEANS

Heat the beans in the microwave or on the stove top.

1 bag salad greens
Favorite salad toppings
Favorite low-fat or nonfat salad dressing

GREEN SALAD

Place the salad greens in serving bowls. Add toppings and drizzle with dressing.

1 bag tortilla chips

TORTILLA CHIPS

Beef Teriyaki Marinade

WHITE RICE · CORN ON THE COB

Prep Time: 5 minutes • Total Time: 20 minutes

1½ cups sugar

Dash pepper

6 tablespoons soy sauce

1 green onion, chopped

2 tablespoons oil

1 clove garlic (minced)

¼ teaspoon ground mustard

Remaining tri-tip from Day 3, sliced

BEEF TERIYAKI MARINADE

In a shallow dish combine all of the ingredients except the roast and mix well. Add the beef and mix. Stir-fry the mixture.

Serves 4 to 6.

---

3 cups water

3 cups instant rice

WHITE RICE

Bring the water to a boil. Stir in the rice; cover and remove from the heat. Let stand for 5 minutes or until the water is absorbed. Fluff with a fork.

Serves 6.

---

6 ears fresh or frozen corn

CORN ON THE COB

Fresh or frozen—your choice. If frozen, follow the package directions. For fresh, boil water, add the corn, and cook for 5 to 8 minutes, until tender. Do not over-cook.

Serves 6.

 **Time Saver** *Defrost mushroom casserole from Week 2 for tomorrow.*

Chicken and Broccoli

MUSHROOM CASSEROLE · DINNER ROLLS

Prep Time: 30 minutes • Total Time: 1 hour 15 minutes

2   heads broccoli, cooked
8   chicken breast halves, cooked and diced
2   10½-ounce cans cream of chicken soup
Juice of ½ lemon
¾   cup mayonnaise
½   cup grated Cheddar cheese

CHICKEN AND BROCCOLI

Put the broccoli on the bottom of greased casserole. Layer the chicken on top. Mix together the soup, lemon juice, and mayonnaise, and pour over the chicken. Top with grated cheese. Bake at 325° for 45 minutes to 1 hour.

Serves 6.

MUSHROOM CASSEROLE (FROM WEEK 2)

Heat in the microwave at half-power for 4 to 5 minutes.

1   package prepared dinner rolls
Butter

DINNER ROLLS

Warm the rolls and serve with butter.

Time Saver *Reserve 2 chicken breasts for Day 5.*

Swiss Steak

NOODLES · SPINACH CASSEROLE

Prep Time: 30 minutes • Total Time: 1 hour 15 minutes

2	tablespoons flour
1	teaspoon garlic salt
1/8	teaspoon pepper
1/2	teaspoon oregano
1 1/2	pounds round steak
2	tablespoons oil
1	onion, sliced
1/2	cup Burgundy wine
1	16-ounce can stewed tomatoes
2	tablespoons chopped parsley
1	4-ounce can sliced or button mushrooms

SWISS STEAK

Mix the flour, garlic salt, pepper, and oregano. Put the meat on a board and sprinkle half the mixture on one side and pound into meat. Turn the meat, top with the remaining flour mixture, and pound in. Cut in 4 serving pieces and brown slowly and well on both sides in heated oil. Add the onions the last 5 minutes of browning and cook until soft. Add wine and tomatoes and cover; boil slowly until the meat is almost fork-tender, or bake in a 350° oven. Add the undrained mushrooms and parsley and cook for 10 to 15 minutes longer.

Serves 4.

1	package egg noodles

NOODLES

Cook as directed on the package for 4 to 6 servings.

1	pound cottage cheese
3	eggs
1	10-ounce package chopped spinach, thawed and drained
1/4	pound Cheddar cheese
1/4	cup margarine
3	tablespoons flour

SPINACH CASSEROLE

Mix the cottage cheese, eggs, and spinach in a bowl. Cut the Cheddar cheese and margarine into coarse pieces and add. Mix in the flour. Place in a 1 1/2-quart casserole and bake at 350° for 10 to 15 minutes.

Serves 4 to 6.

Time Saver *Chop an additional 4 tablespoons parsley for Day 3.*

Broiled Salmon with Caper Sauce

TARRAGON POTATO TOSS · SLICED CARROTS AND ZUCCHINI

Prep Time: 20 minutes • Total Time: 45 minutes

4   salmon steaks
1   large lemon or lemon juice
1   tablespoon lemon pepper
1   clove garlic, minced
1   tablespoon drained capers

BROILED SALMON WITH CAPER SAUCE

Heat a broiler. Sprinkle the salmon with lemon juice, lemon pepper, and garlic. Broil the salmon in a broiler pan for 10 to 15 minutes or until the fish flakes easily with a fork, turning once. Top with capers if desired.

Serves 4.

1½   pounds potatoes, quartered
½   teaspoon salt
1   tablespoon olive oil
2   tablespoons chopped fresh tarragon
¼   teaspoon pepper

TARRAGON POTATO TOSS

In a saucepan over high heat bring the potatoes and enough salted water to cover to a boil. Cook for 15 to 20 minutes until tender. Drain and place in a serving bowl. Add the remaining ingredients. Toss to coat.

Serves 4.

6 to 8 carrots, sliced
1   egg, beaten
3   zucchini, sliced
1   cup bread crumbs
3   tablespoons oil

SLICED CARROTS AND ZUCCHINI

Dip the carrots and zucchini in egg. Dredge in the bread crumbs. In a skillet heat the oil and fry until crisp-tender.

Serves 4 to 6.

Sausage Supper

DINNER ROLLS

Prep Time: 10 minutes • Total Time: 30 minutes

1   head cabbage, wedged
2   medium onions, halved
6 to 8 carrots, peeled and chunked
2   medium or small boiled potatoes,
    halved or quartered, depending on
    size
4   Polish sausages
2   medium apples, quartered

SAUSAGE SUPPER

Place a stainless steel steamer in a 3-quart saucepan. Fill with water to the bottom of the steamer. Fit with cabbage, onions, carrots, and potatoes and lay the sausages on top. Cover and cook for 20 minutes at medium-hot temperature. Add the apples and cook for 5 minutes longer. Serve with butter or sour cream. Salt and pepper to taste.

Serves 4.

---

1   package prepared dinner rolls
Butter

DINNER ROLLS

Warm the rolls and serve with butter.

Green Chili Chicken Casserole

MEXICAN RICE · REFRIED BEANS

Prep Time: 15 minutes • Total Time: 1 hour

2 whole chicken breasts, skinned
1 10½-ounce can cream of
   mushroom soup
1 cup low-fat plain yogurt
1 cup grated Cheddar cheese
1 4-ounce can diced green chilies
1 package flour tortillas

GREEN CHILI CHICKEN CASSEROLE

Combine the chicken, soup, yogurt, cheese, and chilies. Mix by hand. Grease an 8-inch square pan. Layer, starting with the chicken mixture, then the tortillas. Bake at 350° for 25 minutes.

Serves 4.

1 package instant rice
1 cup salsa

MEXICAN RICE

Cook the rice as directed for 6 to 8 servings. Once cooked, add the salsa. Mix well.

Serves 6 to 8.

1 16-ounce can refried beans
¼ cup shredded Cheddar cheese

REFRIED BEANS

Heat the refried beans on low heat. Sprinkle with shredded cheese.

Serves 4.

Mustard-Apricot Pork Chops

ASPARAGUS WITH ALMONDS

Prep Time: 20 minutes • Total Time: 40 minutes

⅓ cup apricot preserves
2 tablespoons Dijon mustard
4 pork loin chops (½ to ¾-inch thick)
3 green onions, chopped
Hot cooked rice for 6

MUSTARD-APRICOT PORK CHOPS

In a small saucepan over low heat cook and stir the preserves and mustard until the preserves are melted. Set aside. Place the pork chops on a lightly greased broiler pan and broil 4 inches from the heat for 5 minutes. Brush with half of the glaze; turn the chops. Broil for 5 minutes longer. Brush with the remaining glaze. Broil 2 to 4 minutes more or until the meat juices run clear. Top with the onions. Serve over rice.

Serves 4.

4 teaspoons olive or vegetable oil, divided
2 tablespoons slivered almonds
1 pound fresh asparagus, cut into 2-inch pieces
¼ cup water
1 teaspoon sugar
¼ teaspoon salt
Dash pepper
1 teaspoon lemon juice

ASPARAGUS WITH ALMONDS

In a skillet heat 1 teaspoon of oil and sauté the almonds until lightly browned. Remove and set aside. In the same skillet sauté the asparagus in the remaining oil for 1 minute. Add the water, sugar, salt, and pepper; bring to a boil. Reduce the heat and cover. Simmer for 3 to 4 minutes or until the asparagus is tender. Drain. Sprinkle with lemon juice; top with almonds.

Serves 3 to 4.

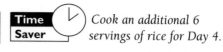

Crock Pot *next day—read ahead!* **Time Saver** *Cook an additional 6 servings of rice for Day 4.*

Easy Pot Roast

GREEN SALAD · DINNER ROLLS

Prep Time: 5 minutes • Total Time: 5 to 7 hours

| 4-pound beef roast
4 to 6 potatoes, quartered
6 to 8 carrots, cut in chunks
| envelope onion soup mix
| 10½-ounce can cream of mush-
room soup

EASY POT ROAST

Sprinkle the roast with salt and pepper. Combine with the potatoes and carrots in a slow cooker. Prepare the soup mix according to the package directions. Stir in the mushroom soup. Add to the slow cooker. Cook on low all day.

Serves 4 to 8.

| bag salad greens
Favorite salad toppings
Favorite low-fat or nonfat dressing

GREEN SALAD

Place salad greens in serving bowls. Add toppings and drizzle with dressing.

| package prepared dinner rolls
Butter

DINNER ROLLS

Warm the rolls and serve with butter.

 Time Saver *Save 1 pound of roast for Day 4.*

Italian Grilled Cheese

SAUSAGE BEAN SOUP

Prep Time: 15 minutes • Total Time: 30 minutes

4   slices Italian bread (1-inch thick)
4   slices mozzarella cheese
3   eggs
½   cup milk
¾   teaspoon Italian seasoning
½   teaspoon garlic salt
⅔   cup Italian-seasoned bread crumbs

ITALIAN GRILLED CHEESE

Cut a 3-inch pocket in each slice of bread. Place a slice of cheese in each pocket. In a bowl beat the eggs, milk, Italian seasoning, and garlic salt. Soak the bread in the egg mixture for 2 minutes on each side. Coat with bread crumbs. Cook on a greased hot griddle until golden brown on both sides.

Serves 4.

¾   pound bulk Italian sausage
½   cup chopped onion
1   garlic clove, minced
1   15-ounce can black beans, rinsed and drained
1   15½-ounce can butter beans, rinsed and drained
1   14½-ounce can diced tomatoes, undrained
1   14½-ounce can beef broth
1   tablespoon minced fresh basil
2   tablespoons grated Parmesan cheese

SAUSAGE BEAN SOUP

In a large saucepan cook the sausage, onion, and garlic until the sausage is browned. Drain. Add the beans, tomatoes, broth, and basil. Cover and simmer for 10 minutes. Sprinkle each serving with Parmesan cheese.

Serves 4 to 6.

Oriental Beef

WHITE RICE

Prep Time: 15 minutes • Total Time: 25 minutes

1 pound lean beef from Day 2
2 tablespoons soy sauce
Several drops of corn oil
1 tablespoon cornstarch
1 tablespoon sugar
Pepper to taste
2 tablespoons soy sauce
1 clove garlic, crushed
1/2 cup sliced onion
1/2 cup chopped green bell pepper
4 tablespoons corn oil
3/4 cup beef broth
1/2 cup diagonally sliced celery
1 tablespoon cornstarch

ORIENTAL BEEF

Slice the beef into 2-inch strips. Combine with 2 tablespoons soy sauce, several drops of corn oil, 1 tablespoon cornstarch, sugar, and pepper in a bowl; mix well. In a skillet stir-fry the vegetables in 2 tablespoons of oil for 5 minutes or until crisp-tender. Cover and steam for several minutes.

Remove the vegetables to a plate. Add 2 tablespoons of oil and the garlic, and stir-fry until brown. Stir in the beef mixture. Stir-fry until the beef is tender. Add the mixture of remaining ingredients. Cook until thickened, stirring constantly. Add the vegetables. Cook until heated through.

Serves 4.

---

2 cups water
2 cups instant rice

WHITE RICE

Bring the water to a boil. Stir in the rice; cover and remove from the heat. Let stand for 5 minutes or until the water is absorbed. Fluff with a fork.

Serves 4.

Time Saver *To save time on Day 5, prepare the chicken tonight.*

Crock Pot next day—read ahead!

Stuffed Chicken Rolls

STUFFING MIX · GREEN BEANS

Prep Time: 15 minutes • Total Time: All day

6	large boneless, skinless chicken breasts
6	slices fully cooked ham
6	slices Swiss cheese
¼	cup all-purpose flour
¼	cup grated Parmesan cheese
½	teaspoon rubbed sage
¼	teaspoon paprika
¼	teaspoon pepper
¼	cup vegetable oil
1	10¾-ounce can cream of chicken soup, undiluted
½	cup chicken broth

Chopped fresh parsley (optional)

STUFFED CHICKEN ROLLS

Flatten the chicken to ⅛-inch thickness. Place a slice of ham and Swiss cheese on each breast. Roll up and tuck in the ends. Secure with a toothpick. Combine the flour, Parmesan cheese, sage, paprika, and pepper, and coat the chicken on all sides. Cover and refrigerate for 1 hour. In a large skillet brown the chicken in oil over medium-high heat. Transfer to a 5-quart slow cooker. Combine the soup and broth; pour over the chicken. Cover and cook on low for 4 to 5 hours. Remove the toothpicks. Garnish with parsley, if desired.

Serves 6.

1	package instant stuffing mix

STUFFING MIX

Prepare the stuffing as directed on the package.

1	16-ounce can green beans

GREEN BEANS

Heat the green beans as directed on the can.

Crock Pot
next day—read ahead!

Bavarian Beef

NOODLES · VEGETABLES

Prep Time: 20 minutes • Total Time: 10 hours 20 minutes or 5 hours 20 minutes

1	2½ to 3-pound boneless beef chuck pot roast
1	tablespoon cooking oil
4	carrots, sliced (2 cups)
2	cups chopped onions
2	large kosher-style dill pickles, chopped (¾ cup)
2	stalks celery, sliced (1 cup)
½	cup dry red wine or beef broth
½	cup German-style mustard
½	teaspoon coarse ground black pepper
¼	teaspoon ground cloves
2	bay leaves
2	tablespoons all-purpose flour
2	tablespoons dry red wine or beef broth

BAVARIAN BEEF

Trim the fat from the pot roast. If necessary, cut the roast to fit into a crock cooker. In a large skillet brown the roast slowly on all sides in hot oil. Meanwhile, in the crock cooker place the carrots, onions, ¾ cup pickles, and celery. Place the meat atop the vegetables.

In a small bowl combine the red wine or beef broth, mustard, pepper, cloves, and bay leaves. Pour over the meat. Cover and cook on the low heat setting for 8 to 10 hours or on the high heat setting for 4 to 5 hours.

Remove the meat from the cooker and place on a serving platter; keep warm. For gravy, transfer the vegetables and cooking liquid to a 2-quart saucepan. Skim off the fat. Remove the bay leaves. Stir together the flour and the remaining 2 tablespoons wine or beef broth. Stir into the mixture in saucepan. Cook and stir over medium heat until thickened and bubbly. Cook and stir for 1 minute more. Serve the meat and vegetables with gravy and noodles.

Serves 4 to 6.

1	package egg noodles

NOODLES

Cook noodles for 4 to 6 servings as directed on the package.

1	bag frozen vegetable combination (broccoli, carrots, cauliflower)

VEGETABLES

Cook the vegetables as directed on the package.

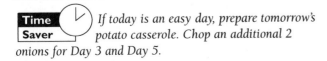

Time Saver *If today is an easy day, prepare tomorrow's potato casserole. Chop an additional 2 onions for Day 3 and Day 5.*

Garlic Turkey Breast

POTATO CASSEROLE · GREEN BEANS

Prep Time: 30 minutes • Total Time: 1 hour

6 to 8 turkey breasts
5 cloves garlic, chopped
1 whole leaf sage
Salt and pepper
Cooking oil

GARLIC TURKEY BREAST

Rinse and dry the turkey. Rub the entire skin surface with a clove of garlic. With a sharp knife, make small random punctures in the turkey about 2 inches apart and stuff each hole with a small piece of garlic and some sage. Salt and pepper the entire turkey and place in a shallow baking pan. Brush the turkey with oil and bake in a preheated 350° oven for 1 hour, basting every 20 to 30 minutes.

Serves 6 to 8.

5 cups cooked potatoes, diced
1/4 cup green onion, minced
1 teaspoon salt
1 small clove garlic, minced or mashed
2 cups creamed cottage cheese
1 cup sour cream
1/2 cup shredded Cheddar cheese
Paprika

POTATO CASSEROLE

In a 2-quart casserole combine the potatoes, onion, salt, garlic, cottage cheese, and sour cream. Top with cheese and sprinkle with paprika. Bake uncovered at 350° for 30 minutes, or until heated through.

Serves 6 to 8.

1 pound green beans or 1 can green beans, drained
1/2 teaspoon oregano
Paprika
Garlic salt

GREEN BEANS

Season the green beans with oregano, paprika, and salt, and heat according to the package directions or boil fresh green beans for about 4 minutes or until bright green and tender.

Serves 4.

Boardwalk Shrimp

CORN-ZUCCHINI BAKE • SLICED TOMATOES WITH ITALIAN DRESSING

Prep Time: 30 minutes • Total Time: 1 hour 30 minutes

1¼ pounds large shrimp, peeled, deveined
¾ cup mayonnaise, divided
¼ teaspoon salt
1 cup corn flakes crumbs
3 tablespoons sweet relish
1 tablespoon chopped parsley
2 teaspoons hot pepper sauce
1 teaspoon Dijon mustard

BOARDWALK SHRIMP

Heat the oven to 425°. Coat a baking sheet with cooking spray. In a bowl combine the shrimp, ¼ cup mayonnaise, and salt; toss well to coat. Place corn flakes crumbs in a large plastic food bag. Add the shrimp, seal, and shake to coat. Arrange the shrimp in a single layer on the prepared baking sheet. Bake 10 minutes, turning once until lightly browned.

Meanwhile in a bowl combine the remaining ½ cup mayonnaise, relish, parsley, hot pepper sauce, and mustard. Serve with the shrimp.

Serves 4 to 6.

3 medium zucchini
¼ cup chopped onion
1 tablespoon butter or margarine
1 10-ounce package frozen whole kernel corn, cooked and drained
1 cup grated Swiss cheese
2 beaten eggs
¼ teaspoon salt
¼ cup fine dry bread crumbs
2 tablespoons grated Parmesan cheese
1 tablespoon butter or margarine, melted

CORN-ZUCCHINI BAKE

Wash, but do not peel, the zucchini. Cut into 1-inch thick slices. Cook covered in a small amount of boiling salted water until tender, 15 to 20 minutes. Drain and mash with a fork.

Cook the onion in 1 tablespoon butter until tender. Combine the zucchini, onion, cooked corn, Swiss cheese, eggs, and salt. Turn the mixture into a 1-quart casserole. Combine the crumbs, Parmesan, and melted butter; sprinkle over the corn mixture. Place the casserole on a baking sheet. Bake uncovered at 350° until a knife inserted off-center comes out clean, about 40 minutes. Let stand for 5 to 10 minutes before serving.

Garnish with cherry tomatoes and parsley, if desired. Serves 6.

SLICED TOMATOES WITH ITALIAN DRESSING

 Time Saver *Chop some extra parsley for Day 5.*

Crab Louis

CRACKERS

Prep Time: 30 minutes • Total Time: 30 minutes

1 head lettuce
2 to 3 cups crabmeat, fresh or canned
2 hard-boiled eggs
1 17-ounce can asparagus
2 large tomatoes

DRESSING:
1 cup mayonnaise
¼ cup catsup or chili sauce
1 teaspoon lemon juice
Salt to taste

CRAB LOUIS

Line 4 large plates with lettuce leaves. Shred the remainder of the head atop. Prepare the crabmeat, reserving the claw meat. Leave the remainder in chunks and arrange on the lettuce. Cut the tomatoes and eggs into wedges, and circle on top the salads. Season with salt. Pour ¼ cup Louis or seafood dressing over each salad. Dash with paprika. Top with claw meat and asparagus. Pass the remaining dressing. Serves 4.

Louis Dressing: To 1 cup of mayonnaise add ¼ cup of catsup or chili sauce. Add 1 teaspoon lemon juice. Salt to taste.

1 package crackers

CRACKERS

French Pork Chops

COMPANY CARROTS · FRENCH BREAD

Prep Time: 30 minutes • Total Time: 1 hour 15 minutes

8   pork chops
Salt and pepper
2   onions, peeled and sliced
1   lemon, sliced
8   tablespoons brown sugar
1   cup catsup
2   bay leaves, crumbled
1/4   teaspoon thyme

FRENCH PORK CHOPS

In a skillet brown the pork chops and drain the fat. Salt and pepper each side. Put a slice of onion, lemon, and 1 tablespoon of brown sugar on each. Combine the catsup and ½ cup of water with the bay leaves and thyme. Pour around the chops. Cook covered over low heat for 45 minutes. Baste once.

Serves 8.

2½   pounds whole carrots, peeled
½   cup mayonnaise
1   tablespoon minced onion
1   tablespoon prepared horseradish
Salt and pepper, to taste
¼   cup finely crushed soda crackers
2   tablespoons butter
Parsley, chopped
Paprika

COMPANY CARROTS

In a microwave cook the carrots in boiling salted water until fork-tender. Reserve ¼ cup of cooking liquid. Cut the carrots lengthwise in narrow strips. Arrange in a 9-inch square baking dish. Set aside. Combine the reserved cooking liquid with the mayonnaise, onion, horseradish, salt, and pepper. Pour the sauce over the carrots. Sprinkle cracker crumbs on top, and dot with butter. Sprinkle with parsley and paprika. Bake at 375° for 20 minutes.

Serves 8.

1   loaf French bread
Butter

FRENCH BREAD

Crock Pot
next day—read ahead!

Chili Beans

CORN BREAD

Prep Time: 30 minutes • Total Time: 2 hours or all day

1½ pounds ground beef
1   pound sirloin or roast, cut in small chunks
1   clove garlic, pressed
1   onion, chopped (white or yellow best)
1   bell pepper, seeded and diced
2   packages chili mix
1   large can pinto beans
1   large can kidney beans
½   cup water
½   cup wine
2   16-ounce cans stewed tomatoes
1   28-ounce can tomatoes (cut tomatoes up but not too much so it looks authentic)

CHILI BEANS

In a skillet brown the beef, garlic, onion, and bell pepper. Drain off the excess fat. Stir in the chili mix. Add the beans, water (more if needed), wine, and tomatoes. Heat to boiling. Reduce the heat and cover. Cook all day in crock pot or simmer for 1½ hours.

Serves 6 to 8.

---

1   box of corn bread mix

CORN BREAD

Prepare as directed on the package.

Time Saver *Chop 1¼ onions for use throughout the week. Dice 2 green bell peppers for Day 4.*

Tuna Casserole

CRUSTY FRENCH BREAD

Prep Time: 20 minutes • Total Time: 50 minutes

I	4-ounce can mushrooms, and liquid
I	10½-ounce can cream of celery soup
I	cup peas
I	6-ounce can tuna, drained
8	ounces noodles, cooked
½	medium onion, chopped
½	cup milk
⅔	cup celery, diced
½	cup grated Jack cheese

TUNA CASSEROLE

Mix all ingredients together except for the cheese and put in a 1½-quart casserole. Sprinkle the cheese on top. Bake at 350° for 25 to 30 minutes.

Serves 4 to 6.

I   loaf crusty French bread
Butter

CRUSTY FRENCH BREAD

Time Saver — *Chop 1 cup celery for Day 4.*
Grate 1 cup Jack cheese for Day 5.
Cook additional 16 ounces of noodles for Day 3.

Crock Pot
next day—read ahead!

Beef Burgundy

SLICED PEACHES · PEAS · DINNER ROLLS

Prep Time: 10 minutes • Total Time: All day

1 to 1½ pounds round steak, cubed
   (fresh or frozen)
1   envelope onion soup mix
¼ to ½ cup red wine
1   10½-ounce can golden mushroom
   soup
1   4-ounce can sliced mushrooms,
   drained
1   16-ounce package noodles, cooked

BEEF BURGUNDY

Combine the steak and the next 4 ingredients in a slow cooker. Cook on low for 6 to 8 hours. Serve over noodles.

Serves 4 to 6.

---

8 to 10 peaches

SLICED PEACHES

---

1   can or bag frozen peas

PEAS

Heat the peas according to the package directions.

---

1   package prepared dinner rolls
Butter

DINNER ROLLS

Warm the rolls and serve with butter.

Excellent Clam Chowder

OYSTER CRACKERS

Prep Time: 15 minutes • Total Time: 30 minutes

½	pound butter
1	cup chopped celery
2	cups chopped onions
2	cups chopped green bell pepper
¾	cup flour
5	cups hot milk
3	6½-ounce cans clams and juice
2	cups cooked potatoes
½	teaspoon thyme

Salt and pepper to taste

EXCELLENT CLAM CHOWDER

In a saucepan melt the butter and sauté the celery, onions, and green pepper until the vegetables are soft. Add the flour and mix until smooth. Add the hot milk and clams with juice. Cook for 10 minutes. Add the potatoes, thyme, salt, and pepper. Mix and simmer on low heat for a few minutes.

Serves 6 to 8.

1	package crackers

OYSTER CRACKERS

Crock Pot
next day—read ahead!

Chicken Tacos

MEXICAN RICE · GREEN SALAD AND TORTILLA CHIPS · REFRIED BEANS

Prep Time: 15 minutes • Total Time: 40 minutes, plus crock pot time

4 boneless, skinless chicken breasts
1 jar salsa
Flour tortillas

SUGGESTED TOPPINGS:
Sour cream
Grated Jack cheese
Lettuce
Diced tomatoes
Guacamole

CHICKEN TACOS

Place the frozen chicken breasts in a slow cooker along with a jar of salsa. As it cooks shred with a fork. Cook for 4 to 5 hours. Serve with flour tortillas and condiments of your choice.

Serves 4.

1 tablespoon oil
1½ cups long grain rice
2 cloves garlic, minced
¼ large onion, chopped
1½ teaspoons cumin
2 beef bouillon cubes
½ 8-oz. can tomato sauce
3½ cups water

MEXICAN RICE

Put the oil in a large frypan. Add the rice. Heat to medium and brown the rice. Stir to brown all sides. Add the garlic, onion, cumin, and bouillon cubes. Add ½ can of tomato sauce. Simmer to mix in. Add water and stir in. Cover and simmer for 25 minutes.

Serves 4.

1 bag salad greens
Favorite low-fat or nonfat salad dressing
Favorite tortilla chips

GREEN SALAD AND TORTILLA CHIPS

Tossed green salad with your choice dressing. Your choice of chips.

1 large can refried beans

REFRIED BEANS

Heat the beans in a microwave-safe bowl or on the stove in a saucepan.

Serves 4.

Roast Turkey

BROCCOLI-STUFFING BAKE · BAKED YAMS

Prep Time: 20 minutes • Total Time: 2 hours 20 minutes

1   3- to 5-pound turkey
Salt, pepper, paprika
1   tablespoon butter, melted

ROAST TURKEY

In a large foil-lined pan arrange the turkey. Season with salt and pepper. Wrap foil loosely around the turkey and secure the edges. Roast in a 375° oven for 1 hour. Turn back the foil and baste with juices. Brush with butter and sprinkle with paprika. Roast until done, about 1 hour more.

Serves 6 to 8.

2   cups milk
1   cup grated sharp American cheese
4   beaten eggs
3   cups herb-seasoned stuffing croutons
1   10-ounce package frozen chopped broccoli, thawed
¼   teaspoon salt

BROCCOLI-STUFFING BAKE

In a saucepan heat and stir together the milk and cheese until blended; remove from the heat. In a mixing bowl gradually stir the hot mixture into the eggs. Add the stuffing croutons, broccoli, and salt, mixing well. Turn the mixture into a greased 1½-quart casserole. Bake uncovered at 325° for 45 minutes.

Serves 6 to 8.

4   yams
¼   cup brown sugar
¼   cup butter

BAKED YAMS

Serve with butter and brown sugar.

Time Saver *Reserve leftover turkey for Day 4.*

Sausage Au Gratin

STRING BEAN CASSEROLE · DINNER ROLLS

Prep Time: 30 minutes • Total Time: I hour 20 minutes

12 medium potatoes

2 8-ounce jars cheese spread

2 cups sour cream

2 tablespoons instant minced onion

I tablespoon dried parsley flakes

I teaspoon salt

I 12-ounce package fully cooked smoked sausage links, sliced

1½ cups soft bread crumbs

I tablespoon melted butter

¼ teaspoon paprika

SAUSAGE AU GRATIN

In a covered kettle cook the potatoes in boiling salted water to cover until tender, about 30 minutes. Drain and cool. When cool enough to handle, peel and slice the potatoes.

Meanwhile, in a large bowl blend together the cheese spread and sour cream. Stir in the instant minced onion, parsley flakes, and salt. Fold in the sliced potatoes and sliced sausages. Turn into a 13 x 9-inch baking dish. Bake uncovered at 350° for 40 to 45 minutes.

Toss together the bread crumbs, melted butter, and paprika. Sprinkle on top of the casserole. Bake until lightly browned, about 10 minutes longer.

Serves 12.

¼ cup butter

I bunch scallions, chopped

I tablespoon flour

I cup sour cream

I package sliced processed Swiss cheese

3 10-ounce packages frozen string beans

I teaspoon sugar

STRING BEAN CASSEROLE

In a skillet melt the butter and sauté the scallions. Add the flour and sour cream and 3 slices of cheese. Blend to make a smooth sauce. Layer the beans and sauce in a 1½ or 2-quart buttered casserole dish. Top with more cheese slices. Bake at 350° for 40 to 45 minutes.

Serves 8 to 10.

I package prepared dinner rolls

Butter

DINNER ROLLS

Warm the rolls and serve with butter.

Hot Crab-Stuffed Tomatoes

SLICED FRENCH BREAD

Prep Time: 30 minutes • Total Time: 1 hour

½   cup butter
⅔   cup flour
2⅔ cups milk (a little sherry wine may be substituted for some of the milk)
2   cups flaked crabmeat
1   large pimento, minced
1   large stalk celery, diced
⅓   cup blanched and quartered almonds
⅓   green pepper, minced
4   hard-boiled eggs, cut up
2   teaspoons salt
6   tomatoes

HOT CRAB-STUFFED TOMATOES

In a saucepan melt the butter and blend in the flour. Gradually blend in the milk and cook for 10 minutes. Cut the tops off the tomatoes and scoop out the centers. Pour the stuffing into centers of large tomatoes. Sprinkle with buttered crumbs and bake at 350° for 30 minutes. Serve on lettuce leaves.

Serves 6.

1   loaf French bread, sliced
Butter

SLICED FRENCH BREAD AND BUTTER

Turkey Broccoli Casserole

SLICED PEARS · BAKED GARLIC POTATOES

Prep Time: 30 minutes • Total Time: 1 hour 10 minutes

1   10-ounce package frozen chopped broccoli, cooked and well drained
1   cup grated Parmesan cheese (save a little for topping)
6   cups cooked turkey pieces
1   10½-ounce can cream of celery soup, undiluted
¼   cup milk
½   cup mayonnaise
1   tablespoon Worcestershire sauce
½   cup whipped topping

TURKEY BROCCOLI CASSEROLE

Place the broccoli on the bottom of a buttered 9 x 13-inch casserole. Sprinkle with cheese. Put turkey pieces over this.

Mix together the soup, milk, mayonnaise, and Worcestershire, then fold in the whipped cream. Pour over the turkey; sprinkle with the remaining cheese. Bake at 425° for 10 to 15 minutes.

Place under a broiler to brown.

Serves 6 to 8.

Pears

SLICED PEARS

1   pound small white potatoes (about 1½-inch in diameter)
4   cloves fresh garlic, minced
4   tablespoons olive oil
¼   cup chopped parsley
2   teaspoons coarse salt
¼   teaspoon freshly ground pepper
Butter or margarine

BAKED GARLIC POTATOES

Wash and dry the potatoes. Arrange in a casserole in 2 layers. Combine the garlic, oil, parsley, salt, and pepper. Pour over the potatoes and toss to coat with oil mixture. Cover and bake at 425° for 40 minutes.

Turn the potatoes to recoat in oil, then bake another 30 minutes.

Cut the potatoes open and squeeze the ends to fluff them up. Serve with butter or margarine.

Serves 6.

Fresh Tomato Soup

JOSEFINAS · GREEN SALAD

Prep Time: 20 minutes • Total Time: 1 hour 15 minutes

2　tablespoons olive oil
2　tablespoons butter
2　medium onions, chopped
2　pounds tomatoes (6), quartered
1　6-ounce can tomato paste
2　teaspoons dry crushed basil, or 2 tablespoons fresh
1　teaspoon dry crushed thyme, or 4 teaspoons fresh
3　cubes chicken bouillon, dissolved in
3　cups boiling water

FRESH TOMATO SOUP

In a saucepan heat the olive oil and butter and sauté the onion. Add all the other ingredients. Bring to a boil, reduce the heat, and simmer for 40 minutes.

Put the soup through a blender/processor. Strain. Add salt and pepper to taste.

This is good served hot or cold and freezes beautifully. Serves 6.

1　cup soft butter
1　clove garlic, pressed
1　cup canned, chopped green chilies
French rolls or baguettes, thinly sliced
½　pound Monterey Jack cheese, grated
1　cup mayonnaise

JOSEFINAS

In a small bowl combine the butter, garlic, and chilies, and mix well. Spread on the bread. Mix the Monterey Jack and mayonnaise, and spread topping over the butter mixture to the edges of the bread slices. Broil.

Yields 5 dozen.

1　bag salad greens
Favorite salad toppings
Favorite low-fat or nonfat dressing

GREEN SALAD

Place salad greens in serving bowls. Add toppings and drizzle with dressing.

Cavatelli

GREEN SALAD · GARLIC BREAD

Prep Time: 15 minutes • Total Time: Microwave - 20 minutes; oven - 35 minutes

1	teaspoon olive oil
1	12-ounce Italian sausage
¼	cup green onions, chopped
2	cloves garlic, minced
2½	cups spiral or wagon wheel noodles
1	12-ounce jar spaghetti sauce, with mushrooms
1	8-ounce can tomato sauce
1	cup grated mozzarella cheese

CAVATELLI

Sauté the sausage, onion, and garlic in oil. Cook the noodles according to package directions. Combine the noodles and sausage mixture in a 2-quart casserole. Mix in the spaghetti sauce and tomato sauce. Toss in half of the cheese. Sprinkle the remaining cheese on top. Bake at 375° for 20 minutes.

For a quick cook, microwave on high for 5 minutes. Serves 4 to 6.

---

1 bag salad greens
Favorite salad toppings
Favorite salad dressing

GREEN SALAD

Place salad greens in serving bowls. Add toppings and drizzle with dressing.

---

1 loaf ready-to-heat garlic bread

GARLIC BREAD

Heat as directed on the package.

Beefed-up Skillet Dinner

POTATOES · DINNER ROLLS

Prep Time: 25 minutes • Total Time: 40 minutes

1 pound cubed sirloin steak
Salt and pepper to taste
Vegetable oil
1 16-ounce package frozen mixed broccoli, carrots, and cauliflower
1 10½-ounce can cream of mushroom soup
⅓ cup light sour cream
1 4-ounce jar chopped pimento
1 teaspoon pepper
1 2.8-ounce can French fried onions
1 cup grated Swiss cheese

BEEFED-UP SKILLET DINNER

Cut the steak into strips or 1-inch cubes; sprinkle with salt and pepper to taste. Brown on all sides in a skillet sprayed with oil. Add the vegetables, soup, sour cream, pimento, pepper, half the onions and half the cheese; mix well. Simmer for 10 minutes. Top with the remaining onions and cheese. Cook until the cheese melts.

Serves 4.

6 to 8 potatoes, peeled
Salt

POTATOES

Boil the peeled potatoes in salted water for 10 minutes. Serves 6 to 8.

1 package prepared dinner rolls
Butter

DINNER ROLLS

Warm the rolls and serve with butter.

Spicy and Sweet Pork Chops

GREEN BEAN CASSEROLE · APPLESAUCE

Prep Time: 20 minutes • Total Time: 1 hour 5 minutes

2   tablespoons vegetable oil
4   thickly sliced pork chops
4   slices pineapple
2   maraschino cherries, cut into halves
½   cup apricot preserves
¼   cup soy sauce
¼   cup white wine
Orange slices and watercress

SPICY AND SWEET PORK CHOPS

Preheat the oven to 350°. In a skillet brown the pork chops on both sides in oil. Arrange in a 9-inch square shallow baking dish. Place the pineapple slices and cherry halves on each pork chop.

In a small bowl combine the preserves, soy sauce, and wine; mix well. Pour over the pork chops. Bake covered for 45 minutes or until the pork chops are cooked through. Arrange on a serving platter. Serve with sauce. Garnish with orange slices and watercress.

Serves 4.

---

1   10½-ounce can condensed cream of mushroom soup
¾   cup milk
⅛   teaspoon pepper
2   16-ounce cans cut green beans, drained
1   2.8-ounce can French fried onions

GREEN BEAN CASSEROLE

In a 1½-quart casserole mix the soup, milk, and pepper. Stir in the beans and half of the French fried onions. Bake uncovered at 350° for 30 minutes, stir. Top with the remaining onions and bake 5 more minutes or until golden.

Serves 4 to 6.

---

1   jar applesauce

APPLESAUCE

Chicken Vegetable Casserole

SAVORY RICE

Prep Time: 15 minutes • Total Time: 35 minutes

3 cups loose-pack frozen cut broccoli or Italian-style mixed vegetables

4 boneless, skinless chicken breasts

2 tablespoons mayonnaise

⅓ cup fine dry Italian seasoned bread crumbs

3 tablespoons grated Parmesan cheese

⅛ teaspoon paprika

CHICKEN VEGETABLE CASSEROLE

In a large strainer rinse the vegetables with warm water to thaw. Place in a 2-quart round casserole. Rinse the chicken and pat dry. Fold the pieces in half and brush on all sides with mayonnaise. Combine the bread crumbs and cheese. Roll the chicken in the crumb mixture, coating well. Arrange the chicken on top of the vegetables with the thickest portions toward the edge. Sprinkle with paprika and the remaining crumb mixture. Microwave with rice 20 minutes on high or 10 to 12 minutes alone.

Serves 4.

1½ cups water

1 teaspoon instant chicken bouillon granules

1½ cups quick cooking rice

1 tablespoon margarine

1 teaspoon dried parsley flakes

¼ teaspoon dried thyme, crushed

SAVORY RICE

In a microwaveable casserole combine all ingredients and microwave on high for 3 to 5 minutes. Let stand covered for 5 minutes. Stir to fluff.

Serves 4.

Time Saver *Hard-boil 2 eggs for use on Day 5.*

Baked Halibut

SPINACH SALAD · GARLIC BREAD · CARROTS AND ZUCCHINI

Prep Time: 10 minutes • Total Time: 40 minutes

4   large halibut fillets (not steaks)
Lemon and herb seasoning
¼   cup butter or margarine
Juice of 1 lemon
Parmesan cheese
1   package fresh pasta (angel hair)

BAKED HALIBUT

Place fillets in a baking dish; sprinkle both sides with lemon and herb seasoning. Melt the butter and lemon juice together. Pour over the fish. Bake at 350° for 30 minutes. Sprinkle generously with Parmesan cheese. Bake until browned slightly. Meanwhile, cook the fresh pasta. Serve the fillets on pasta with drippings poured over as sauce.

Serves 4.

1   bag spinach salad
1   red onion, sliced
1   jar bacon bits
2   hard-boiled eggs
Red wine vinaigrette or poppy seed
    dressing

SPINACH SALAD

Place the spinach salad mix in a salad bowl. Add sliced red onions, bacon bits, and eggs. Serve with a red wine vinaigrette or poppy seed dressing.

Serves 4 to 6.

1   loaf ready-to-heat garlic bread

GARLIC BREAD

Bake as directed on the package.

Carrots and zucchini

CARROTS AND ZUCCHINI

Sauté carrots and zucchini sliced lengthwise in butter, enough for your family.

Baked Ham

SPINACH-CHEESE CASSEROLE

Prep Time: 30 minutes • Total Time: 1 hour 50 minutes

1 12-ounce can beer
1 8-pound bone-in ham

BAKED HAM

Pour the beer over the ham. Bake the ham at 325° for approximately 60 minutes. Baste and return to a 375° oven for 20 minutes.

Serves 6 to 8.

2 slices bacon
½ cup chopped carrots
¼ cup chopped onion
1 11-ounce can condensed Cheddar cheese soup
2 10-ounce packages frozen chopped spinach, thawed and drained
1 cup cooked rice
¼ cup milk

SPINACH-CHEESE CASSEROLE

In a 2-quart saucepan cook the bacon until crisp; drain, reserving drippings. Crumble the bacon and set aside. In the reserved drippings cook the carrots and onion until the onion is tender. Stir in the soup, spinach, rice, and milk. Turn the mixture into a 1-quart casserole. Bake covered at 375° until heated through, 35 to 40 minutes. Sprinkle with the crumbled bacon.

Serves 6 to 8.

Time Saver *Reserve 16 thin slices of ham for Day 3. Reserve ham hock for Day 5. Chop an additional 4 onions for use throughout the week. Cook an additional 3 cups of rice for Day 3. Cook an additional 2 strips of bacon for Day 2.*

Cutlets with Jack

ITALIAN SKILLET ZUCCHINI · SLICED FRENCH BREAD

Prep Time: 30 minutes • Total Time: 1 hour 15 minutes

2   teaspoons dry cheese or Parmesan, grated
1/2 cup dry bread crumbs
Salt and pepper
2   eggs
4   veal or turkey cutlets, pounded thin between waxed paper
5   tablespoons butter
Italian tomato sauce, bottled
1/4 pound Monterey Jack cheese, sliced

CUTLETS WITH JACK

Add dry cheese to the bread crumbs. Add salt and pepper to the eggs and beat. Dip the cutlets into the eggs, then coat with the bread crumbs, and sauté in butter until browned on both sides. Place in an 8 x 11-inch buttered shallow pan, top with the tomato sauce, then with thinly sliced Jack cheese. Bake at 325° for 15 minutes until the cheese is browned.

Serves 4.

1   small onion, minced
2   strips bacon, diced
1/8 teaspoon Italian herbs
1   pound zucchini, thinly sliced
3/4 teaspoon salt
1   tablespoon water

ITALIAN SKILLET ZUCCHINI

Sauté the onion, bacon, and herbs together until the onion is lightly browned. Add the zucchini and sauté 2 to 3 minutes, stirring gently. Sprinkle with salt, add water, and cover. Cook over low heat for 10 minutes. Add another tablespoon of water, if necessary. Zucchini should be slightly crisp when done.

Serves 4.

1   loaf French bread, sliced
Butter

SLICED FRENCH BREAD

Mandarin Ham Rolls

COMPANY CARROTS · SLICED FRENCH BREAD

Prep Time: 30 minutes • Total Time: 1 hour 30 minutes

2   11-ounce cans mandarin orange
    sections, drained
3   cups cooked rice
2/3 cup mayonnaise
4   tablespoons chopped pecans
4   tablespoons snipped parsley
2   tablespoons sliced green onion,
    with tops
16 slices boiled ham (8 ounces)
1/2 cup orange marmalade
2   tablespoons lemon juice
1/2 teaspoon ground ginger

MANDARIN HAM ROLLS

Reserve 8 orange sections; chop the remainder and combine with the cooked rice, mayonnaise, pecans, parsley, and onion. Divide the mixture among the ham slices. Roll up the ham around the filling. Place seam side down in a 10 x 6-inch baking dish. Combine the marmalade, lemon juice, and ginger; brush some over the ham rolls. Bake uncovered at 350° for 25 to 30 minutes, brushing occasionally with the remaining sauce. Garnish with the reserved orange sections.

Serves 8.

2 1/2 pounds whole carrots, peeled
1/2 cup mayonnaise
1   tablespoon onion, minced
1   tablespoon prepared horseradish
Salt and pepper to taste
1/4 cup crushed crackers
2   tablespoons butter
Parsley, chopped
Paprika

COMPANY CARROTS

Cook the carrots in boiling salted water until fork-tender. Reserve 1/4 cup of cooking liquid. Cut the carrots lengthwise in narrow strips. Arrange in a 9-inch square baking dish. Set aside. Combine the reserved cooking liquid with mayonnaise, onion, horseradish, salt, and pepper. Pour over the carrots. Sprinkle cracker crumbs on top. Dot with butter. Sprinkle with parsley and paprika. Bake at 350° for 35 minutes.

Serves 8.

1   loaf French bread, sliced
Butter

SLICED FRENCH BREAD

Crab Florentine

GREEN SALAD · FRENCH BREAD

Prep Time: 30 minutes • Total Time: 1 hour 15 minutes

2 10-ounce packages frozen chopped spinach
1 10½-ounce can cream of mushroom soup
2 cups grated Cheddar cheese (reserve 1 cup)
¼ cup cream or rich milk
¼ cup dry sherry
1 teaspoon Worcestershire sauce
Dash pepper
1 pound crabmeat
½ cup fine, dry bread crumbs
2 tablespoons butter, melted
Paprika

CRAB FLORENTINE

Cook the spinach without salt; drain thoroughly. In a saucepan combine the mushroom soup, 1 cup of cheese, cream, sherry, Worcestershire, and pepper. Stir over low heat until the cheese melts and the ingredients are blended. Mix ½ cup of the sauce with the drained spinach and spread in a greased 10 x 6-inch baking dish. Place the crabmeat evenly over the spinach and cover with the remaining sauce. Mix the crumbs and melted butter and sprinkle over the casserole. Top with the remaining cheese and dust with paprika. Bake at 350° for 25 to 30 minutes.

Serves 6.

1 bag salad greens
Favorite salad toppings
Favorite low-fat or nonfat dressing

GREEN SALAD

Place salad greens in serving bowls. Add toppings and drizzle with dressing.

1 loaf French bread
Butter

FRENCH BREAD

Microwave Minestrone Soup

GARLIC BREAD

Prep Time: 30 minutes • Total Time: 50 minutes

Dash olive oil
1 large onion, chopped
1 ham hock
3 to 4 zucchini, chopped
1 cup elbow macaroni, cooked
2 carrots, thinly sliced
1 turnip, thinly sliced
1 teaspoon dry basil
1½ cups savory cabbage
1 28-ounce can tomatoes
1 stalk celery, chopped
1 bay leaf
Salt and pepper to taste

MICROWAVE MINESTRONE SOUP

Preheat the broiler. Toss the onion slices in a dash of olive oil and arrange in a broiler tray. Broil until toasty brown, 4 to 6 minutes on each side. Tip the onions into a large, casserole-type dish and add the remaining ingredients. Cover in water. Cover and microwave on full power for 20 minutes. Remove the ham from the hock. Remove the bay leaf and hock. Salt and pepper to taste.

Serves 6.

½ cup butter, melted
¼ cup garlic, crushed
1 loaf French bread, cut lengthwise

GARLIC BREAD

Spread butter and garlic on the bread. Broil in the oven until crusty and golden.

Serves 4 to 6.

Chicken Roll-ups

NOODLES · GREEN BEAN CASSEROLE

Prep Time: 25 minutes • Total Time: 1 hour 25 minutes

8	chicken breasts, split and boned
1½	pounds Jack or mozzarella cheese
2	cups sour cream
4	slices bacon
2	10½-ounce cans tomato soup
2	4-ounce cans mushrooms, drained

CHICKEN ROLL-UPS

Place chicken breasts on the counter, skin side down. Place a piece of cheese about ½-inch thick in the middle of each and roll up. Place in casserole dish. Top each with ½ slice of bacon. Grate the remaining cheese and mix with the soup, sour cream, and mushrooms. Pour over the chicken breasts and bake uncovered at 350° for 1 hour.

Serves 8.

1	package wide egg noodles

NOODLES

Prepare wide egg noodles as directed on the package for 8 servings.

1	10¾-ounce can cream of mushroom soup
Dash	pepper
2	14½-ounce cans any style green beans, drained
½	cup milk
1	teaspoon soy sauce
1	2.8-ounce can French fried onions

GREEN BEAN CASSEROLE

Conventional: In 1½-quart casserole, combine the soup, milk, soy sauce and pepper. Stir in beans and ½ can fried onions. Bake at 350° for 25 minutes; stir. Top with remaining onions. Bake 5 minutes.

Microwave: Prepare as above in microwave-safe casserole. Cover; microwave on high for 7 minutes or until hot, stirring halfway through cooking. Sprinkle with remaining onions. Microwave uncovered for 1 minute.

Serves 6.

Crock Pot
next day—read ahead!

SALAD · FRENCH BREAD

Prep Time: 20 minutes • Total Time: 2 hours or all day

1   tablespoon olive oil
1   clove garlic, minced
½   medium onion, chopped
1   pound ground beef
1   8-ounce can tomato sauce
1   6-ounce can tomato paste
½   cup each: dry white wine and
      water
1   teaspoon oregano
1   teaspoon basil
1   teaspoon parsley
½   teaspoon each: salt, pepper, sugar

SPAGHETTI

In a large skillet heat the oil and cook the garlic and onion until soft. Add the beef and brown. Then stir in the tomato sauce, paste, wine, water, and spices. Mix well. Simmer on the stove for 1½ hours or place in a slow cooker on low all day.

Serves 6.

1   package spaghetti

SPAGHETTI NOODLES

Cook enough for your family, as directed on package.

1   bag salad greens
Favorite salad toppings
Favorite low-fat or nonfat dressing

SALAD

Place salad greens in serving bowls. Add toppings and drizzle with dressing.

1   loaf French bread
Butter

FRENCH BREAD

fish Sticks and fries

CANNED SLICED FRUIT SALAD

Prep Time: 10 minutes • Total Time: 25 minutes

I box frozen fish sticks
I bag of fries

FISH STICKS AND FRIES

Choose your favorite frozen fish sticks and fries. Place on a cookie sheet and bake as directed. To save time, combine temperatures and cooking times for an average and cook the sticks and fries together.

Lettuce
Cottage cheese
I can fruit of your choice

CANNED SLICED FRUIT SALAD

Make salad cups with a leaf of lettuce and a scoop of cottage cheese and canned fruit of your choice on top.

Hawaiian Kebabs

CORN ON THE COB · RICE PILAF · CRUSTY FRENCH BREAD

Prep Time: 15 minutes • Total Time: 1 hour 35 minutes

1   20-ounce can unsweetened pineapple chunks
2   large green peppers, cut into 1-inch pieces
1   large onion, quartered
12 to 16 medium fresh mushrooms
16 to 18 cherry tomatoes
1½ pounds kebab meat
½   cup soy sauce
¼   cup olive oil
1   tablespoon brown sugar
2   teaspoons ground ginger
1   teaspoon garlic powder
1   teaspoon dry mustard
¼   teaspoon pepper

HAWAIIAN KEBABS

Drain the pineapple, reserving ½ cup of juice. In a large bowl place the pineapple chunks, vegetables, and meat; set aside. In a saucepan combine the reserved pineapple juice with the soy sauce, olive oil, brown sugar, and seasonings; bring to a boil. Reduce the heat and simmer, uncovered, for 5 minutes. Pour over the meat and vegetable mixture; cover and refrigerate for at least 1 hour, stirring occasionally.

Remove the pineapple, meat, and vegetables from marinade and reserve marinade. Alternate the pineapple, green pepper, onion, meat, mushrooms, and tomatoes on skewers. Grill the kabobs for 20 minutes or until soft, turning and basting with marinade frequently.

Serves 8.

6   ears fresh or frozen corn

CORN ON THE COB

Fresh or frozen corn, cooked as directed. If fresh, try them on the barbecue wrapped in foil.

1   package rice pilaf

RICE PILAF

Cook as directed on the package.

1   loaf French bread
Butter
Garlic

CRUSTY FRENCH BREAD OR FRENCH ROLLS

Prepare with butter and garlic and toast in the oven or on the grill.

Family Tacos

REFRIED BEANS · TORTILLA CHIPS

Prep Time: 10 minutes • Total Time: 20 minutes

1 pound ground beef
1 package taco seasonings
¼ cup oil
1 dozen corn tortillas
2 cups grated lettuce
2 cups grated Cheddar cheese
1 diced tomato

FAMILY TACOS

Brown the ground beef in a skillet. Add the taco seasonings as directed. Set aside. Heat oil on medium high heat and fry tortillas to desired crispness. Serve with lettuce, cheese, and tomatoes.

Serves 4 to 6.

---

1 16-ounce can refried beans
Cheddar cheese

REFRIED BEANS

Heat the beans on the stovetop or in the microwave. Garnish with Cheddar cheese.

---

1 bag tortilla chips

TORTILLA CHIPS

Crock Pot
next day—read ahead!

Lemon-Baked Chicken

CHEDDAR-SQUASH BAKE · FRUIT SALAD

Prep Time: 30 minutes • Total Time: 6 to 8 hours

6 to 8 chicken breasts
1 lemon, sliced
1/2 teaspoon lemon pepper

LEMON-BAKED CHICKEN

Place the chicken in a crock pot. Place the lemon around and on the chicken; sprinkle with pepper. Cook 6 to 8 hours.

Serves 6.

2 pounds yellow crookneck summer squash or zucchini
1 cup sour cream
2 beaten egg yolks
2 tablespoons all-purpose flour
2 stiffly beaten egg whites
1 1/2 cups grated Cheddar cheese
4 slices bacon, crisp-cooked, drained and crumbled
1/3 cup fine dry bread crumbs
1 tablespoon butter, melted

CHEDDAR-SQUASH BAKE

Scrub the squash and cut off the ends. Do not peel. Slice to make 6 cups. Cook, covered, in a small amount of boiling salted water until tender, 15 to 20 minutes. Drain well; sprinkle with salt. Reserve a few slices of squash for garnish.

Mix the sour cream, egg yolks, and flour; fold in the egg whites. In a 12 x 7 1/2-inch baking dish layer half the squash, half the egg mixture, and half the cheese; sprinkle bacon atop. Repeat layers of squash, egg, and cheese. Combine the bread crumbs and butter and sprinkle on top. Arrange the reserved squash on top. Bake uncovered at 350° for 20 to 25 minutes. Top with bacon and parsley, if desired.

Serves 8 to 10.

Fresh fruit

FRUIT SALAD

Favorite fruit sliced and mixed.

 Time Saver *Grate an additional 1/4 cup cheese for Day 3.*

Meat Loaf

BAKED POTATOES · BAKED CARROTS

Prep Time: 20 minutes • Total Time: 1 hour 45 minutes

1½ pounds lean hamburger
1 small onion, chopped
3 slices wheat bread
2 eggs
¼ cup oats
1 cup milk
1 tablespoon Worcestershire sauce
1¼ teaspoons garlic salt
¼ teaspoon celery salt, pepper, sage
¼ teaspoon dry mustard

MEAT LOAF

Crumble the meat in a large bowl. Add the chopped onions, torn bread slices, eggs, oats, milk, Worcestershire sauce, and seasonings. Transfer to a greased glass loaf pan. Cook at 350° for 45 to 50 minutes. Let set 5 minutes before serving for a firmer loaf.

Serves 6.

---

6 large potatoes

BAKED POTATOES

Prick the potatoes in several places. Bake with the meat loaf.

---

12 carrots, peeled and sliced

BAKED CARROTS

Bake the carrots with the meat loaf and potatoes.

 Time Saver *Chop an additional 3 onions for Day 5.*

Crab Gratin

SPINACH TOMATOES · FRENCH BREAD

Prep Time: 30 minutes • Total Time: 1 hour

2	tablespoons butter
2	tablespoons flour
1⅓	cups milk
¼	cup grated sharp Cheddar cheese
¼	cup grated Swiss cheese
1	teaspoon salt
⅛	teaspoon pepper
1	tablespoon dry sherry
24 to 30	asparagus spears, cooked (fresh or frozen)
½	pound crab in big chunks
Parmesan cheese	

CRAB GRATIN

Melt the butter. Stir in the flour and add the milk gradually, stirring constantly to make a smooth sauce. Add the cheeses and stir occasionally until melted. Add the seasonings and sherry and let simmer very slowly for 10 minutes. Line a 2-quart casserole with asparagus. Sprinkle well with salt and pepper. Place a layer of crabmeat over the asparagus and thoroughly cover with the sauce. Sprinkle heavily with grated Parmesan cheese. Bake at 375° for about 20 minutes, until the sauce is bubbly and the top turns golden.

Serves 6.

1	10-ounce package frozen chopped spinach
4	large tomatoes
1	beaten egg
¼	cup fine dry Italian seasoned bread crumbs
¼	cup grated Parmesan cheese
¼	teaspoon onion powder
¼	teaspoon crushed dried oregano
Salt and pepper	
Parmesan cheese	

SPINACH TOMATOES

In a 1-quart casserole microwave the spinach, covered, on high for 7 minutes, stirring once. Drain and squeeze out the excess water. Set aside. Meanwhile, cut a ¼-inch slice off the top of each tomato. Scoop out the tomato pulp, leaving a ¼-inch shell. Invert on paper towels to drain. In a medium mixing bowl stir together the egg, bread crumbs, Parmesan cheese, onion powder, oregano, and ¼ teaspoon of pepper. Stir in the spinach. Sprinkle the insides of the tomato shells with salt and pepper. Fill each with some of the spinach. Top with Parmesan cheese. Place in an 8-inch square baking dish. Microwave uncovered on 100% power (high) for 4 to 6 minutes or until heated through, giving dish a half turn once.

Serves 4.

1	loaf French bread
Butter	

FRENCH BREAD

Chicken Breasts with White Wine

NOODLES · ZUCCHINI

Prep Time: 20 minutes • Total Time: 30 minutes

2 tablespoons margarine
6 boneless/skinned breasts
8 ounces sliced fresh mushrooms
1 cup white wine
½ teaspoon tarragon
½ teaspoon salt
1 tablespoon flour

CHICKEN BREASTS WITH WHITE WINE

In a large skillet melt the margarine. Add the chicken and sauté until brown. Add the mushrooms and sauté another several minutes. Add ¾ cup of white wine, tarragon, and salt. Reduce the heat and simmer covered for 20 minutes.

Stir the flour into the remaining ¼ cup white wine. Stir into the chicken-mushroom mixture. Cook until thickened and smooth.

Serves 6.

---

1 package egg noodles

NOODLES

Cook as directed on the box for 6 servings.

---

5 medium zucchini
Salt and pepper, to taste

ZUCCHINI

Cut the zucchini into large pieces. In a pot, cover with water. Boil until tender. Season to taste.

Serves 4 to 6.

Chili

SLICED PEACHES · FRENCH BREAD

Prep Time: 30 minutes • Total Time: 35 minutes

2   pounds ground beef
1   medium onion, chopped
1   green pepper, chopped
1   clove garlic, minced
1   15-ounce can red kidney beans
1   14½-ounce can tomatoes, cut up
1   10½-ounce can condensed tomato soup
2   teaspoons chili powder
⅛   teaspoon pepper
1   bay leaf

TOPPING SUGGESTIONS:
Crushed crackers
Sour cream
Grated cheese
Chopped fresh tomato

CHILI

Crumble the ground beef into a 2-quart casserole, then stir in the onion, green pepper, and garlic. Microwave covered for 5 to 6 minutes or until the beef is done, stirring once to break up the meat; drain. Stir in the kidney beans, undrained tomatoes, soup, chili powder, pepper, and bay leaf. Microwave for 5 minutes, stir. Reduce to medium power and microwave covered for 20 minutes, stirring twice. Remove the bay leaf.

Serves 6.

---

1   can sliced peaches

SLICED PEACHES

---

1   loaf French bread
Butter

FRENCH BREAD

Baked Ham

BOILED POTATOES AND CARROTS · CRESCENT ROLLS

Prep Time: 15 minutes • Total Time: 1 hour 30 minutes

1 5-pound canned ham	**BAKED HAM** Bake the ham at 350° according to the package directions, or 1 hour 30 minutes. Save 3 slices for use on Day 2.

4 to 6 russet potatoes 4 to 6 carrots Butter Salt and pepper to taste	**BOILED POTATOES AND CARROTS** Peel and boil the potatoes and carrots. Serve with butter and salt and pepper.

1 to 2 cans refrigerator crescent rolls	**CRESCENT ROLLS** Bake according to the package directions.

Rolled Stuffed Meat Loaf

MIXED VEGETABLES · DINNER ROLLS

Prep Time: 10 minutes • Total Time: 1 hour 10 minutes

1½ pounds lean ground beef
1 egg, slightly beaten
1 teaspoon salt
¼ teaspoon pepper
3 slices cooked ham from Day 2
2 slices mozzarella cheese
½ cup chopped green olives

ROLLED STUFFED MEAT LOAF

In a large bowl combine the ground beef, egg, salt, and pepper; mix well. Pat into a ½-inch-thick 8 x 11-inch rectangle on waxed paper. Arrange ham slices crosswise on the beef mixture and top with cheese slices. Sprinkle with chopped olives. Roll up as for jelly-roll, sealing the edge. Place seam side down in 5 x 9-inch glass loaf pan. Insert a microwave meat thermometer into the center of loaf. Microwave on high for 5 minutes or to 105° on the thermometer. Microwave on medium for 16 minutes or to 135° on thermometer. Microwave on medium-low for 4 minutes or to 155° on thermometer. If using a conventional oven, bake at 350° for 1 hour.

Serves 6.

---

1 bag frozen mixed vegetables

MIXED VEGETABLES

Prepare the vegetables as directed on the package.

---

1 package prepared dinner rolls
Butter

DINNER ROLLS

Warm the rolls and serve with butter.

Beef Stroganoff

GREEN BEANS · CREAMED CORN

Prep Time: 15 minutes • Total Time: 40 minutes

1	12-ounce sirloin steak
2	tablespoons corn oil
4	4-ounce cans sliced mushrooms
1	medium onion, chopped
2	cups beef broth
2	tablespoons Worcestershire sauce
1/2	cup tomato sauce
1/2	teaspoon paprika
2	cups instant rice
1/2	cup sour cream

BEEF STROGANOFF

Cut the steak into thin strips. In a skillet heat the oil and brown the steak strips. Add the mushrooms and onion. Sauté for 3 minutes or until onion is tender. Add the broth, Worcestershire sauce, tomato sauce, and paprika. Bring to a boil. Cook for 3 minutes. Stir in the rice. Let stand, covered, for 5 minutes. Stir in the sour cream.

Serves 4.

	Frozen green beans
1/8	cup slivered almonds
1/4	cup onions, chopped

GREEN BEANS

Cook with onions and slivered almonds according to the package directions.

2	16-ounce cans creamed corn

CREAMED CORN

Heat as directed on the can.

Student Supper

DINNER ROLLS

Prep Time: 20 minutes • Total Time: 40 minutes

1 pound ground beef
1 egg, beaten
1 cup seasoned bread crumbs
2 tablespoons butter
1 medium onion, chopped
1 4-ounce can sliced mushrooms
1/2 cup chopped green bell pepper
1 16-ounce can sliced potatoes
1/2 cup chopped celery
1 10 1/2-ounce can golden mushroom soup
1 cup grated Cheddar cheese
1/3 cup milk
1 bay leaf
1 4-ounce can sliced olives
1/4 teaspoon garlic salt
1/4 teaspoon black pepper
1/4 teaspoon paprika

STUDENT SUPPER

In a large bowl mix together the beef, egg, and breadcrumbs. In a large skillet melt the butter and sauté the beef mixture until browned.

Add the onion, mushrooms, bell pepper, potatoes, celery, soup, and Cheddar.

Add the remaining ingredients and mix well. Simmer for about 15 minutes.

1 package prepared dinner rolls
Butter

DINNER ROLLS

Warm the rolls and serve with butter.

Crispy Chicken Strips

MASHED POTATOES · CORN ON THE COB

Prep Time: 30 minutes • Total Time: 1 hour

2 tablespoons mayonnaise
1 tablespoon Dijon mustard
1 teaspoon Worcestershire sauce
½ teaspoon paprika
¼ teaspoon salt
¼ teaspoon pepper
½ teaspoon ground red pepper, divided
1 pound boneless, skinless chicken strips
½ cup cracker meal or bread crumbs
4 tablespoons margarine
2 tablespoons lemon juice
1 tablespoon parsley, chopped

CRISPY CHICKEN STRIPS

Heat the oven to 400°. Coat a baking sheet with cooking spray. In a bowl combine the mayonnaise, mustard, Worcestershire sauce, paprika, salt, pepper, and ¼ teaspoon of red pepper; add the chicken strips and toss well to coat. On waxed paper combine the cracker meal and remaining red pepper. Dredge the chicken strips in the mixture to coat. Arrange in a single layer on the prepared baking sheet. Bake for 20 minutes, turning once, until golden.

Meanwhile in a saucepan over low heat, melt the margarine and stir in the lemon juice and parsley. Drizzle over the chicken strips. If less spicy chicken is desired, decrease the red pepper by half.

6 to 8 potatoes
4 tablespoons butter
Salt, pepper
Milk
Butter substitute powder

MASHED POTATOES

Peel and boil the potatoes until soft, approximately 10 minutes. Add salt before cooking. Drain. Mash with butter and salt and pepper. With a large spoon whip with a little milk until creamy. Add butter substitute for more flavor.

1 box frozen corn

CORN ON THE COB

Cook as directed on the package.

· SWISS CHICKEN CUTLETS · STEAMED WHITE RICE · ROLLS ·

· BAKED POTATOES · CHUCK TRI-TIP ROAST ·

· BROCCOLI RICE CASSEROLE · UPSIDE-DOWN PIZZA · CORN CHIPS ·

· BAKED HAM · GREEN SALAD · MEXICAN STEAK & BEANS ·

· MEXICAN LASAGNA · RICE PILAF · HOT CHICKEN SALAD ·

Winter

· PORK CHOPS A L'ORANGE · STEAMED VEGETABLES ·

· EASY CHICKEN DISH · BISCUITS · CARROT-RICE BAKE ·

· CRUNCH SPINACH SALAD · PEPPERED RIB EYE STEAKS ·

· MASHED POTATOES · GRANDMA'S MEATBALLS · GREEN BEANS ·

· CREPES PUERTO VALLARTA · VEGETABLE

MEDLEY · POT LUCK POTATOES · GREEN SALAD · GRILLED

CHEESE SANDWICHES · MANICOTTI · GARLIC

TOAST · COPPER PENNIES · ASPARAGUS WITH SAUCE ·

· CROCK POT SPLIT PEA SOUP · WHITE RICE ·

· SPINACH WITH VINEGAR · PIZZA ROLL · SLICED

FRUIT · BEEF RAGOUT · VEGETABLE MEDLEY · PEAS ·

· SPICY WINE POT ROAST ·

· BEEF BURGUNDY ·

· TWICE-BAKED SWEET POTATOES ·

WEEK 8

Day	Main Dish			
Day 1	Mexican Steak & Beans	Salad	Jalapeño Rice	Tortilla Chips
Day 2	Chicken Stir-Fry	White Rice		
Day 3	Sloppy Joes	Corn Chips	Stovetop Baked Beans	
Day 4	Old-Fashioned Beef Stew	Biscuits		
Day 5	Rustic Lasagna	Green Salad	Garlic Bread	

WEEK 7

Day	Main Dish			
Day 1	Baked Virginia Ham	Mustard Ring	Sliced Oranges	
Day 2	Easy Chicken Dish	Potluck Potatoes	Green Salad	
Day 3	Crock Pot Split-Pea Soup	French Bread		
Day 4	Crepes Puerto Vallarta	Vegetable Medley	Green Salad	
Day 5	Pizza Roll	Green Salad	Sliced Fruit	

WEEK 6

Day	Main Dish			
Day 1	Pork Chops a l'Orange	Fettuccine Noodles	Steamed Vegetables	Garlic Bread
Day 2	Grandma's Meatballs	Mashed Potatoes	Green Beans	
Day 3	Hot Chicken Salad	Dinner Rolls		
Day 4	Mexican Lasagna	Refried Beans	Green Salad	Tortilla Chips
Day 5	Peppered Rib Eye Steaks	Rice Pilaf	Crunchy Spinach Salad	

WEEK 5

Day	Main Dish			
Day 1	Spicy Wine Pot Roast	Dinner Rolls		
Day 2	Sour Cream–Chili Bake	Fruit Salad	Breadsticks	
Day 3	Fish & Chip Bake	Green Salad		
Day 4	Pizza	Fruit Salad	Relish	
Day 5	Stuffed Pork Roast	Carrot-Rice Bake	Sliced Apples	

WINTER MENUS AT A GLANCE

WEEK 1

Day 1	Swiss Chicken Cutlets	White Rice	Green Beans	Dinner Rolls
Day 2	Chuck/Tri-tip Roast	Dinner Rolls		
Day 3	Monterey Chicken Breasts	Vegetable Medley	White Rice	
Day 4	Chimichangas	Mexican Rice	Green Salad	Tortilla Chips
Day 5	Sweet Mustard Sauced Fish	Hash Browns	Green Salad	

WEEK 2

Day 1	Beef Stew	Corn Bread	Fruit Salad
Day 2	Lemon Basil Chicken	Potato Dish	Cider Peas & Apples
Day 3	Turkey Strips with Apricot Sauce	Stuffed Acorn Squash	French Bread
Day 4	Broccoli Rice Casserole	Fruit Sections	
Day 5	Garlic Prawns	String Beans Oriental	Rice

WEEK 3

Day 1	Low-fat Chicken Enchiladas	Mexicana Corn	Refried Beans	
Day 2	Baked Ham	Mac 'n' Cheese	Baked Beans	Applesauce
Day 3	Upside-down Pizza	Green Salad		
Day 4	Ham and Potato Casserole	Microwave Cauliflower & Peas	Dinner Rolls	
Day 5	Zucchini Boats	Corn Chips	Sliced Peaches	

WEEK 4

Day 1	Baked Chicken Breasts	Carrot-Rice Bake	Fruit Cup Salad
Day 2	Seafood Bisque	Asparagus with Sauce	Biscuits
Day 3	Manicotti	Copper Pennies	Garlic Toast
Day 4	Noodle, Cheese & Meat Casserole	Green Beans with Garlic	Breadsticks
Day 5	Potato Soup	Grilled Cheese Sandwiches	

WEEK 13

Day 1	Spaghetti	Green Salad	Garlic Bread
Day 2	Shepherd's Pie	Sliced Peaches	Salad
Day 3	Smothered Steak	Mashed Potatoes	Green Beans
Day 4	Sausage Casserole	Carrots & Zucchini	
Day 5	Chicken Veggie Casserole	Savory Rice	

WINTER MENUS AT A GLANCE

WEEK 9

Day 1	Cavatelli	Green Salad	Garlic Bread	
Day 2	Chicken Supreme	Green Beans	Flaky Biscuits	
Day 3	Beef Burgundy	White Rice	Peas	Dinner Rolls
Day 4	Smothered Pork Chops	Applesauce	Rice	Steamed Vegetables
Day 5	Chicken Tacos	Mexican Rice	Refried Beans	Green Salad & Chips

WEEK 10

Day 1	Baked Ham	Vegetable Medley	Dinner Rolls
Day 2	Monterey Spaghetti Casserole	Green Salad	
Day 3	Beef Ragout	Carrots	
Day 4	Saucy Pork Chops	Twice-Baked Sweet Potatoes	Green Salad
Day 5	Ham & Mac Bake	Green Beans	Sliced Pears

WEEK 11

Day 1	Spareribs "Cooked Easy"	Rice	Green Salad
Day 2	Pork Chops O'Brien	Green Beans	Dinner Rolls
Day 3	Mom's Meat Loaf	Mac 'n' Cheese	Applesauce
Day 4	Stuffed Chicken Pasta	Corn on the Cob	Green Salad
Day 5	Excellent Clam Chowder	French Bread	

WEEK 12

Day 1	Cranberry Pork Roast	Broccoli-Rice Casserole	Sliced Apples
Day 2	Beefy Onion Pie	Spinach with Vinegar	Breadsticks
Day 3	Chicken Soup	Sliced French Bread	
Day 4	Worcestershire Burgers	Fresh Fruit Salad Cups	
Day 5	Enchiladas	Spanish Rice	Refried Beans

Swiss Chicken Cutlets

WHITE RICE · GREEN BEANS WITH BACON AND ONION · DINNER ROLLS

Prep Time: 20 minutes • Total Time: 35 minutes

2 thin slices Swiss cheese
4 chicken breasts
Kitchen string
2 tablespoons flour
1/2 teaspoon black pepper
1 tablespoon butter
1/2 cup chicken broth
1/4 cup dry white wine
1/4 teaspoon dried oregano
Chopped fresh parsley and fresh
    oregano sprigs, for garnish

SWISS CHICKEN CUTLETS

Cut each cheese slice in half; place half on top of each cutlet. Starting with a short end, tightly roll up cutlets, jellyroll style. Tie securely with string. On waxed paper, combine the flour and pepper. Mix well. Add the cutlets and toss gently to coat.

In a large non-stick skillet melt butter over medium heat. Add cutlets and cook until golden, about 3 minutes, turning frequently. Add the broth, wine, and dried oregano to skillet. Increase the heat, and bring to a boil. Reduce the heat to medium-low; simmer until the chicken is cooked through and the sauce is slightly thickened, about 10 to 12 minutes. Place on a serving plate; remove string. Garnish with parsley and oregano sprigs.

Serves 4.

2 cups water
2 cups instant rice

STEAMED WHITE RICE

Bring the water to a boil. Stir in the rice; cover and remove from the heat. Let stand 5 minutes or until the water is absorbed. Fluff with a fork.

Serves 4.

2 cans green beans
2 slices bacon
1/4 large onion, chopped

GREEN BEANS WITH BACON AND ONION

Cook the green beans with diced bacon and onion according to the directions on the can.

1 package prepared dinner rolls
Butter

DINNER ROLLS

Warm the rolls and serve with butter.

Time Saver *Prepare 6 extra servings of rice for Day 3.*
Chop 1/2 onion for use on Day 4.

Crock Pot
next day—read ahead!

Chuck or Tri-tip Roast

DINNER ROLLS

Prep Time: 10 minutes • Total Time: 3—4 hours or all day

1	large tri-tip/chuck roast
Salt, pepper, cumin	
Garlic powder	
1	package onion soup mix
1	bag baby carrots
6	potatoes
½	cup water

CHUCK OR TRI-TIP ROAST

Season the roast; add the soup mix. In the bottom of a crock pot place the peeled and chunked carrots and potatoes along with the water; wrap the roast tightly in foil (twice) and place in the crock pot. Cook on low all day or on high 3 to 4 hours. If you don't have a crock pot, try a casserole with lid in the oven all day at 200°.

Serves 4 to 6.

1	package prepared dinner rolls
Butter	

DINNER ROLLS

Warm the rolls and serve with butter.

 Time Saver *Reserve 3 cups shredded roast for Day 4.*

Monterey Chicken Breasts

VEGETABLE MEDLEY · WHITE RICE

Prep Time: 20 minutes • Total Time: 50 minutes

8	boneless, skinless chicken breasts
2	4-ounce cans whole green chilies, drained
1	block (4 ounces) Monterey Jack cheese
1/2	cup dry bread crumbs
1/4	cup grated Parmesan cheese
2	teaspoons chili powder
1/2	teaspoon garlic salt
1/2	teaspoon ground cumin
1/4	teaspoon pepper
2	tablespoons butter, melted
1	jar salsa (optional)

MONTEREY CHICKEN BREASTS

Flatten the chicken to ¼-inch thickness. Remove the seeds from the chilies and cut into 8 pieces. Cut the cheese in 8 1½ x ½-inch sticks. Place 1 cheese stick and 1 piece of chili in the center of each chicken breast. Fold short sides over and roll up along long sides to enclose filling (secure with a toothpick, if necessary).

In a shallow bowl combine the bread crumbs, Parmesan cheese, chili powder, garlic salt, cumin, and pepper. Dip the chicken in butter, then roll in the crumb mixture. Place in a greased 13 x 9-inch baking dish, seam side down. Bake uncovered at 400° for 25 to 30 minutes or until the chicken juices run clear.

Remove the toothpicks. Serve with salsa, if desired. Serves 8.

1	16-ounce package frozen mixed vegetables

VEGETABLE MEDLEY

Prepare as directed on the package.

2	cups water
2	cups instant rice

WHITE RICE

Bring the water to a boil. Stir in the rice; cover and remove from the heat. Let stand 5 minutes or until the water is absorbed. Fluff with a fork.

Serves 4.

Chimichangas

MEXICAN RICE · GREEN SALAD · TORTILLA CHIPS

Prep Time: 25 minutes • Total Time: 50 minutes

1	pound roast (3 cups shredded) from Day 2
1	16-ounce jar salsa
1	16-ounce can refried beans
1	4-ounce can diced green chilies
1	envelope taco sauce mix
16	8-inch flour tortillas
16	ounces grated Jack cheese
1	cup sour cream
1	tub guacamole

CHIMICHANGAS

In a large skillet combine the meat, salsa, beans, chilies, and seasoning mix. Cook on medium. Heat the tortillas in another skillet 30 seconds each side. Place 1/2 cup of meat mixture on edge of each tortilla, top with cheese and roll up. Should make 16. Set out those you wish to serve and wrap the remainder in foil and place in the freezer. Bake at 350° for 10 minutes or until crisp. For frozen ones, bake 30 minutes. Serve with sour cream and guacamole.

1	tablespoon oil
1 1/2	cups long grain rice
2	cloves garlic, minced
1/4	large onion, chopped
1 1/2	teaspoons cumin
2	beef bouillon cubes
1	6-ounce can tomato sauce
3 1/2	cups water

MEXICAN RICE

Put the oil in a large skillet. Add the rice. Heat to medium and brown the rice, stirring to brown all sides. Add the garlic, onion, cumin, and bouillon cubes. Add 1/2 can of tomato sauce. Simmer to mix in. Add water. Stir in; cover and simmer for 25 minutes.

Serves 4 to 6.

1 bag salad greens
Favorite salad toppings
Favorite nonfat or low-fat dressing

GREEN SALAD

Place salad greens in serving bowls. Add toppings and drizzle with dressing.

Tortilla chips

TORTILLA CHIPS

Your choice of chips.

Sweet Mustard Sauced Fish

HASH BROWNS · GREEN SALAD

Prep Time: 20 minutes • Total Time: 1 hour

1½ pounds frozen fish fillets
2 tablespoons honey
½ cup salsa
2 tablespoons mustard
2 tablespoons mayonnaise

SWEET MUSTARD SAUCED FISH

Place the fish in a 13 x 9 x 2-inch baking dish. Bake uncovered at 450° for 4 to 6 minutes per ½-inch thickness. Drain off the liquid.

Stir together the salsa, mayonnaise, honey, and mustard. Spoon over the fish and bake for 2 to 3 minutes longer, until the sauce is warm. Serves 6.

---

1 large package frozen hash browns

HASH BROWNS

Prepare as directed on the package.

---

1 bag salad greens
Favorite salad toppings
Favorite low-fat or nonfat dressing

GREEN SALAD

Place salad greens in serving bowls. Add toppings and drizzle with dressing.

Crock Pot
next day—read ahead!

Beef Stew

CORN BREAD · FRUIT SALAD

Prep Time: 20 minutes • Total Time: 8 hours

1½ pounds lean beef, cut in 1½-inch cubes

4 carrots, cut in half

1 small onion, cut up

3 potatoes, peeled and cubed

2 stalks celery, cut in diagonal pieces

¼ teaspoon pepper

2 teaspoons salt

½ teaspoon dried basil

1 10½-ounce can condensed tomato soup

½ soup can of water

BEEF STEW

Place the beef—no need to brown it—in a crock pot. Sprinkle with seasonings. Top with vegetables. Combine soup and water and pour over all. Cover tightly. Cook for 6 to 8 hours.

Serves 5 to 6.

---

1 box corn bread mix

CORN BREAD

Prepare the corn bread mix as directed on the package.

Favorite fruit

FRUIT SALAD

Dice your favorite fruit and mix.

 Thaw potatoes for Day 2's meal.

Time
Saver

Crock Pot
next day—read ahead!

Lemon Basil Chicken

POTATO DISH · CIDER PEAS AND APPLES

Prep Time: 30 minutes • Total Time: 2 hours or 1 hour in microwave

4   tablespoons butter or margarine, divided
8   chicken breasts, skinned and boned
1   cup chicken broth
2   teaspoons grated lemon peel
3   tablespoons chopped fresh basil
2   tablespoons lemon juice

LEMON BASIL CHICKEN

In a wide non-stick frying pan melt 1 tablespoon of butter over medium-high heat. Add the chicken and cook, turning until lightly browned on both sides (about 3 minutes total). Add the broth, lemon peel, basil, and lemon juice. Reduce the heat, cover, and simmer just until the thickest portion of the chicken is no longer pink when slashed with a knife, 10 to 12 minutes.

Transfer the chicken to warm platter and keep warm. Bring the cooking liquid to a boil over high heat and boil until reduced by about 2/3. Add any accumulated juices from the chicken. Add the remaining 3 tablespoons of butter. Stir constantly until the butter is melted. If the sauce is too thin to coat a spoon, reduce the heat slightly and boil gently, shaking and swirling the pan constantly until the sauce thickens. Pour around the chicken.

Note: All ingredients can be combined and cooked in a crock pot all day.

Serves 8.

continued on next page

continued from previous page

I	2-pound package frozen hash browns
I	10½-ounce can cream of potato soup
I	10½-ounce can cream of mushroom soup
I	cup sour cream
I	large onion, chopped
½	cup chopped green bell pepper

Dash paprika, flaked parsley
Grated Cheddar cheese

POTATO DISH

Almost thaw the potatoes. Combine the soups, sour cream, onion, and green pepper and add to the potatoes. Turn into a greased pan. Top with paprika, flaked parsley, and grated cheese. Bake at 300° for 1½ to 2 hours or microwave on high for 35 minutes.

Serves 8.

3	cups frozen peas
I	medium apple, cored and thinly sliced, chopped
⅓	cup apple juice
I	teaspoon cornstarch

CIDER PEAS AND APPLES

Place a steamer basket in a saucepan and add water until just below the basket; bring to boiling. Add the peas to the steamer basket; cover and steam for 5 minutes. Add the apple, and steam for 2 to 4 minutes more or until the apples are just tender.

Meanwhile, in a medium saucepan combine the apple cider or juice and cornstarch. Cook and stir until the mixture is thickened and bubbly. Cook for 1 minute more, stirring often. Add the peas and apples, tossing them gently together to evenly coat with sauce.

Serves 4.

Time Saver *Reserve 4 breasts for Day 4. Chop an additional 2 onions for use throughout the week. Squeeze a whole lemon, reserving juice for Day 5.*

Turkey Strips

APRICOT SAUCE · STUFFED ACORN SQUASH · FRENCH BREAD

Prep Time: 30 minutes • Total Time: 50 minutes

1 package turkey breast fillets (3 to a package)
1/3 cup flour
Salt and pepper, to taste
1 egg, beaten, with 1/4 cup milk
1 cup dried bread crumbs
1/2 cup butter

TURKEY STRIPS

Rinse and pat the turkey fillets dry. With a meat mallet, pound down to about 1/2-inch thick. Remove the membrane down the middle of each fillet and cut into 3-inch strips. Combine the flour, salt, and pepper. Dip the strips in flour, then egg mixture; roll in bread crumbs. Place in a jellyroll pan or cookie sheet (with sides) in which margarine has been melted. Arrange in a single layer. Bake at 350° for 12 minutes. Turn once.

Serve with Apricot Sauce. Can be the main dish or an appetizer.

1/2 cup apricot jam
1/4 cup chili sauce
1 tablespoon vinegar
1 teaspoon cornstarch

APRICOT SAUCE

Mix all ingredients. Cook over medium heat, stirring constantly until thickened and clear.

2 acorn squash
1/4 cup water
1/2 cup brown sugar
1/2 teaspoon cinnamon
1/4 cup chopped onion (optional)
1 cup sour cream
1 tablespoon parsley, chopped
1/4 cup bread crumbs
1 tablespoon butter

STUFFED ACORN SQUASH

Split the squash, clean, and microwave cut side down in the water for 15 minutes. Scrape out the shell and mash. Add the remaining ingredients except the bread crumbs and butter. Spoon back into the shells. Mix the bread crumbs and butter and sprinkle on squash. Bake at 350° until hot and crumbs are toasted.

Serves 4.

1 loaf French bread
Butter

FRENCH BREAD

Broccoli Rice Casserole

FRUIT SECTIONS

Prep Time: 20 minutes • Total Time: 50 minutes

¼	cup chopped onion
¾	cup chopped celery
3	tablespoons butter
2	packages chopped frozen broccoli (fresh may be used)
1	10½-ounce can cream of mushroom soup
4	cups cooked rice
1	10½-ounce can cream of chicken soup
1	small jar processed cheese
4	cups diced cooked chicken

BROCCOLI RICE CASSEROLE

Sauté the onion and celery in butter. Mix the remaining ingredients together. Add the onion and celery. Pour into a 9 x 13-inch baking dish (sprayed with cooking spray). Bake at 350° for 30 minutes.

Serves 10.

5	oranges, peeled and sectioned
5	grapefruit, peeled and sectioned

FRUIT SECTIONS

Toss together and serve.

 Time Saver *Prepare extra rice for a side dish for Day 5.*

Garlic Prawns

STRING BEANS ORIENTAL · RICE

Prep Time: 25 minutes • Total Time: 55 minutes

1	pound prawns
1	cup butter
2	tablespoons olive oil
1/3	cup parsley, chopped
6	cloves garlic
2	shallots
1	tablespoon lemon juice
2	tablespoons white wine
1	tablespoon brandy

Salt and pepper

GARLIC PRAWNS

Clean and drain the prawns; pat dry. In a skillet heat the butter and olive oil. Add the parsley, garlic, and shallots. Mix in the prawns. Add the wine, lemon, and brandy. Salt and pepper, to taste. When the prawns turn pink (very short time), you are ready to enjoy.

Serves 4.

1	package frozen French-style green beans
1/2	medium onion, chopped
1/4	cup butter or margarine
1/4	cup flour
1	cup milk
1/3	cup grated Cheddar cheese
1/2	teaspoon salt
1/4	teaspoon pepper
1	5-ounce can water chestnuts
1	5-oz. can sliced mushrooms
1	teaspoon soy sauce
1/8	cup sliced almonds

STRING BEANS ORIENTAL

Cook the beans in salted water until barely tender; drain. Sauté the onion in butter; add the flour and blend. Slowly add the milk and cheese. Cook until thick. Add the seasonings and beans, water chestnuts, and mushrooms. Pour into a 2-quart buttered casserole. Top with sliced almonds. Bake uncovered at 375° for 30 minutes.

Serves 5.

RICE FROM DAY 4

Low-Fat Chicken Enchiladas

MEXICANA CORN · REFRIED BEANS

Prep Time: 20 minutes • Total Time: 40 minutes

4	chicken breasts
3	tablespoons butter
1	teaspoon minced garlic
1	medium onion, chopped
1	tablespoon flour
1	tablespoon cornstarch
1	14-ounce can chicken broth
1	4-ounce can chopped green chilies
1	14½-ounce can diced tomatoes
2	cups sour cream
2	cups grated mozzarella cheese
10	small flour tortillas

LOW-FAT CHICKEN ENCHILADAS

Boil the chicken; shred. Combine the butter, garlic, and onion; cook until soft. Add flour, cornstarch, chicken broth, and green chilies; stir until bubbly and smooth. Add the chicken; remove from the heat. Combine the tomatoes, sour cream, and half of the cheese; add to the chicken mixture. Spoon the sauce onto the tortillas, roll up, and place in casserole dish sprayed with cooking spray; pour the remaining sauce over all. Sprinkle the remaining cheese on top. Bake at 350° until hot and bubbly, 15 to 20 minutes.

2	16-ounce cans whole kernel corn, drained
8	ounces cream cheese, cubed
2	tablespoons salsa
1	cup grated Cheddar cheese

MEXICANA CORN

Combine the corn and cream cheese in a saucepan. Cook over medium heat until the cream cheese is melted, stirring frequently. Add the salsa and Cheddar cheese. Heat to serving temperature. Serves 6.

1	16-ounce can refried beans
½	cup grated Cheddar cheese

REFRIED BEANS

Heat the beans in a skillet on the stovetop or in a microwave-safe dish. Garnish with grated cheese.

Time Saver *Chop additional onion for Days 4 and 5. Grate an additional cup of mozzarella for Day 3. Grate an additional 2 cups Cheddar cheese for Days 4 and 5.*

Baked Ham

MAC 'N' CHEESE · BAKED BEANS · APPLESAUCE

Prep Time: 15 minutes • Total Time: 1 hour 25 minutes

1   canned or boneless ham
1   12-ounce can beer

HAM GLAZE:
½   cup packed brown sugar
½   teaspoon dry mustard
2   tablespoons orange juice

BAKED HAM

Place the ham in a roasting pan. Score the ham and pour 1 cup of beer over it. Bake at 350° for 40 minutes.

In a small bowl combine all of the glaze ingredients. Glaze the ham with the mixture and cook 30 minutes more.

1   box macaroni and cheese

MAC N' CHEESE

Follow the package directions.

1   16-ounce can baked beans

BAKED BEANS

Heat as directed on the can.

1   jar applesauce of your choice

APPLESAUCE

Serve the applesauce warm or cold.

Time Saver *Reserve 2 cups ham for use on Day 4.*

Upside-Down Pizza

GREEN SALAD

Prep Time: 15 minutes • Total Time: 25 minutes

2 pounds ground beef
1 8-count can crescent rolls
1 jar pizza sauce
Grated Parmesan cheese
1 cup grated mozzarella cheese

UPSIDE-DOWN PIZZA

Preheat the oven to 350°. Brown the ground beef in a skillet, stirring until crumbly; drain. Reserve half for use on Day 5. Stir in the pizza sauce. Simmer for 5 minutes. Spread the mixture in an 11 x 13-inch baking pan. Sprinkle with mozzarella cheese. Place the crescent roll dough on top, sealing perforations. Sprinkle with Parmesan cheese. Bake for 8 to 10 minutes or until golden brown.

Variations: Add any other of your favorite toppings (i.e. olives, mushrooms, onions, pepperoni, etc.)

Serves 4 to 6.

1 bag salad greens
Favorite salad toppings
Favorite low-fat or nonfat dressing

GREEN SALAD

Place salad greens in serving bowls. Add toppings and drizzle with dressing.

 **Time Saver** *Reserve 1 pound ground beef for Day 5.*

Ham and Potato Casserole

MICROWAVE CAULIFLOWER AND PEAS · DINNER ROLLS

Prep Time: 20 minutes · Total Time: 1 hour 10 minutes

1   32-ounce bag frozen hash browns, thawed
4   tablespoons butter, melted
½   cup chopped onion
1   10½-ounce can cream of chicken soup
1   8-ounce carton sour cream
1   cup grated mild Cheddar cheese
2   cups cubed ham from Day 2

TOPPING:
2   cups corn flakes
2   tablespoons butter, melted

HAM AND POTATO CASSEROLE

Mix together the hash browns, butter, onions, soup, sour cream, cheese, and ham and turn into 9 x 13-inch pan. Bake for 30 minutes at 350°. Stir, then add the topping. Bake for an additional 20 to 30 minutes, or until hot and bubbly, and the potatoes are tender.

Serves 6.

1   head cauliflower
½   cup mayonnaise
1   teaspoon prepared mustard
Garlic salt, to taste
½   cup grated Cheddar cheese
1   10-ounce package frozen peas

MICROWAVE CAULIFLOWER AND PEAS

Wash the cauliflower. Cut off enough core end to make the cauliflower stand level; place in a microwave-safe dish. Microwave tightly covered with plastic wrap on high for 8 minutes or until crisp-tender.

Mix the mayonnaise, mustard, and garlic salt in a bowl. Spread over the cauliflower; sprinkle with cheese.

Microwave the peas using the package directions. Spoon onto the dish around the cauliflower. Microwave until the cheese is melted.

Serves 6 to 8.

1   package prepared dinner rolls
Butter

DINNER ROLLS

Warm the rolls and serve with butter.

Zucchini Boats

CORN CHIPS · SLICED PEACHES

Prep Time: 30 minutes • Total Time: 1 hour

1	pound ground beef from Day 3
1/2	cup bread crumbs
1	egg, beaten
1/2	teaspoon garlic salt
1/2	teaspoon chopped onion
1/2	teaspoon thyme
1/2	teaspoon salt
1/2	teaspoon pepper
4	zucchini
1/2	cup grated Cheddar cheese

ZUCCHINI BOATS

Preheat the oven to 350°. Combine the browned ground beef from Day 3 with the bread crumbs, egg, and seasonings in a bowl; mix well. Cut the zucchini into halves lengthwise. In a saucepan cook in boiling water for 15 minutes. Scoop out the pulp, leaving a thin shell. Stir the pulp into the ground beef mixture. Spoon the mixture into the zucchini shells; arrange on a baking sheet. Bake for 20 minutes. Sprinkle with cheese. Bake for 5 minutes longer until cheese is melted.

Serves 6 to 8.

1	bag corn chips

CORN CHIPS

1	16-ounce can sliced peaches

SLICED PEACHES

Baked Chicken Breasts

CARROT-RICE BAKE · FRUIT CUP SALAD

Prep Time: 30 minutes • Total Time: 1 hour

6   chicken breasts
1/2 cup honey
1 to 2 teaspoons curry powder
1/4 cup prepared mustard
Salt and pepper
1/4 cup softened margarine

BAKED CHICKEN BREASTS

Place the chicken in a shallow pan. Mix the remaining ingredients well and pour over the chicken. Bake at 350° for 45 minutes. Baste 2 or 3 times.

Serves 6.

4   cups water
1   tablespoon instant chicken bouillon
     granules
1   teaspoon salt
2   cups chopped carrots
1 1/2 cups regular rice
2   tablespoons butter or margarine
1/2 teaspoon dried thyme, crushed
1/2 cup grated sharp American cheese

CARROT-RICE BAKE

In a saucepan bring the water, bouillon granules, and salt to boiling. Stir in the carrots, rice, butter, and thyme; return to boiling. Turn the mixture into a 2-quart casserole. Bake covered at 350° for 15 minutes, stir.

Sprinkle with cheese. Bake uncovered about 5 minutes longer. Garnish with parsley, if desired.

Serves 8.

Romaine lettuce
Cottage cheese
1   16-ounce can sliced peaches

FRUIT CUP SALAD

Arrange the lettuce leaves on salad plates. Add a scoop of cottage cheese and top with peaches.

Serves 4 to 6.

Seafood Bisque

ASPARAGUS WITH SAUCE · BISCUITS

Prep Time: 30 minutes • Total Time: 55 minutes

---

2   10½-ounce cans cream of celery soup

1   10½-ounce can tomato bisque soup

2   cans evaporated milk (use 1 can to measure half and half)

½   can half and half

1   6-ounce can shrimp, rinsed in water

1   6-ounce can crab, well drained

1   6-ounce can clams, with juice

1   teaspoon curry powder

2   tablespoons sherry

SEAFOOD BISQUE

In a saucepan combine all of the ingredients. Bring to a near boil, but DO NOT BOIL.

Serves 10.

1¼   teaspoons lemon juice

½   cup sour cream

¼   teaspoon salt

¼   cup mayonnaise

½   teaspoon paprika

1   bunch steamed asparagus

ASPARAGUS WITH SAUCE

Combine all ingredients except the asparagus. Mix well. Pour over the asparagus and serve.

Yields ¾ cup sauce.

---

2   cups flour

3   teaspoons baking powder

½   teaspoon salt

1   cup milk

¼   cup oil

BISCUITS

Mix the flour, baking powder, and salt. Add the milk and oil, and mix well. Drop onto a greased cookie sheet. Bake at 450° for 10 minutes.

Makes about 10 biscuits.

 Time Saver *Prepare Copper Pennies for tomorrow's meal, refrigerate.*

Manicotti

COPPER PENNIES · GARLIC TOAST

Prep Time: 30 minutes • Total Time: 55 minutes

1½ pounds ground beef
1 clove garlic, crushed
½ cup mayonnaise
1 cup creamed cottage cheese
1 cup grated mozzarella cheese
1 16-ounce jar spaghetti sauce
½ teaspoon salt
8 manicotti shells, cooked and drained
½ teaspoon dried oregano leaves
Parmesan cheese

MANICOTTI

Brown the beef and garlic; drain fat. Reserve 1 pound of beef for Day 4. In a bowl mix the mayonnaise, cottage cheese, and mozzarella; stir in the beef. Fill each manicotti shell with about ¼ cup of cheese-meat filling. Place in a baking dish and cover with sauce. Sprinkle with oregano and Parmesan. Cover with foil. Bake at 350° for 15 minutes. Remove the foil and bake 10 minutes longer.

Serves 4.

4½ cups carrots, sliced in ¼-inch thick rounds
1 medium bell pepper, sliced
1 10½-ounce can condensed tomato soup
⅔ cup sugar or increase to 1 cup
¾ cup vinegar
1 teaspoon Worcestershire sauce
⅜ cup salad oil
1 teaspoon dry mustard
½ teaspoon salt
2 medium onions, thinly sliced and separated

COPPER PENNIES

Cook the carrots separately until tender; drain. In a saucepan put the green pepper, tomato soup, sugar, vinegar, Worcestershire sauce, oil, dry mustard, and salt; cook until the pepper is tender. Cool and pour over the carrots and onions.

Makes 5 cups.

Note: Use frozen cut carrots to omit the slicing step. Purchase 1 large package of carrots.

¼ cup butter, melted
⅛ cup minced garlic
8 slices French bread
Dash chopped parsley

GARLIC TOAST

Spread butter and garlic on bread. Sprinkle with parsley. Bake in the oven with the manicotti for the final 10 minutes.

Time Saver *Reserve 1 pound browned beef for Day 4.*

Noodle, Cheese, and Meat Casserole

GREEN BEANS WITH GARLIC · BREADSTICKS

Prep Time: 30 minutes • Total Time: 1 hour 20 minutes

1	pound lean ground meat from Day 3
1	onion, diced
½	bell pepper, diced
1	16-oz. can stewed tomatoes
1	8-ounce can tomato sauce
1	package frozen peas
1	8-ounce package egg noodles, cooked and drained
1	8-ounce package Parmesan cheese

NOODLE, CHEESE, AND MEAT CASSEROLE

Sauté the meat, onion, and bell pepper together. Spread in the bottom of a 3-quart casserole. Pour the tomatoes and tomato sauce over the meat. Put thawed peas over the sauce and noodles on top of the peas. Sprinkle with Parmesan. Cover with foil and bake at 350° for 35 minutes with foil on and 15 minutes with foil off.

Serves 4 to 6.

10	ounces frozen green beans
¼	cup white wine
2	tablespoons butter
1	tablespoon garlic, minced

GREEN BEANS WITH GARLIC

Cook the green beans as directed on the package using wine instead of water. Add butter and garlic.

Serves 4.

1	package seasoned breadsticks

BREADSTICKS

 Time Saver *Chop an additional 2 onions for use on Day 5.*

 Crock Pot *next day—read ahead!*

Potato Soup

GRILLED CHEESE SANDWICHES

Prep Time: 30 minutes • Total Time: 1 hour 10 minutes

4   potatoes, peeled and diced
2   onions, chopped
¼   cup butter or margarine
4   cups water
1   stalk celery, chopped
2   teaspoons chicken bouillon powder
Pinch nutmeg
Dash hot pepper sauce
1   cup hot milk (or evaporated milk)

POTATO SOUP

In a heavy kettle combine the potatoes, onions, and butter; cook, stirring frequently, until the butter is melted and the vegetables are well coated. Add water, celery, bouillon, nutmeg, and hot pepper sauce; cook until the potatoes are very tender, about 20 minutes. Process in a blender or put through a sieve. Stir in the milk.

Serves 4 to 6.

10   slices bread, toasted
⅛   cup butter, melted
Mayonnaise
5   slices cheese

GRILLED CHEESE SANDWICHES

Heat a skillet or griddle. Spread butter on one side of bread. Put cheese in between 2 slices. Spread a thin coat of mayonnaise on the outside of the bread. Grill until the cheese is melted.

Serves 5.

Mexican Steak and Beans

SALAD · JALAPENO RICE · TORTILLA CHIPS

Prep Time: 30 minutes • Total Time: I hour 10 minutes

1 tablespoon flour
1/2 to I teaspoon chili powder
1/2 pound round steak, sliced into 1-inch pieces
Salt and pepper
1 tablespoon oil
1/2 cup water
1 jar chili sauce
3/4 cup sliced celery
1 medium onion, chopped
2 carrots, cut diagonally into 1/2-inch slices
1 small green bell pepper, cut into 1/2-inch strips
1/8 teaspoon cumin
1 8-ounce can kidney beans, drained

MEXICAN STEAK AND BEANS

Mix the flour and chili powder in a dish. Salt and pepper the meat. Coat the meat with flour mixture. Heat the oil and brown the meat over medium heat for 10 minutes. Drain the fat. Stir in the water, chili sauce, and the rest except the beans. Boil. Simmer for 1 hour. Add the kidney beans and simmer for 10 minutes.

Serves 4 to 6.

1 bag salad greens
Favorite salad toppings
Favorite low-fat or nonfat dressing

SALAD

Place salad greens in serving bowls. Add toppings and drizzle with dressing.

1 teaspoon chopped onion
2 cups uncooked rice
1/2 cup canola oil
3 whole jalapeno peppers
4 cups water
1 pound processed American cheese, chopped
1/4 cup margarine

JALAPENO RICE

In a large saucepan mix all ingredients. Simmer for 30 to 40 minutes or until the rice is tender.

Serves 8.

TORTILLA CHIPS

Time Saver *Marinate tomorrow's chicken tonight.*

Chicken Stir-fry

WHITE RICE

Prep Time: 20 minutes • Total Time: 2 hours 30 minutes

¼ cup orange juice
1½ tablespoons cornstarch
1 pound skinless, boneless chicken breasts, cut into strips
¾ cup chicken broth
1½ tablespoons soy sauce
2½ teaspoons vegetable oil
1 clove garlic, minced
1½ teaspoons ground ginger
1½ cups snow peas
1 medium red bell pepper, cut into thin strips (about 1 cup)
¾ cup sliced green onion
1 cup frozen broccoli, thawed
1 medium carrot, thinly sliced

CHICKEN STIR-FRY

In a shallow glass bowl combine the orange juice and cornstarch; mix well. Stir in the chicken. Cover and chill for 2 hours.

Drain the chicken and discard the juice mixture. In a small bowl combine the broth and soy sauce. Set aside. In a wok or large non-stick skillet heat the oil over medium heat. Add garlic and ginger and stir-fry for 30 seconds. Add the chicken, and stir-fry for 3 minutes. Add the vegetables and stir-fry until crisp-tender, about 5 minutes. Stir in the broth mixture. Place White Rice on each serving plate and top with the chicken mixture, dividing evenly.

Serves 4.

2 cups water
2 cups instant rice

WHITE RICE

Bring the water to a boil. Stir in the rice; cover and remove from the heat. Let stand 5 minutes or until the water is absorbed. Fluff with a fork.

Serves 4.

Time Saver *Use pre-cut vegetables from produce section of the supermarket.*

Sloppy Joes

CORN CHIPS · STOVETOP BAKED BEANS

Prep Time: 20 minutes • Total Time: 40 minutes

1	pound ground beef
½	cup chopped onion
¼	cup chopped green pepper
¼	cup chopped celery
⅛	teaspoon pepper
1	8-ounce can tomato sauce
¼	cup catsup
1	tablespoon vinegar
1	tablespoon sugar
1	teaspoon salt
1½	teaspoons Worcestershire sauce
1	package hamburger buns

SLOPPY JOES

In a skillet brown the meat. Add the vegetables. Cook until the vegetables are tender. Add the remaining ingredients; mix well. Cover. Simmer 20 minutes. Serve over hamburger buns.

Serves 6.

1	bag corn chips

CORN CHIPS

1	large can pork and beans
¼	cup brown sugar
¼	onion, diced
1	tablespoon mustard
2	slices bacon, cut in pieces
1	tablespoon catsup

STOVETOP BAKED BEANS

In a saucepan combine all of the ingredients. Cook for 20 minutes on simmer.

Old-Fashioned Beef Stew

BISCUITS

Prep Time: 25 minutes • Total Time: 1 hour 45 minutes

1	pound lean beef chuck, trimmed and cut into 1-inch cubes
2	tablespoons all-purpose flour
2	teaspoons vegetable oil
2	large yellow onions, thinly sliced (about 3 cups)
2	cups sliced mushrooms
2	cloves garlic, minced
2	teaspoons reduced-sodium tomato paste
2	cups reduced-sodium beef broth
4	cups sliced carrots
2	medium russet potatoes, thinly sliced (about 2 cups)
1	cup 1-inch green bean pieces
1	tablespoon cornstarch
1	tablespoon cold water
1/4	cup chopped fresh parsley

OLD-FASHIONED BEEF STEW

Coat the beef with flour, shaking off the excess. In a large non-stick pot heat the oil over medium-high heat. Add the beef and sauté until browned, about 6 minutes. Place on a plate. Add the onions and mushrooms to the pot, and sauté for 6 minutes. Add the garlic and cook, stirring for 1 minute. Pour off the fat. Return the beef to the pot; stir in the tomato paste, then the broth. Add just enough water to cover, and bring to a boil. Reduce the heat to low, and simmer until beef is tender, about 1 hour and 15 minutes. Skim off any foam.

Add the carrots, potatoes, and green beans. Cover partially. Simmer for 15 minutes. In a small bowl mix the cornstarch and cold water; stir into the stew. Increase the heat and boil, uncovered, for 1 minute. Sprinkle with parsley and serve.

Serves 6.

2	or more cans biscuits

BISCUITS

Prepare as directed on the can.

Rustic Lasagna

GREEN SALAD · CRUSTY GARLIC BREAD

Prep Time: 30 minutes • Total Time: 45 minutes

9   lasagna noodles
2   8-ounce cans tomato sauce
1   clove garlic, minced
1/4 teaspoon dried oregano
1   10-ounce package frozen chopped broccoli, thawed and squeezed of excess moisture
1   cup shredded carrots
1   15- to 16-ounce carton ricotta cheese
1/4 cup grated Parmesan cheese
1   cup grated mozzarella cheese

RUSTIC LASAGNA

Cook the lasagna noodles according to the package directions. While the noodles are cooking, preheat the oven to 350°. Spray a 9 x 13-inch baking dish with vegetable cooking spray; set aside. In a small bowl combine the tomato sauce, garlic, and oregano. Mix well. In a medium bowl combine the broccoli, carrots, ricotta, and Parmesan. Mix well. Drain the noodles in a colander. Spread 1/2 cup of tomato sauce in the bottom of a prepared dish. Place 3 noodles on top of the tomato sauce. Spread 1/2 of the broccoli mixture over the noodles. Spoon 1/2 cup of tomato sauce over the broccoli; place 3 noodles on top. Spread with remaining broccoli mixture. Top with 1/2 cup of tomato sauce. Top with the remaining noodles and tomato sauce; sprinkle mozzarella over the top. Bake until bubbling, about 45 minutes. Place on a wire rack and cool for about 15 minutes. Cut into squares.

Serves 8.

1   bag salad greens
Favorite salad toppings
Favorite lowfat or nonfat dressing

GREEN SALAD

Place salad greens in serving bowls. Add toppings and drizzle with dressing.

continued on next page

2 cloves garlic, minced
2 teaspoons olive oil
2 tablespoons chopped fresh parsley
2 teaspoons dried thyme
¾ teaspoon dried marjoram
½ teaspoon paprika
2 tablespoons grated Parmesan cheese
2 small loaves (4 ounces each) Italian or French bread

CRUSTY GARLIC BREAD

Preheat the oven to 350°. In a small bowl combine the garlic and oil. Mix well. In another small bowl combine the parsley, thyme, marjoram, and paprika. Add Parmesan and mix well. Cut each loaf crosswise into diagonal slices, without cutting all the way through. Brush the cut sides of the slices with garlic oil. Sprinkle herb mixture between slices. Wrap each loaf in foil and place on a baking sheet. Bake until heated through, about 10 to 15 minutes. Unwrap the loaves. Serve immediately.

Makes 10 slices.

Baked Virginia Ham

MUSTARD RING · SLICED ORANGES

Prep Time: 20 minutes • Total Time: 1 hour 30 minutes

1   teaspoon dry mustard
2   cups apple cider
2 to 3 tablespoons sherry
1   pound dark brown sugar
1   4- to 5-pound ham

BAKED VIRGINIA HAM

Mix together the dry mustard, cider, sherry, and brown sugar. Pour over the ham. Bake at 350° for 70 minutes.

¼   cup water
¾   cup sugar
¼   teaspoon salt
1   tablespoon dry mustard
¼   teaspoon pepper
¾   cup vinegar
½   teaspoon turmeric
2   tablespoons Knox gelatin, softened
    in ½ cup cold water
4   eggs, well beaten, set aside
½   pint whipping cream

MUSTARD RING

In the top of a double boiler combine the water, sugar, salt, dry mustard, pepper, vinegar, and turmeric. Cook, stirring constantly, until thickened. Add the gelatin and stir until dissolved. Then add the eggs, and blend well. Combine all. Cool. Fold in the whipped cream. Put into an 8½-inch ring mold. Chill.

Note: To double the recipe add 1 extra tablespoon of gelatin.

Serves 10 to 12.

Oranges

SLICED ORANGES

 Time Saver *Save 12 thin slices for Day 4. Use rest of leftover ham on Day 3.*

Easy Chicken Dish

POTLUCK POTATOES · GREEN SALAD

Prep Time: 20 minutes • Total Time: 1 hour 50 minutes

1 3- to 4-pound chicken Onion salt to taste 1 6-ounce can frozen orange juice Sesame seeds	**EASY CHICKEN DISH** Skin the chicken and cut into pieces. Place in a casserole dish. Sprinkle onion salt over the chicken. Pour thawed orange juice over all. Sprinkle sesame seeds on top. Bake uncovered at 350° for 1 hour and 30 minutes. Serves 6.

EASY CHICKEN DISH

Skin the chicken and cut into pieces. Place in a casserole dish. Sprinkle onion salt over the chicken. Pour thawed orange juice over all. Sprinkle sesame seeds on top. Bake uncovered at 350° for 1 hour and 30 minutes.

Serves 6.

1   2-pound package frozen hash brown potatoes
½   cup melted butter or margarine
¼   teaspoon pepper
1   teaspoon salt
½   cup chopped onion
1   cup cream of chicken soup
1   pint sour cream
2   cups grated Cheddar cheese
2   cups crushed corn flakes
¼   cup melted butter or margarine

POTLUCK POTATOES

Combine all ingredients except the crushed corn flakes and ¼ cup of butter or margarine. Pour into a 9 x 13-inch baking dish. Combine the corn flakes and melted butter and put on top of the casserole. Bake at 350° for 45 minutes. Can be frozen and reheated.

Serves 6.

1   bag salad greens
Favorite salad toppings
Favorite low-fat or nonfat dressing

GREEN SALAD

Place salad greens in serving bowls. Add toppings and drizzle with dressing.

Time Saver *Grate an additional 3 cups of cheese for use on Day 4. Chop an additional onion for Day 3.*

Crock Pot *next day—read ahead!*

Crock Pot Split-Pea Soup

SLICED FRENCH BREAD

Prep Time: 20 minutes • Total Time: 10 hours

2   tablespoons butter
1   cup minced onion
6   cups water
1/8   teaspoon dried marjoram
2   cups or 1 pound green split peas
4   whole cloves
1   bay leaf
Ham from Day 1
1   cup finely chopped celery
1   cup diced or grated carrots
1/8   teaspoon savory
1/2   teaspoon salt or garlic salt
1/4   teaspoon pepper
1/4   teaspoon garlic powder or 2 to 3
     cloves crushed garlic

CROCK POT SPLIT-PEA SOUP

Put all ingredients in a crock pot and cook on low for 8 to 10 hours, or on high for 3 hours, then low for 3 hours. Make the day before serving for better flavor and to thicken. Warm up on low to medium.

Serves 6.

1   loaf French bread, sliced
Butter

SLICED FRENCH BREAD

Crock Pot
today!

Crepes Puerto Vallarta

VEGETABLE MEDLEY · GREEN SALAD

Prep Time: 30 minutes • Total Time: 1 hour 15 minutes

12	thin slices ham from Day 1
12	slices Monterey Jack cheese
12	crepes
1	can whole green chilies
3	cups grated Cheddar cheese
2	8-ounce cans tomato sauce

CREPES PUERTO VALLARTA

Lay ham and Monterey Jack cheese on each crepe and roll up. Place a generous slice of green chili on top. Arrange the rolled crepes in well-greased baking dish. Sprinkle grated cheese over all. When ready to bake, pour tomato sauce over everything. Bake at 350° for about 20 minutes.

Serves 6.

4	zucchini
1	large onion
2	yellow crookneck squash
8	mushrooms
1/4	cup salad oil
1	package Italian salad seasoning mix
2	tablespoons vinegar
	Parmesan cheese

VEGETABLE MEDLEY

Thinly slice the vegetables, in any combination desired. Place in an 8 x 11-inch baking dish.

Combine the remaining ingredients and mix well. Pour over vegetables. Bake covered at 350° for 35 minutes or microwave on high, covered with plastic wrap, for 10 to 15 minutes. Sprinkle top with grated Parmesan cheese.

Alternative: Put vegetables in lightly greased dish and sprinkle seasoning mix on top, omitting oil and vinegar.

Serves 6.

1 bag salad greens
Favorite salad toppings
Favorite low-fat or nonfat dressing

GREEN SALAD

Place salad greens in serving bowls. Add toppings and drizzle with dressing.

Pizza Roll

GREEN SALAD · SLICED FRUIT

Prep Time: 30 minutes • Total Time: 1 hour 5 minutes

½ pound ground beef
1 package refrigerated pizza dough
1 envelope spaghetti sauce mix
1 cup water
1 6-ounce can tomato paste
½ cup grated mozzarella cheese

PIZZA ROLL

Brown the ground beef; drain. Add the spaghetti sauce envelope. Mix in the tomato paste with 1 cup of water. Simmer for 10 minutes, cool slightly. Roll out the dough to an 8 x 16-inch rectangle. Spread on the sauce and sprinkle with mozzarella cheese. Roll up. Bake at 400° for 15 to 20 minutes.

Serves 6.

1 bag salad greens
Favorite salad toppings
Favorite low-fat or nonfat dressing

GREEN SALAD

Place salad greens in serving bowls. Add toppings and drizzle with dressing.

Favorite sliced fruit, mixed

SLICED FRUIT

Pork Chops a l'Orange

BUTTERED FETTUCCINE NOODLES · STEAMED VEGETABLES · GARLIC BREAD

Prep Time: 20 minutes • Total Time: 35 minutes

1   pound thinly sliced pork chops, fat
    trimmed
2   teaspoons butter or margarine
Salt and lemon pepper, to taste
2   teaspoons rosemary
Juice of 1 orange
Sections of 1 orange

PORK CHOPS A L'ORANGE

In a skillet brown the pork chops in butter for 2 minutes on each side. Sprinkle with rosemary, salt, and lemon pepper. Cook for 5 minutes on each side. Add the orange juice and sections to the pork chops. Simmer for several minutes longer or until done, stirring to scrape the pan. Arrange on a serving platter. Place orange sections on the pork chops; pour pan drippings over the top.

Serves 4.

1   package fettuccine noodles

BUTTERED FETTUCCINE NOODLES

Prepare according to the package directions.

Fresh or frozen vegetables of your
choice

STEAMED VEGETABLES

Steam or cook as directed.

1   loaf ready-to-heat garlic bread

GARLIC BREAD

Heat as directed on the package.

Grandma's Meatballs

MASHED POTATOES · GREEN BEANS

Prep Time: 20 minutes • Total Time: 40 minutes

2   pounds ground beef
2 to 3 handfuls of corn flakes
½   onion, chopped (save other ½ for sauce)
2   tablespoons flour
1   16-oz. can stewed tomatoes
1   8-oz. can tomato sauce
1   teaspoon sugar
Salt and pepper

GRANDMA'S MEATBALLS

Mix the ground beef and corn flakes and shape into balls. Fry until done. Remove from the pan and brown ½ onion. Add the flour, stewed tomatoes, and tomato sauce. Add a little water and let simmer. Add the sugar, salt, and pepper. Simmer until done, about 15 minutes.

Serve the sauce over the meatballs. If you like your sauce less chunky, put the tomatoes through your blender or food processor.

6   medium to large potatoes
Salt and pepper
Butter
Milk

MASHED POTATOES

Peel the potatoes, dice, and boil until cooked in salted water, approximately 10 minutes. Mash with salt, pepper, butter, and milk.

Serves 6.

Frozen or canned green beans

GREEN BEANS

Cook as directed on the package or can.

Time Saver *Hard-boil 8 eggs for Day 3 and Day 5. Chop an additional tablespoon of onion for use with Day 3's salad. Prepare salad for Day 3.*

Hot Chicken Salad

DINNER ROLLS

Prep Time: 5 minutes • Total Time: 20 minutes

4   cups chopped cooked chicken
    breasts
2   tablespoons lemon juice
2   tablespoons chopped pimentos
1   tablespoon minced onion (or
    finely chopped)
2½ cups diced celery
¾   cup mayonnaise
1   teaspoon salt
¾   cup sour cream or cream of
    chicken soup
4   hard-boiled eggs, sliced
1   cup grated Jack cheese
1½ cups crushed potato chips
½   cup slivered almonds

HOT CHICKEN SALAD

Combine the chicken, lemon juice, pimentos, onions, celery, mayonnaise, salt, sour cream, and eggs and place in a 9 x 13-inch pan or casserole. Sprinkle Jack cheese, potato chips, and almonds on the top. Refrigerate overnight.

Bake at 425° for 15 minutes.

1   package prepared dinner rolls
Butter

DINNER ROLLS

Warm the rolls and serve with butter.

Mexican Lasagna

REFRIED BEANS · GREEN SALAD · TORTILLA CHIPS

Prep Time: 20 minutes • Total Time: 45 minutes

1½ pounds ground beef
1 teaspoon seasoned salt
1 package taco seasoning mix
2 8-ounce cans tomato sauce
1 4-ounce can chopped green chilies
8 ounces ricotta cheese
2 eggs
9 soft corn tortillas
10 ounces Monterey Jack cheese, grated

MEXICAN LASAGNA

In a skillet brown the beef. Drain off the fat. Add the seasoned salt, taco seasoning mix, tomato sauce, and chilies. Simmer uncovered for 10 minutes.

Combine the ricotta and eggs. In a 9 x 13-inch pan spread ⅓ of the meat over 3 tortillas, cut in strips, and spread with ⅓ of the cheese-egg mixture. Sprinkle ⅓ of the Jack cheese over. Repeat the layers. Bake at 350° for 20 minutes or until it bubbles.

Let stand 10 minutes. Cut in squares and serve. Serves 4.

---

1 16-ounce can refried beans

REFRIED BEANS

Cook the refried beans as directed on the can.

---

1 bag salad greens
Favorite salad toppings
Favorite lowfat or nonfat dressing

GREEN SALAD

Place salad greens in serving bowls. Add toppings and drizzle with dressing.

---

1 bag tortilla chips

TORTILLA CHIPS

Peppered Rib Eye Steak

RICE PILAF · CRUNCHY SPINACH SALAD

Prep Time: 30 minutes • Total Time: 1 hour

PEPPERED RIB EYE STEAK

4 beef rib eye steaks (1½-inch thick)
1 tablespoon olive oil
2 teaspoons dried ground oregano
1½ teaspoons pepper
1 teaspoon salt
1 tablespoon garlic powder
1 teaspoon lemon pepper
1 tablespoon paprika
1 teaspoon ground red pepper
2 teaspoons dried ground thyme
Orange slices (optional)
Parsley sprig (optional)

Brush the steaks lightly with olive oil. In a small bowl combine all seasonings. Sprinkle seasonings over steaks and press into both sides. Cover and chill for 1 hour. Grill or broil the steaks, turning once, over medium-hot coals 14 to 18 minutes for rare, 18 to 22 minutes for medium, or 24 to 28 minutes for well-done. Place on a warm serving platter; cut across the grain into thick slices. Garnish with orange slices and parsley, if desired.

Serves 8.

RICE PILAF

1 box rice pilaf

Prepare as directed on the box.

CRUNCHY SPINACH SALAD

1 bunch fresh torn spinach
2 cups fresh bean sprouts
1 8-ounce can sliced water chestnuts, drained
4 hard-boiled eggs, chopped
6 bacon strips, cooked and crumbled
1 small onion, thinly sliced

DRESSING:
½ cup packed brown sugar
⅓ cup vinegar
½ cup vegetable oil
⅓ cup catsup
1 tablespoon Worcestershire sauce

In a large bowl combine the spinach, bean sprouts, water chestnuts, eggs, bacon, and onion. In a bottle or jar combine all dressing ingredients. Cover and shake well to mix. Just before serving, pour the dressing over the salad and toss.

Serves 8.

Crock Pot
next day—read ahead!

Spicy Wine Pot Roast

DINNER ROLLS

Prep Time: 20 minutes • Total Time: 10 hours

1   3- to 4-pound beef pot roast
Salt and pepper
¼   cup catsup
¼   cup dry red wine
1   small onion, chopped
2   teaspoons Dijon-style mustard
1   package brown gravy mix
1   teaspoon Worcestershire sauce
1   cup water
⅛   teaspoon garlic powder
5   potatoes, peeled and quartered
6 to 8 carrots, 2 to 3-inch long
3   onions, quartered

SPICY WINE POT ROAST

Sprinkle the meat with salt and pepper; place in a crock pot. Combine the remaining ingredients except the vegetables; pour over the meat. Cover and cook on low 8 to 10 hours.

Remove the meat and slice. If desired, thicken the sauce with flour dissolved in a small amount of water and serve over meat. Last 2 hours of cooking, add the potatoes, carrots, and onions.

Serves 6 to 7.

1   package prepared dinner rolls
Butter

DINNER ROLLS

Warm the rolls and serve with butter.

Time Saver *Chop an additional small onion for use on Day 4.*

Sour Cream–Chili Bake

BREADSTICKS · FRUIT SALAD

Prep Time: 30 minutes • Total Time: 1 hour

---

1   pound ground beef
1   15-ounce can pinto beans, drained
1   10-ounce can hot enchilada sauce
1   8-ounce can tomato sauce
1   cup grated sharp American cheese
1   tablespoon instant minced onion
1   6-ounce package corn chips
1   cup sour cream
½   cup grated sharp American cheese

SOUR CREAM–CHILI BAKE

In a skillet brown the ground beef. Drain off the fat. Stir in the drained beans, enchilada sauce, tomato sauce, 1 cup of American cheese, and instant minced onion. Set aside 1 cup of the corn chips, and coarsely crush the remaining chips. Stir the crushed chips into the meat mixture. Turn into a 1½-quart casserole. Bake covered at 375° for 30 minutes.

Spoon sour cream atop the casserole. Sprinkle with the remaining American cheese. Sprinkle reserved chips around the edge of casserole. Bake uncovered for 2 to 3 minutes.

Serves 6.

---

1   package breadsticks

BREADSTICKS

Favorite fruit

FRUIT SALAD

Your favorite fruit, including oranges and grapefruit, sliced and mixed.

Time Saver *Grate an additional ½ cup cheese for Day 5.*

Fish and Chip Bake

GREEN SALAD

Prep Time: 30 minutes • Total Time: 1 hour 25 minutes

Packaged instant mashed potatoes
(enough for 8 servings)
2   10-ounce packages frozen chopped
spinach, cooked and well drained
1   cup sour cream
Dash pepper
2   16-ounce packages frozen perch
fillets, thawed
1/2   cup milk
1   cup herb-seasoned stuffing mix,
crushed
4   tablespoons butter or margarine,
melted
Lemon slices

FISH AND CHIP BAKE

Prepare the potatoes according to package directions, except reduce the water by 1/4 cup. Stir in the drained spinach, sour cream, and pepper. Turn into a 10 x 6 x 2-inch baking dish.

Skin the fish fillets. Dip one side of each fillet in milk, then in crushed stuffing mix. Fold the fillets in half, coating side out. Place on top of the potato mixture. Drizzle with melted butter. Bake uncovered at 350° until the fish flakes easily when tested with a fork, 30 to 35 minutes. Serve with lemon slices.

Serves 8 to 10.

1   bag salad greens
Favorite salad toppings
Favorite low-fat or nonfat dressing

GREEN SALAD

Place salad greens in serving bowls. Add toppings and drizzle with dressing.

Pizza

FRUIT SALAD · CUT RELISH

Prep Time: 30 minutes • Total Time: 1 hour 5 minutes

1   pound pork sausage
1   loaf frozen bread dough, thawed
1   8-ounce can tomato sauce
1   tablespoon finely chopped onion
1/2   teaspoon salt
1/2   teaspoon oregano
1/4   teaspoon pepper
2   cups grated Jack cheese
Black olives, chopped
Canned mushrooms, chopped
1   6-ounce can Ortega chilies,
    chopped

PIZZA

In a skillet brown the sausage; drain off the excess fat. Spread the thawed bread dough on a greased pizza pan or oblong pan. Mix the tomato sauce, onion, and seasonings; spread over the dough. Next put on the sausage; top with cheese and the optional toppings. Bake at 425° for 20 to 25 minutes.

Serves 4 to 5.

Favorite fruits

FRUIT SALAD

Slice and mix your favorite fruits.

Carrots
Celery

CUT RELISH

Stuffed Pork Roast

CARROT-RICE BAKE · SLICED APPLES

Prep Time: 30 minutes • Total Time: 1 hour 40 minutes

2 cups fresh bread crumbs

4 cloves garlic, minced

¼ cup chopped parsley

1 egg white

1 tablespoon each: chopped fresh rosemary and sage, or 1 teaspoon each dried

Kitchen string

2 pounds center-cut boneless pork loin roast

¾ teaspoon salt, divided

½ teaspoon pepper

STUFFED PORK ROAST

Heat the oven to 325°. In a large bowl combine the bread crumbs, garlic, parsley, egg white, rosemary, sage, and ¼ teaspoon salt. With a sharp knife, make 6 evenly spaced 1½-inch-deep slits lengthwise along the top, bottom, and sides of the pork roast. Stuff the crumb mixture into slits. Tie the pork securely at 1-inch intervals with kitchen twine. Place on a rack set in a roasting pan. Sprinkle with pepper and the remaining ½ teaspoon of salt. Roast for 1 hour or until a thermometer inserted into the meat, not stuffing, registers 155°. Let stand, covered, at least 10 minutes before carving.

Serves 4 to 6.

4 cups water

1 tablespoon instant chicken bouillon granules

1 teaspoon salt

2 cups chopped carrots

2 tablespoons butter or margarine

½ teaspoon dried thyme, crushed

1½ cups rice

½ cup grated sharp American cheese (2 ounces)

CARROT-RICE BAKE

In a saucepan bring the water, bouillon granules, and salt to boiling. Stir in the carrots, rice, butter, and thyme, and return to boiling. Turn the mixture into a 2-quart casserole. Bake covered at 325° for 25 minutes; stir.

Sprinkle with cheese. Bake uncovered about 5 minutes longer. Garnish with parsley, if desired.

Serves 8.

Apples

SLICED APPLES

Cavatelli

GREEN SALAD · GARLIC BREAD

Prep Time: 15 minutes • Total Time: Microwave 20 minutes; oven 35 minutes

1 teaspoon olive oil 12 ounces Italian sausage 1/4 cup green onions, chopped 2 cloves garlic, chopped 2 1/2 cups spiral or wagon wheel noodles 1 12-ounce jar spaghetti sauce, with mushrooms 1 8-ounce can tomato sauce 1 cup grated mozzarella cheese	**CAVATELLI** In a skillet heat the oil and sauté the sausage, onion, and garlic. Cook the noodles according to the package directions. Combine the noodles and sausage mixture in a 2-quart casserole. Mix the spaghetti sauce and tomato sauce. Toss in half of the cheese. Sprinkle the remainder on top. Bake at 375° for 20 minutes. For a quick cook, microwave on high 5 minutes. Serves 4 to 6.

1 bag salad greens Favorite salad toppings Favorite low-fat or nonfat dressing	**GREEN SALAD** Place salad greens in serving bowls. Add toppings and drizzle with dressing.

1 loaf ready-to-heat garlic bread	**GARLIC BREAD** Prepare the bread as directed on the package.

Chicken Supreme

GREEN BEANS · FLAKY BISCUITS

Prep Time: 10 minutes • Total Time: 1 hour 10 minutes

4	chicken breasts, boneless
1	cup grated Jack or Swiss cheese
1	can cream of chicken soup
½	cup water
½	cup margarine
2	cups herb stuffing mix

CHICKEN SUPREME

Place the chicken breasts in a shallow baking dish and cover with cheese. Mix the soup and water. Pour over the chicken. Melt the margarine and add the stuffing. Pour over the top. Bake at 350° for 1 hour, or cover and microwave 12 to 15 minutes on high or until cooked through.

Serves 4.

Frozen or canned green beans

GREEN BEANS

Cook the beans as directed on the can or package.

---

1 to 2 large cans flaky biscuits
Butter

FLAKY BISCUITS

Cook as directed on the can.

Crock Pot
next day—read ahead!

Beef Burgundy

WHITE RICE · PEAS · DINNER ROLLS

Prep Time: 10 minutes · Total Time: All day

1 to 1½ pounds round steak, cubed
1 10½-ounce can golden mushroom soup
1 4-ounce can sliced mushrooms, drained (optional)
1 envelope onion soup mix
¼ to ½ cup rose or Burgundy

BEEF BURGUNDY

Combine the steak and next 4 ingredients in a slow cooker. Cook on low for 6 to 8 hours.

Serve over White Rice.

3 cups water
3 cups instant rice

WHITE RICE

Bring the water to a boil. Stir in the rice; cover and remove from the heat. Let stand 5 minutes or until the water is absorbed. Fluff with fork.

Serves 6.

1 can or package frozen peas

PEAS

Serve as directed.

1 package prepared dinner rolls
Butter

DINNER ROLLS

Warm the rolls and serve with butter.

Time Saver *Cook enough extra rice for Day 4.*

Smothered Pork Chops

APPLESAUCE · STEAMED RICE · STEAMED BROCCOLI, CARROTS, CAULIFLOWER

Prep Time: 25 minutes • Total Time: 45 minutes

6	pork chops, boned
2	tablespoons catsup
½	cup chicken broth
¼	teaspoon ground ginger
⅓	cup honey
1	clove garlic, minced
¼	cup soy sauce

SMOTHERED PORK CHOPS

Preheat the electric skillet at 350°. Sear the pork chops on both sides. Reduce the temperature to 225–250°.

In a bowl combine the remaining ingredients in a bowl and mix well. Pour over the pork chops. Simmer, covered, stirring frequently for 20 minutes until the sauce thickens.

Serves 4 to 6.

1	jar old-fashioned-style applesauce with cinnamon

APPLESAUCE

Serve warm or cold, according to taste.

WHITE RICE FROM DAY 3

1	large bag frozen mixed broccoli, carrots, and cauliflower

STEAMED BROCCOLI, CARROTS, CAULIFLOWER

Steam or follow package directions.

Crock Pot
next day—read ahead!

Chicken Tacos

MEXICAN RICE · GREEN SALAD AND TORTILLA CHIPS · REFRIED BEANS

Prep Time: 15 minutes • Total Time: 40 minutes, plus crock pot time

---

4   boneless, skinless chicken breasts
1   jar salsa
Flour tortillas

SUGGESTED TOPPINGS:
Sour cream
Grated Jack cheese
Lettuce
Diced tomatoes
Guacamole

CHICKEN TACOS

Place the frozen breasts in a slow cooker along with the jar of salsa. As it cooks, shred with a fork. Cook for 4 to 5 hours. Serve with flour tortillas and condiments of your choice.

Serves 4 to 6.

---

1   tablespoon oil
1½ cups long grain rice
2   cloves garlic, minced
¼   large onion, chopped
1½ teaspoons cumin
2   beef bouillon cubes
1   small can tomato sauce
3½ cups water

MEXICAN RICE

Put the oil in a large skillet. Add the rice. Heat to medium and brown the rice, stirring to brown all sides. Add the garlic, onion, cumin, and bouillon cubes. Add ½ can of tomato sauce. Simmer to mix in. Add the water. Stir in, cover, and simmer for 25 minutes.

Serves 4 to 6.

---

1   bag salad greens
Favorite salad toppings
Favorite low-fat or nonfat dressing

GREEN SALAD

Place salad greens in serving bowls. Add toppings and drizzle with dressing.

Tortilla chips

TORTILLA CHIPS

---

1   16-ounce can refried beans

REFRIED BEANS

Heat the refried beans in the microwave or on the stovetop in a saucepan.

Baked Ham

VEGETABLE MEDLEY · DINNER ROLLS

Prep Time: 25 minutes • Total Time: 1 hour 25 minutes

¼ cup prepared mustard	**BAKED HAM**
½ cup firmly packed brown sugar	
2 tablespoons honey	
1 5-pound boneless cooked ham	

BAKED HAM

Mix the mustard, sugar, and honey to make the glaze. Bake ham in 325° oven for 30 minutes. Remove from the oven, score, spread with glaze, and bake an additional 30 minutes at 350°.

Serves 6 to 8.

---

4 zucchini
1 large onion
8 mushrooms
¼ cup salad oil
1 package Italian salad seasoning mix
2 tablespoons vinegar

VEGETABLE MEDLEY

Thinly slice the vegetables, in any combination desired. Place in a 8 x 11-inch baking dish.

Combine the remaining ingredients and mix well. Pour over vegetables. Bake covered at 350° for 35 minutes or microwave on high, covered with plastic wrap, for 10 to 15 minutes. Sprinkle top with grated Parmesan cheese.

Alternative: Put vegetables in lightly greased dish and sprinkle seasoning mix on top, omitting oil and vinegar.

Serves 6.

---

1 package prepared dinner rolls
Butter

DINNER ROLLS

Warm the rolls and serve with butter.

Time Saver — *Reserve 2 cups of ham for Day 5.*

Monterey Spaghetti Casserole

GREEN SALAD

Prep Time: 20 minutes • Total Time: 1 hour

1   egg, beaten
1   cup sour cream
1/4 cup grated Parmesan cheese
1/4 teaspoon garlic powder
2   cups grated Monterey Jack cheese
4   ounces spaghetti, cooked in unsalted water and drained
1   10-ounce package frozen chopped spinach, thawed
1   2.8-ounce can French fried onions, divided

MONTEREY SPAGHETTI CASSEROLE

Preheat oven to 350°. In a medium bowl combine the egg, sour cream, Parmesan cheese, and garlic powder. Stir in the Monterey Jack, hot spaghetti, spinach, and half of the onions. Pour into an 8-inch square baking dish. Bake covered for 30 minutes. Top with the remaining onions and bake uncovered for 5 minutes.

Serves 4 to 6.

1   bag salad greens
Favorite salad toppings
Favorite low-fat or nonfat dressing

GREEN SALAD

Place salad greens in serving bowls. Add toppings and drizzle with dressing.

Crock Pot
next day—read ahead!

Beef Ragout

CARROTS

Prep Time: 30 minutes • Total Time: All day

1½ pounds top round, 1-inch thick
1 10½-ounce can condensed Cheddar cheese soup
¼ cup dried minced onion
3 tablespoons tomato paste
½ teaspoon lemon pepper
2 cups small mushrooms, halved
9 ounces frozen Italian green beans
½ cup buttermilk
9 ounces fettuccine

BEEF RAGOUT

Trim the fat from the steak, and cut into 1-inch pieces. Spray a pan, heat over medium heat and cook the steak, half at a time, until brown. Place the meat in a 3½- or 4-quart crock pot.

In a medium bowl combine the soup, onion, tomato paste, and lemon pepper. Pour the mixture over the meat. Add the mushrooms. Cook on low for 8 to 10 hours (or on high for 4 to 5 hours). Turn the heat to high. Add the frozen green beans and buttermilk. Stir, cover, and cook for 30 minutes more.

Meanwhile, cook the fettuccine. Serve the meat over fettuccine.

Serves 6.

---

1 16-ounce can carrots

CARROTS

Heat the carrots as directed on the can.

Saucy Pork Chops

TWICE-BAKED SWEET POTATOES · GREEN SALAD

Prep Time: 30 minutes • Total Time: 1 hour 45 minutes

Oil
6   pork chops, ³/₄-inch thick
Salt and pepper
1   medium onion, thinly sliced
1   10¹/₂-ounce can condensed cream
    of chicken soup
¹/₄ cup catsup
2 to 3 teaspoons Worcestershire sauce

SAUCY PORK CHOPS

In a skillet heat the oil and brown the chops on both sides. Drain and season with salt and pepper. Top with onion slices. Combine the remaining ingredients; pour over the chops. Cover and simmer for 45 to 60 minutes or until done.

Remove the chops to a platter, spoon the sauce over, and serve.

8   sweet potatoes (about 4¹/₂ pounds)
¹/₂ cup low-fat sour cream
3   tablespoons chopped fresh chives
1   teaspoon grated orange peel
¹/₂ teaspoon salt

TWICE-BAKED SWEET POTATOES

With a fork, randomly prick the potatoes all over. Cook in the microwave on high for 15 to 20 minutes until tender, turning occasionally. Let cool slightly.

Meanwhile, heat the oven to 400°. Slice off the top one-third of each potato lengthwise and reserve for another use. Scoop out the pulp into a large bowl, leaving ¹/₄-inch of shell intact. With a fork, mash the pulp. Stir in the sour cream, chives, orange peel, and salt. Spoon the mixture into the shells, or, if desired, place the mixture in a pastry bag fitted with a star tip and pipe into the shells. Arrange the potatoes on a baking sheet. Bake for 10 minutes or until lightly browned and heated through.

Serves 8.

1   bag salad greens
Favorite salad toppings
Favorite low-fat or nonfat dressing

GREEN SALAD

Place salad greens in serving bowls. Add toppings and drizzle with dressing.

Ham and Mac Bake

GREEN BEANS · SLICED PEARS

Prep Time: 30 minutes • Total Time: 1 hour 5 minutes

3½ ounces elbow macaroni (1 cup)
¼ cup butter or margarine
¼ cup all-purpose flour
2 tablespoons brown sugar
2 tablespoons prepared mustard
¼ teaspoon salt
Dash pepper
2 cups milk
2 cups cubed ham from Day 1
2 medium apples, peeled and thinly sliced (2 cups)
1½ cups soft bread crumbs (2 slices)
2 tablespoons butter or margarine, melted

HAM AND MAC BAKE

Cook the macaroni in boiling salted water just until tender, 8 to 10 minutes; drain. In a large saucepan melt the ¼ cup butter. Blend in the flour, brown sugar, mustard, salt, and pepper. Add the milk all at once. Cook and stir until thickened and bubbly. Stir in the cooked macaroni, ham, and apple slices. Turn the mixture into a 2-quart casserole. Combine the bread crumbs and the 2 tablespoons melted butter and sprinkle over the casserole. Bake uncovered at 350° for about 35 minutes.

Serves 6.

---

1 10-ounce package frozen green beans

GREEN BEANS

Prepare the green beans as directed on the package.

---

1 16-oz. can sliced pears

SLICED PEARS

Spareribs "Cooked Easy"

RICE · GREEN SALAD

Prep Time: 25 minutes • Total Time: I hour

½ cup vinegar
½ cup soy sauce
½ cup packed brown sugar
4 cloves garlic, chopped
3 pounds spareribs (boneless, country-style)
2 tablespoons cornstarch
I 6-ounce can pineapple juice

SPARERIBS "COOKED EASY"

Bring the vinegar, soy sauce, brown sugar, garlic, and spareribs to a boil. Reduce the heat and simmer for about 45 minutes, stirring occasionally. Make the cornstarch paste with 2 tablespoons cornstarch and the can of pineapple juice. Pour over the meat and cook for 15 minutes.

Serves 6 to 8.

3 cups water
3 cups rice

RICE

Bring the water to a boil. Stir in the rice; cover and remove from the heat. Let stand 5 minutes or until the water is absorbed. Fluff with fork.

Serves 6.

I bag salad greens
Favorite salad toppings
Favorite low-fat or nonfat dressing

GREEN SALAD

Place salad greens in serving bowls. Add toppings and drizzle with dressing.

Pork Chops O'Brien

GREEN BEANS · DINNER ROLLS

Prep Time: 20 minutes • Total Time: 1 hour 5 minutes

6	pork loin chops (½-inch thick)
1	tablespoon cooking oil
1	10½-ounce can condensed cream of celery soup, undiluted
½	cup milk
½	cup sour cream
¼	teaspoon pepper
1	cup (4 ounces) grated Cheddar cheese, divided
1	2.8-ounce can French fried onions, divided
1	24-ounce package frozen hash brown potatoes, thawed
½	teaspoon seasoned salt

PORK CHOPS O'BRIEN

In a skillet over medium-high heat brown the pork chops in oil. Set aside. Combine the soup, milk, sour cream, pepper, ½ cup of cheese, and ½ cup of onions. Fold in the potatoes. Spread in a greased 9 x 13-inch baking dish. Arrange the chops on top, sprinkle with seasoned salt. Cover and bake at 350° for 40 to 45 minutes or until the pork is tender.

Uncover and sprinkle with the remaining cheese and onions. Return to the oven for 5 to 10 minutes, or until the cheese melts.

Serves 6.

1	bag frozen green beans

GREEN BEANS

Prepare the green beans as directed on the package.

1	package prepared dinner rolls
Butter	

DINNER ROLLS

Warm the rolls and serve with butter.

Mom's Meat Loaf

MOM'S MACARONI AND CHEESE · APPLESAUCE

Prep Time: 30 minutes • Total Time: 1 hour 30 minutes

MEAT LOAF:

1½ pounds ground beef
1 teaspoon salt
½ cup chopped onion
¼ teaspoon pepper
½ cup chopped bell pepper
½ cup milk
¾ cup oats
¼ cup tomato sauce
1 egg
1 teaspoon mustard
2 teaspoons Worcestershire sauce

SAUCE:

1 cup tomato sauce
¼ cup brown sugar, packed
1 teaspoon Worcestershire sauce
1 tablespoon mustard
¼ cup catsup

MOM'S MEAT LOAF

In a large bowl combine the meat loaf ingredients. Mix together and form into a loaf. Put in an oblong pan. In a separate bowl combine the sauce ingredients. Mix well and pour over the loaf. Bake at 350° for 1 hour.

Serves 4 to 6.

continued on next page

continued from previous page

1½ cup uncooked elbow macaroni

5 tablespoons butter or margarine, divided

3 tablespoons all-purpose flour

1½ cups milk

1 cup grated Cheddar cheese

2 ounces processed American cheese, cubed

½ teaspoon salt

¼ teaspoon pepper

2 tablespoons dry bread crumbs

MOM'S MACARONI AND CHEESE

Cook the macaroni according to the package directions. Drain. Place in a greased 1½-quart baking dish. Set aside.

In a saucepan melt 4 tablespoons of butter over medium heat. Stir in the flour until smooth. Gradually add the milk and bring to a boil. Cook and stir for 2 minutes; reduce the heat. Stir in the cheeses, salt, and pepper until the cheese is melted. Pour over the macaroni and mix well. Melt the remaining butter, and add the bread crumbs. Sprinkle over the casserole. Bake uncovered at 350° for 35 minutes.

Serves 6.

1 jar old-fashioned–style chunky cinnamon applesauce

APPLESAUCE

Serve hot or cold.

Time Saver *Chop 2 additional onions for Day 5. Chop entire bell pepper for use on Day 5.*

Stuffed Chicken Pasta

SPAGHETTI NOODLES · CORN ON THE COB · GREEN SALAD

Prep Time: 15 minutes • Total Time: 1 hour 30 minutes

6 boneless, skinless chicken breasts 1 pound sliced mozzarella cheese 1 16-ounce jar spaghetti sauce	**STUFFED CHICKEN PASTA**

STUFFED CHICKEN PASTA

6   boneless, skinless chicken breasts
1   pound sliced mozzarella cheese
1   16-ounce jar spaghetti sauce

Slice the chicken breasts in the middle lengthwise and stuff with sliced cheese. Place them in a large casserole dish and cover with spaghetti sauce. Bake at 350° for 1 hour. Serve over spaghetti noodles.

Serves 6.

SPAGHETTI NOODLES

1   pound spaghetti noodles
Butter

Follow the package directions for the number of servings desired and start cooking noodles about 20 minutes before the chicken is due out of the oven. Add butter.

Serves 6 to 8.

CORN ON THE COB

1   bag frozen corn on the cob

Prepare enough for your family. Cook as directed on the package.

GREEN SALAD

1   bag salad greens
Favorite salad toppings
Favorite low-fat or nonfat dressing

Place salad greens in serving bowls. Add toppings and drizzle with dressing.

Excellent Clam Chowder

FRENCH BREAD

Prep Time: 20 minutes • Total Time: 45 minutes

1   cup butter
1   cup celery, chopped
2   cups chopped onions
2   cups chopped green pepper
¾   cup flour
5   cups hot milk
3   6½-ounce cans clams and juice
2   cups cooked potatoes
½   teaspoon thyme
Salt and pepper, to taste

EXCELLENT CLAM CHOWDER

In a saucepan heat the butter and sauté the celery, onions, and green pepper until the vegetables are soft. Add the flour and mix until smooth. Add the hot milk, clams, and juice. Cook for 10 minutes. Add the potatoes, thyme, salt, and pepper. Mix and simmer on low heat for a few minutes.

Serves 6.

1   loaf French bread
Butter

FRENCH BREAD

Serve soup with a loaf of warmed crusty French bread and butter. You could even buy the small ones to use for soup bowls.

Crock Pot
next day—read ahead!

Cranberry Pork Roast

BROCCOLI-RICE CASSEROLE · SLICED APPLES

Prep Time: 20 minutes • Total Time: 10 hours

4   pounds pork roast or pork loin
Salt and pepper
1/4 cup honey
1   teaspoon grated orange peel
1   cup ground or finely chopped
    cranberries
1/8 teaspoon ground clove
1/8 teaspoon ground nutmeg

CRANBERRY PORK ROAST

Sprinkle the roast with salt and pepper. Place in a slow cooker. Combine the remaining ingredients; pour over the roast. Cover and cook on low for 8 to 10 hours.

Serves 6 to 8.

1   package frozen chopped broccoli or
    cauliflower mix
1   cup instant rice
1   8-ounce jar processed American
    cheese
1   can condensed cream of mushroom
    soup
1   cup water

BROCCOLI RICE CASSEROLE

Cook the broccoli according to the package instructions, but cut the cooking time in half. Drain well. Mix the broccoli with the remaining ingredients and turn into a 1½-quart baking dish. Bake at 350° for 45 minutes.

Serves 6.

Apples

SLICED APPLES

Beefy Onion Pie

SPINACH WITH VINEGAR · BREADSTICKS

Prep Time: 30 minutes • Total Time: 1 hour 20 minutes

1/4 cup butter
1 1/2 cups thinly sliced onion
   (3 medium)
1/4 cup chopped green bell pepper
2 cups chopped cooked beef
1 cup sour cream
2 tablespoons all-purpose flour
3/4 teaspoon salt
1/8 teaspoon pepper
1 beaten egg
2 tablespoons snipped parsley
2 tablespoons chopped pimento
1 9-inch pastry shell

BEEFY ONION PIE

In a skillet melt the butter and cook the onion and green pepper until tender. Stir in the beef and remove from the heat. Combine the sour cream, flour, salt, and pepper; blend in the egg, parsley, and pimento. Stir into the onion-beef mixture and mix well. Turn the beef mixture into the pastry shell. Bake uncovered at 375° until the crust is golden, about 30 minutes.

Makes 6 servings.

---

1 bunch spinach, boiled or 1 can
   spinach, heated
Red wine vinegar

SPINACH WITH VINEGAR

Splash the spinach with red wine vinegar.
Serves 4.

---

1 package breadsticks

BREADSTICKS

Grammy's Chicken Soup

SLICED FRENCH BREAD

Prep Time: 15 minutes • Total Time: 1 hour 15 minutes

3 chicken breasts
2 potatoes
1 onion, chopped
1 clove garlic
2 stalks celery, chopped
2 chicken bouillon cubes
2 to 3 carrots, chopped
½ cup white rice
1 package dry chicken soup mix
½ teaspoon cumin
Salt and pepper to taste

GRAMMY'S CHICKEN SOUP

In a large pot combine all of the ingredients and bring to a boil. Remove the chicken breasts after 10 minutes and shred the chicken with fork. Return to the pot and continue to cook all on medium-high for 1 hour.

Serves 6.

1 loaf French bread

SLICED FRENCH BREAD

Worcestershire Burgers

FRESH FRUIT SALAD CUP

Prep Time: 15 minutes • Total Time: 30 minutes

1   pound ground beef
¼   cup Worcestershire sauce
2   tablespoons honey
2   teaspoons Worcestershire sauce
1   package hamburger buns

WORCESTERSHIRE BURGERS

Mix the hamburger with 1/4 cup of Worcestershire sauce. Shape into burgers. Place the burgers on a cookie sheet. Broil until done, turning once.

Meanwhile combine the honey and remaining Worcestershire sauce. Glaze the burgers with the mix. Serve on buns with the remaining glaze mix.

Serves 4 to 6.

Coconut
Apples
Strawberries
Pineapple
Bananas
Grapes
Nuts

FRESH FRUIT SALAD CUP

Clean and chop the fruit. Mix and garnish with coconut. Serve in individual cups.

Enchiladas

SPANISH RICE · REFRIED BEANS

Prep Time: 30 minutes • Total Time: 1 hour 30 minutes

½ pound ground beef
12 corn tortillas
3 tablespoons cooking oil
1 large can enchilada sauce
1 4-ounce can black olives, chopped
1⅓ cups grated Cheddar cheese
1 large onion, chopped

ENCHILADAS

Brown the ground beef, drain. Dip each tortilla in oil, quickly fry until soft, drain, and dip in sauce. Put a little of the olives, enchiladas, cheese, and onions on each tortilla. Reserve some cheese for topping. Roll up and place in a line in a 9 x 11-inch casserole dish. Repeat. Cover with the remaining cheese and enchilada sauce. Bake in a 450° oven for 10 to 15 minutes until cheese is melted.

Serves 6.

---

1 package long grain rice
½ cup salsa

SPANISH RICE

Prepare rice as directed on the package for 6 to 8 people. When cooked, stir in the salsa.

Serves 6 to 8.

---

1 16-ounce can refried beans

REFRIED BEANS

Prepare the beans as directed on the can.

Crock Pot
next day—read ahead!

Spaghetti

GREEN SALAD · GARLIC BREAD

Prep Time: 20 minutes • Total Time: skillet - 2 hours; slow cooker - 8 hours

1 tablespoon olive oil	**SPAGHETTI**
½ medium onion, chopped	In a large skillet heat the oil and cook the onion and
1 clove garlic	garlic until soft. Add the beef and brown, then stir in the
1 pound ground beef	tomato sauce, tomato paste, wine, water, and spices.
1 8-ounce can tomato sauce	Mix well. Simmer on the stovetop 1 hour and 30 min-
1 6-ounce can tomato paste	utes or place in a slow cooker on low all day.
½ cup each: dry white wine and water	Serves 6.
1 teaspoon oregano	
1 teaspoon basil	
½ teaspoon each: salt, pepper, sugar	
1 teaspoon parsley	

---

1 package spaghetti noodles

SPAGHETTI NOODLES

Cook enough noodles for your family, following the package directions.

---

1 bag salad greens
Favorite salad toppings
Favorite low-fat or nonfat dressing

GREEN SALAD

Place salad greens in serving bowls. Add toppings and drizzle with dressing.

---

1 loaf ready-to-heat garlic bread

GARLIC BREAD

Bake as directed on the package.

Time Saver *Chop an entire onion for use on Day 2 and Day 3.*

Shepherd's Pie

SLICED PEACHES

Prep Time: 20 minutes • Total Time: 45 minutes

6 potatoes
2 pounds ground beef
¼ cup chopped onions
2 16-ounce cans corn, drained
Butter
Salt and pepper
Milk
¼ cup grated Cheddar cheese

SHEPHERD'S PIE

Peel the potatoes and put in a large saucepan with salted water to cover. Boil for 10 minutes or until soft enough to mash. In a skillet fry the ground beef in skillet, adding salt and pepper to taste. Add the chopped onion and cook until soft. Pour the beef and onion mixture into a casserole dish, adding the canned corn. Mash the potatoes with butter, milk, salt, and pepper. Scoop the potatoes and spread on top of the beef and corn mixture. Sprinkle the top with grated cheese. Bake at 350° for 20 minutes.

Serves 6.

Romaine lettuce
Cottage cheese
1 16-ounce can peaches, chilled

SLICED PEACHES SALAD

Arrange the lettuce leaves on salad plates. Add a scoop of cottage cheese and top with sliced peaches.

Time Saver *Grate an additional 2¼ cups Cheddar cheese for use on Day 4.*

Smothered Steak

MASHED POTATOES · GREEN BEANS

Prep Time: 20 minutes • Total Time: 2 hours

1½ pounds round steak, tenderized
Salt and pepper
Flour
1 tablespoon oil
¼ onion, chopped
1 clove garlic, pressed
1 4-ounce can sliced mushrooms, undrained
1 10½-ounce can cream of mushroom soup
2 tablespoons Worcestershire sauce
1 teaspoon catsup
1 teaspoon steak sauce

SMOTHERED STEAK

Tenderize the round steak and season with salt and pepper. Flour the meat and brown in oil. Add the onion and garlic. Add the undrained mushrooms, soup, water, Worcestershire, catsup, and steak sauce. Cover the meat with the liquid, adding enough water to do so. Simmer until tender, about 1 hour and 30 minutes.

Serves 4.

8 potatoes
Margarine or butter
Salt and pepper
Milk

MASHED POTATOES

Peel and dice the potatoes. Place in a saucepan with 1 teaspoon salt, cover with water and bring to a boil. Boil for at least 10 minutes, until soft enough for mashing. Drain off the water and add margarine or butter to taste (2 to 4 tablespoons). Mash, adding salt and pepper. For extra-smooth potatoes, add 2 tablespoons milk or more after mashing and whip until fluffy. Serve with gravy from the Smothered Steak.

Serves 4 to 6.

2 cans cut green beans
2 slices bacon
Freeze-dried onion or fresh diced onion, if desired

GREEN BEANS

In a large saucepan place the green beans, bacon (cut up), and onion. Cook according to the directions on the can.

 Make tomorrow's casserole and refrigerate.

Sausage Casserole

CARROTS AND ZUCCHINI

Prep Time: 30 minutes • Total Time: 1 hour 10 minutes

1½ pounds regular sausage
1 4-ounce can chilies
3 eggs
1½ cups milk
½ teaspoon salt
½ teaspoon chili powder
4 slices sourdough bread, buttered and cubed
2¼ cups grated Cheddar cheese

SAUSAGE CASSEROLE

In a skillet brown the sausage and drain. Add the chilies. In a separate bowl beat the eggs and add milk, salt, and chili powder in a separate bowl. In a 9 x 13-inch dish place half of the bread cubes. Cover with half of the grated cheese, then half of the meat mixture. Repeat layers. Pour the egg mixture over all. Cover and chill overnight.

Bake at 350° for 1 hour. Let set 15 minutes before cutting in squares to serve.

Serves 6.

5 medium-sized carrots
3 small zucchini
2 tablespoons butter
3 cloves fresh garlic, minced
Pinch rosemary
Salt and pepper
Water
1 tablespoon capers

CARROTS AND ZUCCHINI

Slice the carrots and zucchini about ¼-inch thick. In a skillet melt the butter over medium heat. Lightly sauté the garlic, then stir in the carrots and cook 2 minutes. Stir in the zucchini, rosemary, and salt and pepper to taste. Stir until the zucchini is heated through, then add 1 or 2 tablespoons of water and cover the pan. Cook over medium heat until the carrots are barely fork-tender, shaking the pan and stirring occasionally. Do not overcook. Stir in the capers and serve.

Serves 6.

Chicken Vegetable Casserole

SAVORY RICE

Prep Time: 15 minutes • Total Time: 35 minutes

3   cups loose-pack frozen cut broccoli
4   boneless, skinless chicken breasts
2   tablespoons mayonnaise
1/3 cup fine dry Italian seasoned
    bread crumbs
3   tablespoons Parmesan cheese,
    grated
1/8 teaspoon paprika

CHICKEN VEGETABLE CASSEROLE

In large strainer rinse the broccoli with warm water to thaw. Place in a 2-quart round casserole. Rinse the chicken and pat dry. Fold the pieces in half and brush on all sides with mayonnaise. Combine the bread crumbs and Parmesan. Roll the chicken in the crumb mixture, coating well. Arrange the chicken on top of the broccoli with the thickest portions toward the edge. Sprinkle with paprika and the remaining crumb mixture. Microwave with the savory rice for 20 minutes on low or 10 to 12 minutes on high.

Serves 4.

1 1/2 cups water
1   teaspoon instant chicken bouillon
      granules
1 1/2 cups instant rice
1   tablespoon margarine
1   teaspoon dried parsley flakes
1/4   teaspoon dried thyme, crushed

SAVORY RICE

In a microwave-safe casserole combine all ingredients and microwave on high for 3 to 5 minutes. Let stand covered for 5 minutes. Stir to fluff.

Serves 4.

Shopping Lists

· DINNER ROLLS · POTATOES · GROUND BEEF ·

· CREAM OF MUSHROOM SOUP · SOUR CREAM ·

· TACO SEASONING MIX · GREEN BEANS · BUTTER · PORK ROASTS ·

CORN ON THE COB ·

· SALAD OIL · ORANGES · CHICKEN BREASTS ·

· BROCCOLI · SPAGHETTI SAUCE · BABY CARROTS ·

· SMOKED SAUSAGE · ONIONS ·

· BOX INSTANT RICE · SALAD GREENS · GARLIC ·

· MOZZARELLA CHEESE · FLOUR · DOZEN EGGS ·

· REFRIED BEANS · BEEF BOUILLON CUBES · CHOPPED GREEN

CHILIES · CELERY · GREEN PEPPER · SHRIMP ·

· BROWN SUGAR · SOY SAUCE · SNIPPED PARSLEY · PARMESAN

CHEESE · VINEGAR · LEMON JUICE · WHITE SQUASH ·

· CRACKER CRUMBS · ORANGES · MARSALA COOKING WINE ·

· EGG NOODLES · STEWED TOMATOES ·

· PORK CHOPS · BOILED HAM ·

· SLICED WATER CHESTNUTS · CATSUP · PEA PODS ·

· FRENCH FRIED ONIONS ·

· CHERRY TOMATOES ·

Bulk Shopping List

SPRING • WEEKS 1–4

MEATS

5 pounds ground beef

24 boneless, skinless chicken breasts

2½ pounds round steak

2 large pork roasts

CANS/JARS

8 oz. diced green chilies

16 oz. tomato sauce

32 oz. refried beans

Favorite salad dressing for 6 dinners

8 tablespoons vegetable/salad oil

3 10½-oz. cans cream of
mushroom soup

GROCERY

3 envelopes onion soup mix

2 bags corn chips

2 envelopes taco seasoning mix

PRODUCE

15 onions

20 pounds potatoes

24 carrots

3 bags baby carrots

6 cloves garlic

BAKERY

Dinner rolls for 4 dinners

3 dozen flour tortillas

CHECK YOUR STAPLES

4 tablespoons cumin

9 tablespoons salt

3 tablespoons pepper

2 tablespoons parsley

2 tablespoons paprika

DAIRY

6 cups grated Cheddar cheese

2 cups sliced mozzarella cheese

2 large tubs sour cream

5 sticks butter

FREEZER

5 pounds green beans

Shopping List

MEATS

2 large pork roasts–1,3,5

1½ pounds round steak–2

2 slices bacon–2

4 to 6 skinless chicken breasts–4

CANS/JARS

1 cup barbecue sauce–1,5

1 10½-oz. can cream of mushroom soup–2

1 4-oz. can sliced mushrooms–2

2 cans cut green beans–2

1 16-oz. jar salsa–3

1 17-oz. can refried beans–3

1 4-oz. can diced green chilies–3

1 8-oz. can tomato sauce–3

1 large jar spaghetti sauce–4

Favorite salad dressing for 1 dinner–3

GROCERY

1 taco seasoning packet–1

2 cans refrigerator biscuits–1

2 cans refrigerator breadsticks–4

2 envelopes onion soup mix–1,5

1 pound spaghetti noodles–4

1 bag potato chips–5

PRODUCE

2 small bags baby carrots–1,5

12 to 14 potatoes–1,2

4 cloves garlic–1,2,3

1 onion–2,3

1 bunch celery–5

2 heads broccoli–4

Favorite salad greens for 1 dinner–3

Favorite salad toppings for 1 dinner–3

BAKERY

16 8-inch flour tortillas–3

6 to 8 sandwich rolls–5

DAIRY

2 sticks butter–1,2,4

½ cup milk–2

1 pound grated Jack cheese–3

1 pound sliced mozzarella cheese–4

CHECK YOUR STAPLES

Salt–1,2

Pepper–1,2

Cumin–3

1½ cups long grain rice for 1 dinner–3

1 teaspoon steak sauce–2

2 tablespoons oil–2,3

2 beef bouillon cubes–3

2 tablespoons Worcestershire sauce–2

Flour–2

1 teaspoon catsup–2

Shopping List

MEATS

1½ pounds smoked sausage–2

2 pounds ground beef–4

1 pound round steak–5

4 chicken breasts–1

CANS/JARS

1 4-oz. can chopped green chilies–1

1 14-oz. can chicken broth–1

1 14½-oz. can diced tomatoes–1

1 8-oz. can tomato sauce–1

1 16-oz. can refried beans–1

3 6½-oz. cans clams–3

2 16-ounce cans corn–4

Favorite salad dressing for 1 dinner–1

GROCERY

Tortilla chips–1

PRODUCE

4 large onions–1,2,3,4

Salad greens for 1 dinner–1

10 pounds potatoes–2,3,4

1 small bag baby carrots–2

1 bunch celery–3

1 green bell pepper–3

1 bunch green onions–5

Favorite fruit for salad–4

3 cloves garlic–1

BAKERY

14 8-inch flour tortillas–1

1 bag dinner rolls–2

French bread loaf–3

DAIRY

4 sticks butter–1,2,3,4

2 cups grated mozzarella cheese–1

3 cups sour cream–1,2

1 dozen eggs–2

½ gallon milk–3,4

¼ cup grated Cheddar cheese–4

FREEZER

1 bag Oriental vegetables–5

CHECK YOUR STAPLES

Cumin–1

Salt–2,3,4

Pepper–2,3,4

Paprika–2

Thyme–3

2 beef bouillon cubes–1

1 tablespoon cornstarch–1

1 cup flour–1,3

1 cup oil–1,5

½ cup soy sauce–5

1½ cups long grain rice–1

Instant rice for 1 dinner–5

Shopping List

MEATS

- 1 4- to 5-pound boneless pork loin roast–1
- 2 pounds ground beef–2,4
- 6 boneless chicken breasts–3

CANS/JARS

- ½ cup apple jelly–1
- 1 6-oz. can sliced water chestnuts–4
- 1 10½-oz. can cream of mushroom soup–4
- 4 oz. tomato sauce–2
- 1 3-oz. can chow mein noodles–4
- 1 large can tuna–5
- Favorite salad dressing for 1 dinner–2
- 2 10½-oz. cans golden mushroom soup–5
- 1 20-oz. can pineapple chunks–3
- 2 tablespoons lime juice–3

GROCERY

- 1 cup corn chips–1
- 1 box won tons–4
- 1 envelope onion soup mix–3

PRODUCE

- 2 acorn squash–1
- 5 onions–1,3,4,5
- 1 green bell pepper–2
- Salad greens for 1 dinner–2
- Favorite salad toppings for 1 dinner–2
- 1 clove garlic–3
- 6 stalks celery–4,5
- 14 carrots–1,5
- 6 potatoes–1,5
- 4 turnips–5
- Broccoli for 1 dinner–4
- 1½ pounds green beans–3

BAKERY

- Dinner rolls for 3 dinners–1,3,5

DAIRY

- 1 cup sour cream–1
- 8 oz. grated Cheddar cheese–2
- 1 egg–2
- ¼ cup milk–2,4
- 2 sticks butter–1,3,5

FREEZER

- 1 9-inch pie shell–2
- 1½ pounds green beans–3
- 1 10-oz. box peas–4

CHECK YOUR STAPLES

- Parsley–1
- Salt–1,2,3,4
- Garlic salt–1,5
- Cinnamon–1
- Oregano–2
- Pepper–2,3,4
- Dry mustard–2
- Paprika–3
- Chili powder–1
- Seasoned salt–5
- 1 tablespoon cornstarch–3
- ½ cup brown sugar–1
- 1 cup bread crumbs–1,2,3
- 2 tablespoons vinegar–1,3
- ½ teaspoon Worcestershire sauce–2
- 2 tablespoons oil–3
- ½ cup balsamic vinegar–4
- ½ cup catsup–1
- 2 tablespoons grated Parmesan–3

Shopping List

MEATS

1 4- to 5-pound boneless cooked ham–1,4
1 2- to 3-pound whole chicken–2
1 pound ground beef–3
1 pound skinless, boneless chicken
    breasts–5

CANS/JARS

1 10½-oz. can cream of mushroom soup–1
1 2.8-oz. can French fried onions–1
Salad dressing for 3 dinners–2,4,5
1 3-oz. can mushrooms, sliced–3
⅛ teaspoon hot pepper sauce–3
2 cans hominy–3
1 4-oz. can diced green chilies–3
1 10½-oz. can cream of broccoli soup–5

GROCERY

3 cups egg noodles–3
2¼ cups tomato juice–3
1 bag corn chips–3
1 package taco seasoning mix–3

PRODUCE

2 apples–1
2 oranges–1
1 bunch grapes–1
2 green bell peppers–2
6 onions–2,3,4
8 carrots–2
1 bunch celery–2
8 potatoes–2
4 teaspoons chives–2
Salad greens for 3 dinners–2,4,5

Salad toppings for 3 dinners–2,4,5
1 medium tomato–3
2 green onions–3
1 head broccoli–4
Clove garlic–4

DAIRY

1½ sticks butter-2,3,4,5
5 cups milk–1,4,5
1 cup sour cream–3
4 cups grated Cheddar cheese–3,4
6 eggs–4

BAKERY

1 loaf ready-to-heat garlic bread–4

FREEZER

2 9-oz. packages cut green beans–1
1 9-inch deep-dish pie shell–4
1 10-oz. box broccoli cuts–5

CHECK YOUR STAPLES

1½ teaspoons pepper–1,2,5
4 teaspoons salt–2,3,4
1 tablespoon parsley flakes–3
¼ teaspoon nutmeg–4
Dash cayenne pepper–4
1 teaspoon sugar–5
Dash paprika–2
¾ cup honey–1
1 tablespoon mayonnaise–4
4 tablespoons oil–5
1¼ cups instant rice–5
1¼ teaspoons seasoned salt–3

Bulk Shopping List

MEATS

4½ pounds ground beef
30 boneless, skinless chicken breasts

CANS/JARS

3 10½-oz. cans cream of chicken soup
5 10½-oz. cans cream of mushroom soup
¾ cup catsup
Favorite salad dressing for 4 dinners
2 16-oz. cans green beans

GROCERY

1 cup brown sugar

PRODUCE

2 heads garlic
11 onions

BAKERY

4 loaves French bread
Dinner rolls for 2 dinners

DAIRY

13 sticks butter
2½ cups grated mozzarella cheese
5 cups grated Cheddar cheese
2 cups sour cream

CHECK YOUR STAPLES

7 teaspoons salt
6½ teaspoons pepper
1 cup flour
1½ teaspoons oregano
3 tablespoons cornstarch
7 tablespoons Worcestershire sauce
½ cup soy sauce
7 tablespoons vinegar
1⅓ cups grated Parmesan cheese

Shopping List

MEATS

2 pounds ground beef–1
8 slices boiled ham–1
6 boneless, skinned chicken breasts–2,4
4 $\frac{1}{2}$-inch-thick pork chops–3
1 pound uncooked, peeled shrimp–5

CANS/JARS

1 16-oz. can green beans–1
$\frac{1}{3}$ cup Marsala cooking wine–2
$\frac{1}{3}$ cup chicken broth–2
1 14$\frac{1}{2}$-oz. can stewed tomatoes–3
1 large can peas–3
$\frac{1}{2}$ cup tomato juice–1
1 16-oz. can peaches–4
1 16-oz. can carrots–5

GROCERY

1 package egg noodles–2
1 cup cracker crumbs–5

PRODUCE

2 tablespoons snipped parsley–1
3 cloves garlic–1,4
5 carrots–2
1 pound mushrooms, sliced–2
3 onions–3,4,5
1 bunch celery–3,5
2 green bell peppers–3,4
2 tomatoes–4
2 pounds white squash–5

BAKERY

1 loaf ready-to-heat garlic bread–1
$\frac{3}{4}$ cup soft bread crumbs–1
Dinner rolls for 2 dinners–2,5

DAIRY

2 eggs–1
1$\frac{1}{2}$ cups grated mozzarella cheese–1
3 slices mozzarella–1
1 stick butter–2,5

CHECK YOUR STAPLES

Olive oil–2,4
Salt–1,3,5
Pepper–1,2,3,5
Paprika–2
Oregano–1
Seasoned salt–2
2 tablespoons cider vinegar–3
3 tablespoons flour–2
3 tablespoons cornstarch–3,4
$\frac{1}{2}$ cup catsup–3
2 tablespoons Worcestershire sauce–3
1 tablespoon lemon juice–3
2 teaspoons soy sauce–4
1 beef bouillon cube–3
Instant rice for 2 dinners–3,4
2 tablespoons brown sugar–3
2 tablespoons oil–4,5

Shopping List

SPRING • WEEK 6

MEATS

1 6- to 8-pound tri-tip/chuck roast–1

6 chicken breasts–2,4

1 pound ground beef–3

CANS/JARS

1 jar barbecue sauce–1

2 10½-oz. cans cream of mushroom soup–2,3,4

2 5-oz. cans sliced water chestnuts–2,4

1 3-oz. can broiled button mushrooms–2

Favorite salad dressing for 2 dinners–2,5

1 10½-oz. can golden mushroom soup–3

½ cup chicken gravy–4

1 16-oz. can green beans–4

¼ cup bacon bits–4

1 6½-oz. can tuna fish–5

¼ cup sliced black olives–5

¾ cup cooking wine–2

GROCERY

6 cups noodles–3,5

1 bag potato chips–4,5

PRODUCE

3 yellow squash–1

4 onions–1,3,4,5

6 zucchini–1,2

2 red bell peppers–1

1 green bell pepper–2

Salad greens for 2 dinners–2,5

Salad toppings for 2 dinners–2,5

4 to 6 apples–3

1 tablespoon minced pimentos–4

Strawberries–5

1 bunch fresh parsley–4

BAKERY

1 loaf French bread–1

1 loaf white bread–4

DAIRY

2 sticks butter–1,2,4

1 cup cottage cheese–2

8 oz. grated Cheddar cheese–4,5

5 eggs–2,3,4

1 cup sour cream–5

4 tablespoons milk–4

FREEZER

1 10-oz. package chopped spinach–3

1 small bag hash brown potatoes–4

CHECK YOUR STAPLES

Salt–1,2,3,4,5

Pepper–1,2,3,4,5

Thyme–2

Dill seed–2

Garlic powder–3

2 tablespoons Worcestershire sauce–3

Instant rice for 1 dinner–2

Shopping List

MEATS

1 6-pound ham–1,3
6 boneless, skinless chicken breasts–2
5 slices bacon–2,5
1 pound turkey scallops–4

CANS/JARS

2 10½-oz. cans cream of chicken soup–2
1 10½-oz. can cream of mushroom soup–5
1 16-oz. can spinach–2
2 28-oz. cans chopped, peeled
    tomatoes–3,5
¾ cup red cooking wine–4
Salad dressing for 1 dinner–3
1 12-ounce can beer–1

GROCERY

2 tablespoons orange juice–1
12 oz. fettuccine–5
1 envelope onion soup mix–5
1 package mac 'n' cheese–1
1 bag corn chips–3
1 box stuffing mix, instant–4

PRODUCE

Favorite fresh fruit for salad–1
1 onion–2,3,5
2 cloves garlic–3,5
1 bunch chives–5
10 leaves basil–4,5
3 cups fresh green beans–5
4 oz. fresh mushrooms–5

6 ears corn on cob–4
3 stalks celery–3
1 lemon–3
Salad greens for 1 dinner–3
Favorite salad toppings for 1 dinner–3
6 to 8 oranges–2

DAIRY

3 sticks butter–1,3,4,5

BAKERY

1 loaf French bread–5
1 package hamburger buns–3

CHECK YOUR STAPLES

Dry mustard–1
Salt–2,5
Pepper–2,5
Oregano–5
Garlic powder–4
3 bay leaves–3
¾ cup brown sugar–1,3
3 tablespoons cornstarch–3
2 cups instant rice–2
2 tablespoons Worcestershire sauce–3
¼ cup catsup–3
5 tablespoons vinegar–3
¼ cup soy sauce–4
½ cup oil–1,2,4
1 cup grated Parmesan–5

Shopping List

MEAT

1½ pounds ground beef–2
4 fresh or frozen fish fillets–3
12 boneless chicken breasts–1,5

CANS/JARS

1 16-oz. can cranberry sauce–1
2 10½-oz. cans cream of potato soup–4
2 10½-oz. cans mushroom soup–1
1 10½-oz. can cream of chicken soup–3
2 16-oz. cans white asparagus–1
3 8-oz. cans tomato sauce–2
2 tablespoons diced green chilies–5
Salad dressing for 1 dinner–2
1 16-oz. can refried beans–5
1 8-oz. bottle French salad dressing–1
1 cup salsa–5

GROCERY

1 box cheese crackers–1
1 8-oz. package lasagna noodles–2
Peanut butter and crackers–4

PRODUCE

2 tablespoons pimento–1
1 tablespoon parsley–1
1 bulb garlic–1
6 scallions–2
2 tablespoons basil–2,3
7 medium potatoes–3
2 onions–1,5
1 head cauliflower–3
2 heads broccoli–4
Salad greens for 1 dinner–2
Salad toppings for 1 dinner–2

BAKERY

2 loaves French bread–2
Crackers–4
8 to 10 flour tortillas–5

DAIRY

6 sticks butter–1,3,5
8 oz. grated mozzarella cheese–2
1½ cups cottage cheese–2
1 cup sour cream–3
1½ cups grated Cheddar cheese–3,5
4 cups milk–4
1 cup grated Swiss cheese–4
6 oz. cream cheese–5
⅔ cup heavy cream–5
2¼ cups grated Monterey Jack cheese–5

CHECK YOUR STAPLES

Salt–1,2,3
Pepper–1,2,3
Instant minced onion–3,4
Oregano–2
Ground red pepper–2,3
Ground white pepper–3
Onion powder–3
Garlic salt–3
Thyme–3
Ground sage–3
Basil–3
2 teaspoons Worcestershire sauce–1
½ cup mayonnaise–2
Seasoned bread crumbs–3
Oil–5
Rice for 1 dinner–5
⅓ cup grated Parmesan–2

Bulk Shopping List

MEATS

18 boneless pork chops

10 boneless chicken breasts

4 pounds ground beef

CANS/JARS

7 10½-oz. cans cream of mushroom soup

2¾ cups mayonnaise

54 oz. tomato sauce

1 cup honey

Salad dressing for 6 dinners

2½ cups barbecue sauce

GROCERY

3 bags potato chips

PRODUCE

15 onions

10 cloves garlic

28 carrots

BAKERY

Dinner rolls for 6 dinners

DAIRY

1 pound grated Cheddar cheese

¾ cup Jack cheese

¾ cup sour cream

9 sticks butter

CHECK YOUR STAPLES

12½ teaspoons salt

7 teaspoons pepper

2 tablespoons minced dry onion

3 cups flour

½ teaspoon cayenne pepper

1½ teaspoons dry mustard

1 cup grated Parmesan cheese

2½ tablespoons Worcestershire sauce

1 cup olive oil

Shopping List

MEATS

1 6-pound boneless chuck roast–1,3
1 3-pound broiler chicken, cut up–2
1 pound round steak–4
1 pound peeled shrimp–5

CANS/JARS

1 tablespoon Dijon mustard–2
2 cups barbecue sauce–3
1/4 cup dry sherry–4
1 3-oz. can mushrooms–4
1/4 cup brandy–4
1 16-oz. can green beans–4
2 tablespoons steak sauce–4,5
Salad dressing for 1 dinner–5

GROCERY

1 envelope onion soup mix–1
1 bag potato chips–3
12 oz. fettuccine–5
1 box prepared pilaf–4

PRODUCE

2 carrots–1
2 onions–1,5
1 stalk celery–1
Small head cabbage–1
3 lemons–2,5
1 bunch green onion–2
1 bunch asparagus–2
4 large potatoes–2
1 bunch chives–4
4 cloves garlic–5
2 tablespoons parsley–5

Salad greens for 1 dinner–5
Salad toppings for 1 dinner–5

BAKERY

1 loaf ready-to-heat garlic bread–5
Dinner rolls for 1 dinner–1
1 package hamburger buns–3

DAIRY

1/2 cup plain yogurt–2
Sour cream–2
2 sticks butter–1,2,5

FREEZER

1 bag sliced carrots–3

CHECK YOUR STAPLES

Salt–1,2
Pepper–1,2
1 bay leaf–1
Dried minced onion–1
Ground thyme–2
Cayenne pepper–2
Dry mustard–4
Tarragon–5
Garlic powder–2
1 tablespoon vinegar–1
1 1/2 tablespoons Worcestershire sauce–2,5
2 tablespoons cooking oil–4
1/4 teaspoon hot sauce–5
2 tablespoons flour–1
1/2 cup grated Parmesan–2
2 tablespoons horseradish–1
1/4 cup mayonnaise–2

Shopping List

MEAT

1 3- to 4-pound roast beef–1

6 pork chops–2

4 boneless chicken breasts–3

3 cups turkey breast meat–4

CANS/JARS

2 8-oz. cans tomato sauce–2,4

4 10½-oz. cans cream of mushroom
     soup–3,5

Salad dressing for 1 dinner–3

2 cups chicken gravy–4

2 tablespoons dry sherry–4

2 6½-oz. cans tuna–5

1 5-oz. can sliced water chestnuts–5

Favorite steak sauce for roast beef–1

1 can dried onions–3

GROCERY

5 salted soda crackers–1

½ pound linguini–4

1 large package Chinese noodles–5

PRODUCE

1 pound zucchini–1

4 onions–1,2,3,4,5

1 red onion–2

5 stalks celery–1,4,5

2 green bell peppers–1,4

2 cloves garlic–2,4

3 cups spinach–2

1 head lettuce–2

2 oranges–2

1 cucumber–2

5 tablespoons lemon juice–2,5

1 head broccoli–3

Salad greens for 1 dinner–3

Salad toppings for 1 dinner–3

½ pound mushrooms–4

2 large eggplants–4

¼ cup parsley–4

1 tomato–4

½ teaspoon basil–4

4 pounds asparagus–5

BAKERY

Dinner rolls for 2 dinners–1,4

1 package flour tortillas–3

¾ cup soft bread crumbs–4

DAIRY

2⅓ cups grated Cheddar cheese–1,2,3,4

2½ cups milk–1,3

1 cup whipping cream–4

½ cup sour cream–5

2 sticks butter–1,4

CHECK YOUR STAPLES

Salt–1,2,4,5

Pepper–1,2,4

Caraway seeds–2

Paprika–5

Garlic powder–4

1 cup olive oil–2,4

¼ cup honey–2

2 cups mayonnaise–2,5

1 cup brown rice–2

Shopping List

MEATS

1 pound ground beef–1
4 boneless chicken breasts–2
8 hamburger patties–3
6 boneless pork chops–4

CANS/JARS

1 6-oz. can tomato paste–1
$\frac{1}{2}$ cup dry white wine–1
1 8-oz. can tomato sauce–1
Salad dressing for 1 dinner–1
1 10$\frac{1}{2}$-oz. can cream of chicken soup–2
$\frac{1}{2}$ cup barbecue sauce–3
1 17-oz. can baked beans–3
$\frac{1}{2}$ cup chicken broth–4
1 jar applesauce–4
1 16-oz. can fruit salad–5

GROCERY

1 package spaghetti noodles–1
Bag herb stuffing mix–2
2 large cans refrigerated biscuits–2
1 bag potato chips–3
2 boxes Jell-O (any flavor)–3

PRODUCE

1 onion–1
2 cloves garlic–1,4
Salad greens for 1 dinner–1
Favorite salad toppings for 1 dinner–1

1 head lettuce–3,5
1 tomato–3
1 red onion–3

BAKERY

1 loaf ready-to-heat garlic bread–1
1 bag hamburger buns–3

DAIRY

1 cup grated Jack cheese–2
2 cups cottage cheese–5
2 sticks butter–2

FREEZER

1 bag peas–2
1 bag mixed broccoli, carrots, cauliflower–4
1 box fish sticks–5
1 bag French fries –5

CHECK YOUR STAPLES

Salt–1,3
Pepper–1,3
Sugar–1
Oregano–1
Basil–1
Parsley–1
Ground ginger–4
1 tablespoon olive oil–1
$\frac{1}{3}$ cup honey–4
$\frac{1}{4}$ cup soy sauce–4
2 tablespoons catsup–4
Instant rice for 1 dinner–4

Shopping List

MEATS

1 4- to 5-pound boneless, cooked ham–2,4
6 boneless pork chops–3

CANS/JARS

1 7-oz. can white chicken–1
1 can cream of mushroom soup–1
1 can peas–1
1/2 cup orange marmalade–2
1 16-oz. can creamed corn–2
2 16-oz. cans stewed tomatoes–3
1 6-oz. can whole Ortega chilies–4
1 10 1/2-oz. can cream of shrimp soup–5
2 7-oz. cans cooked shrimp–5
Favorite salad dressing for 1 dinner–4

GROCERY

1 bag potato chips–1
18 salted crackers–2

PRODUCE

6 onions–1,3,5
1 clove garlic–1
6 ears of corn–3
2 pounds carrots–4
2 apples–5
Salad greens for 1 dinner–4
Favorite salad toppings for 1 dinner–4
1 lemon–4

BAKERY

Breadsticks–2
2 packages flour tortillas–3,4

DAIRY

2 quarts milk–1,4
1 egg–2
1/2 pound Jack cheese–4
3/4 pound grated sharp Cheddar cheese–4
1 cup sour cream–5
2 sticks butter–1,2,4,5

FREEZER

1 10-oz. package chopped spinach–1
1 10-oz. package broccoli–2
1 10-oz. box peas–5

CHECK YOUR STAPLES

Salt–1,2,4
Pepper–1,2,4
Instant minced onion–2
Crushed red pepper–3
Cumin–3
Dry mustard–4
Dash Accent–4
Curry powder–5
1/2 cup flour–4
Instant rice for 1 dinner–5
1/2 cup mayonnaise–3
1 tablespoon Worcestershire sauce–3
1/2 cup grated Parmesan–3

Shopping List

MEATS

3½ to 4 pounds corned beef–1

1 2½- to 3-pound chicken + 2 chicken
    breasts–2,4

3 pounds ground beef–3

CANS/JARS

2½ tablespoons horseradish–1,5

¼ cup molasses–1

½ cup dry white wine–2

2 17-oz. cans corn–3

2 cans sliced carrots–3

2 15-oz. cans tomato sauce–3

1 16-oz. can chicken broth–4

1 10½-oz. can cream of mushroom soup–5

1 15-oz. can corned beef hash–5

1 16-oz. can green beans–2

Favorite salad dressing for 2 dinners–2,5

PRODUCE

1 head cabbage–1

1 bag carrots–1

30 boiling onions–1,2

1 clove garlic–2

1 tablespoon parsley–2

2 green bell peppers–3

2 onions–3

Basket strawberries–3

4 kiwis–3

4 bananas–3

6 oranges–5

Favorite salad greens for 2 dinners–2,5

Favorite salad toppings for 2 dinners–2,5

Bunch fresh asparagus–4

6 tablespoons pimento–4, 5

BAKERY

Dinner rolls for 3 dinners–1,3,4

DAIRY

1 cup sour cream–2

5 cups milk–2,4

3 cups grated sharp American cheese–3,5

8 eggs–4,5

2 sticks butter–1,3,4

FREEZER

2 9-inch deep-dish pie crusts–5

2 10-oz. bags chopped spinach–5

1 cup frozen peas–4

2 pounds hash browns–3

CHECK YOUR STAPLES

Salt–2,4

Pepper–2,4

2 whole cloves–2

Marjoram–2

Thyme–2

1 bay leaf–2

Baking powder–4

Paprika–4

Cooking oil–4

2¼ cups flour–4,5

1 cup baking mix–2

2 tablespoons red wine vinegar–1

3 tablespoons prepared mustard–1,5

Bulk Shopping List

SUMMER • WEEKS 1–4

MEATS

4½ pounds ground beef

CANS/JARS

Salad dressing for 3 dinners
3 cans cream of mushroom soup
4 2.8-oz. cans French fried onions
3 8-oz. cans sliced mushrooms

GROCERY

2 packages sliced almonds
24 oz. egg noodles

PRODUCE

15 cloves garlic
14 onions
18 apples

BAKERY

Dinner rolls for 2 dinners
4 loaves French bread

DAIRY

10 sticks butter
7 cups grated Cheddar cheese

FREEZER

80 ounces French-cut green beans

CHECK YOUR STAPLES

11 teaspoons salt
5 teaspoons pepper
¾ cup flour
6¼ teaspoons ground ginger
¾ teaspoon garlic powder
¾ teaspoon garlic salt
2½ teaspoons thyme
2½ cups vinegar
3 cups soy sauce
2¾ cups oil
1½ cups catsup
2½ cups lemon juice
23 cups rice
1 cup grated Parmesan cheese

Shopping List

MEATS

3 pounds boneless spareribs–1
4 6-oz. halibut steaks–2
2 pounds flank steak–3
4 boneless chicken breasts–4
1 pound ground beef–5

CANS/JARS

1 6-oz. can pineapple juice–1
Favorite salad dressing for 1 dinner–5
1 16-oz. can bean sprouts–4
1 10½-oz. can cream of mushroom soup–4
2 2.8-oz. cans French fried onions–4
1 16-oz. can pinto beans–5
1 15-oz. can black beans–5
1 10-oz. can tomatoes and green chilies–5
1 jar salsa–5
1 box scalloped potatoes–1
¼ cup nonfat salad dressing–3

GROCERY

2 envelopes fat-free Italian salad dressing
    mix–3
Tortilla chips–5

PRODUCE

4 cloves garlic–1
1 pound asparagus–1
4 onions–2,3,4,5
1 head broccoli–2
2 heads cauliflower–2,3
1 lemon–3
2 cucumbers–3
1 bunch celery–3,4
1 basket cherry tomatoes–3
1 green bell pepper–3,5
1 red bell pepper–3
1 bunch green onions–3

3 red potatoes–3
6 apples–4
Salad greens for 1 dinner–5
Favorite salad toppings for 1 dinner–5

BAKERY

Dinner rolls for 1 dinner–4
1 package 6-inch or 7-inch flour tortillas–5

DAIRY

3 cups grated sharp Cheddar cheese–4,5
1 cup shredded Monterey Jack cheese–5
½ cup milk–4
2 sticks butter–2,3

FREEZER

1 bag French fries–2
2 packages French-cut green beans–4

CHECK YOUR STAPLES

Sesame seeds–1
Ground ginger–1
Ground cumin–1,5
Dill–2
Salt–2,5
Pepper–2,3,5
Italian seasoning–3
Chili powder–5
½ cup brown sugar–1
1½ teaspoons sugar–1
2 tablespoons cornstarch–1
1 tablespoon vinegar–1
¾ cup soy sauce–1
3 tablespoons cooking oil–1,3
4 chicken bouillon cubes–1
1 tablespoon olive oil–2

Shopping List

SUMMER • WEEK 2

MEATS

2½ pounds ground beef–1,5
6 pork chops–2
1 to 2 pounds beef round steak–3
2½ pounds chicken pieces–4

CANS/JARS

1 cup tomato juice–1
1 10½-oz. can cream of chicken soup–2
1 10½-oz. can cream of mushroom soup–2
1 10½-oz. can tomato soup–5
1 6-oz. can sliced water chestnuts–2,4
1 2-oz. can sliced mushrooms–4
2 2.8-oz. cans French fried onions–2,4
Salad dressing for 2 dinners–4,5

GROCERY

½ cup quick oats–1
1 package instant mashed potatoes–1
3 cups egg noodles–2
1 package sliced almonds–2

PRODUCE

3 onions–1,2,3,5
6 peaches–1
3 green onions–2
2 tablespoons parsley–3
6 ears corn–3
1 red bell pepper–4
4 stalks celery–4
Ready-to-serve spinach salad–4
3 zucchini or 9 oz. frozen spinach–5

2 green bell peppers–4,5
Salad greens for 1 dinner–5
Salad toppings for 1 dinner–5

BAKERY

1 loaf ready-to-heat garlic bread–5
Sliced French bread–3

DAIRY

3 eggs–1,4
1⅓ cups grated Cheddar cheese–3,5
1 stick butter–3

FREEZER

2 10-oz. bags French-cut string beans–2
1 6-oz. bag pea pods–4

CHECK YOUR STAPLES

Salt–1,2,3,5
Pepper–1,2,3,5
Garlic salt–3
3 tablespoons shortening–3
Ground ginger–4
Garlic powder–4
Paprika–5
3 teaspoons Worcestershire sauce–2
¾ cup catsup–1,2,4
2 tablespoons oil–2
3 tablespoons soy sauce–4
½ cup rice–4,5
¼ cup flour–3

Shopping List

MEATS

2 pounds chicken wings–1
1 pound ground beef–2
1 pound cooked shrimp, tuna or
    crabmeat–5
2 pounds boneless sirloin steak–4

CANS/JARS

1 14-oz. can beef broth–2
2 5-oz. cans white chunk chicken–3
1 11-oz. can mandarin oranges–3
2 tablespoons orange juice–3
1 8-oz. can sliced mushrooms–2
1 tablespoon orange-flavored liqueur
    (opt.)–4

GROCERY

Egg noodles–2
1/4 cup oats–2
1 can refrigerated bread loaf–2

PRODUCE

Favorite summer vegetables for steaming–1
5 stalks celery–2
2 onions–2,5
6 apples or other fruit for salad–2
1 banana–3
Salad greens–3
2 cloves garlic–2,4
2 melons–5
1 lemon–4
8 cherry tomatoes–4
4 large mushrooms–4
1 red bell pepper–5
1 green bell pepper–4
1 lime–4

1 basket strawberries–4
1 cup grapes–4
1 honeydew melon–4
1 cantaloupe–4

BAKERY

French bread for 2 dinners–3,4
Dinner rolls for 1 dinner–5

DAIRY

1 egg–2
1 cup sour cream–2
3 sticks butter–2

FREEZER

1 10-oz. package green peas–5

CHECK YOUR STAPLES

Garlic powder–1
Ground ginger–1,4
Curry powder–3
Salt–2
Lemon pepper–5
Crushed hot red pepper–4
Instant rice for 1 dinner + 2 cups–1,5
3 tablespoons flour–2
3 1/4 tablespoons lemon juice–1,3,5
1/4 cup sugar–4
2 tablespoons instant chicken bouillon–1
1 1/4 cups mayonnaise–3
1 tablespoon oil–2
1/2 cup catsup–2
2 tablespoons Worcestershire sauce–2
2 tablespoons soy sauce–1,4
1/2 cup honey–1,4

Shopping List

MEATS

1½ pounds ground beef–1
Anchovies (opt.)–1
2 pounds boneless lamb–2
7 chicken breasts–4
2 pounds sliced turkey meat–5

CANS/JARS

2 8-oz. cans tomato sauce–1
2¼ cups chicken broth–2
1 8-oz. can sliced mushrooms–2
1 4-oz. can sliced mushrooms–4
1 10½-oz. can cream of mushroom soup–3
1 large can chow mein noodles–3
1 7-oz. can tuna–3
2 teaspoons sesame oil–4
2 pints dry sherry–4,5
1 5-oz. can sliced water chestnuts–4

GROCERY

1 12-oz. package egg noodles–1
⅓ cup sliced almonds–4
1 envelope dry onion soup mix–5

PRODUCE

3 green onions–1
5 green bell peppers–1,2,3
9 cloves garlic–1,2,4,5
1 head romaine lettuce–1
5 onions–2,4,5
½ cup parsley–2
3 red bell peppers–2
12 mushrooms–2
12 cherry tomatoes–2
12 stalks celery–2,3
6 large tomatoes–3
1 red onion–3
1 cucumber–3
1 orange–5
4 artichokes–5

2 pounds potatoes–5
5 to 6 apples–3

BAKERY

Croutons–1
1 loaf French bread–1

DAIRY

1 8-oz. package cream cheese–1
½ pound cottage cheese–1
¼ cup sour cream–1
1 egg–1
2½ cups milk–3,4
2 cups grated cheese–3,4

FREEZER

1 10-oz. package peas–3
3 10-oz. packages green beans–4

CHECK YOUR STAPLES

Pepper–1,2,3,4
Salt–1,2,3,4,5
Marjoram–2
Thyme–2
Parsley–2
Celery salt–3
Mustard seed–3
Sugar–3
Cayenne–3
Ginger–4
Oregano–5
2⅓ cups oil–1,2,4,5
⅓ cup flour–4
1 teaspoon Worcestershire sauce–1
1 cup lemon juice–1,2
¾ cup vinegar–3
1½ cups soy sauce–4
½ cup honey–4
Instant rice for 1 dinner–4
1 cup wild rice–2

Bulk Shopping List

MEATS

9 pounds ground beef
22 boneless chicken breasts
2 4-pound frying chickens
3½ pounds round steak

CANS/JARS

2 4-oz. cans sliced mushrooms
2 10½-oz. cans cream of chicken soup
2 10½-oz. cans cream of mushroom soup
6¼ cups chicken broth or cubes
3 2.8-oz. cans French fried onions
2 4-oz. cans sliced olives
Salad dressing for 3 dinners
3 10½-oz. cans tomato soup
2 6-oz. cans tomato paste
2 jars applesauce

PRODUCE

10 onions
6 apples
9 cloves garlic

BAKERY

5 loaves French bread
2 packages flour tortillas

DAIRY

4 cups grated Cheddar cheese
11 sticks butter

FREEZER

20 oz. peas

CHECK YOUR STAPLES

1 cup oil
¾ cup olive oil
½ cup lemon juice
¾ cup Worcestershire sauce
1 cup mayonnaise
1 cup vinegar
6 teaspoons mustard
1½ cups grated Parmesan cheese

Shopping List

MEATS

4 large boneless chicken breasts–1
2 pounds ground beef–2
4 pork chops–3
1 pound frankfurters–4

CANS/JARS

2 teaspoons Dijon mustard–1
3¼ cups chicken broth–1
2 16-oz. cans red kidney beans–2
2 small cans chopped olives–2
Catalina salad dressing–2,3
1 10½-oz. can tomato soup–4
1 jar applesauce–4
French salad dressing–5
1 14-oz. can white tuna–5
1 can peas–5
1 6-oz. can chili peppers–2

GROCERY

1 envelope taco seasoning mix–2
1 bag tortilla chips–2
2 cups egg noodles–4

PRODUCE

2 lemons–1,3
1 bunch green onions–1,2,3
1 bunch parsley–1,5
2 pounds green beans–1
2 heads lettuce–2,5
10 tomatoes–2,3,5
6 stalks celery–2,5
2 avocados–2
2 apples–3

1 cucumber–3
1 onion–4
1 large crown summer squash–5
1 green bell pepper–5

BAKERY

1 loaf ready-to-heat garlic bread–5
1 package flour tortillas–2
Dinner rolls for 1 dinner–3

DAIRY

1 cup grated Cheddar cheese–2
1 cup milk–4
Sliced American cheese–4
2 eggs–5
4 sticks butter–1,3,4

FREEZER

1 bag mixed vegetables–4

CHECK YOUR STAPLES

Salt–1
Pepper–1
Savory–1
Thyme–1
Rosemary–1
Marjoram–1
Ground cinnamon–3
¼ cup brown sugar–3
4 tablespoons oil–1,3
2 tablespoons vinegar–3
1 cup rice–1
½ cup mayonnaise–5

Shopping List

MEATS

1½ pounds round steak–1
1 4-pound frying chicken–5
1 pound uncooked large prawns or shrimp,
   shelled and deveined–3
1 pound ground beef–4
¼ pound bacon–4
3 boneless chicken breasts–2

CANS/JARS

½ cup Burgundy wine–1
1 can (1 pound) stewed tomatoes–1
1 large can whole tomatoes–5
1 4-oz. can sliced mushrooms–1
1 10½-oz. can cream of chicken soup–1
1 14-oz. can sliced pineapple–3
⅛ cup Dijon mustard–4
Salad dressing for 2 dinners–1,4
1 4-oz. can sliced olives–2
1 11-oz. can mandarin oranges–2
1 2.8-oz. can French fried onions–5
2 15-oz. cans pinquitos beans–4

GROCERY

1 8-oz. package herb stuffing mix–1
½ cup slivered almonds–2
1 envelope onion soup mix–5

PRODUCE

4 onions–1,2,4,5
2 tablespoons parsley–1
2 pounds yellow summer squash–1
2 carrots–1
2 cloves garlic–4,5
3 pimentos–5
1 green bell pepper–3
1 head broccoli–3

1 head cauliflower–3
Salad greens for 2 dinners–1,4
Salad toppings for 2 dinners–1,4
3 celery sticks–2
1 cup seedless grapes–2
4 to 6 peaches–5

BAKERY

1 loaf French bread–4
Breadsticks–2

DAIRY

24 oz. sour cream–1,5
¼ cup blue cheese, crumbled–4
2 eggs–2
3 sticks butter–1,3,4

FREEZER

1 9-oz. package peas–5
3 10-oz. packages chopped spinach–5

CHECK YOUR STAPLES

Garlic salt–1
Pepper–1,3,4,5
Salt–2,3,4,5
Oregano–1
Paprika–5
Powdered saffron–5
1 bay leaf–5
Chili powder–3
Instant rice for 1 dinner + 2 cups–3,5
2 tablespoons flour–1
½ cup mayonnaise–2
2 tablespoons lemon juice–2
¼ cup olive oil–5
2 tablespoons oil–1
2 chicken bouillon cubes–5
½ tablespoon Worcestershire sauce–4

Shopping List

SUMMER • WEEK 7

MEATS

7 boneless chicken breasts–1,5
3 pounds ground beef–2,3
2 pounds round or cubed steak–4

CANS/JARS

1 can chicken broth–1
1 6-oz. can tomato paste–2
1/2 cup dry red wine–2
4 8-oz. cans tomato sauce–2,3
Favorite salad dressings–2
1 jar applesauce–3
1 10 1/2-oz. can cream of mushroom soup–4
1 2.8-oz. can French fried onions–1
1 4-oz. can sliced mushrooms–4
1 17-oz. can pineapple chunks–5

GROCERY

1 package spaghetti sauce mix–2
12 oz. lasagna noodles–2
3/4 cup oats–3
1 1/2 cups elbow macaroni–3
Instant mashed potatoes–4
1 box rice pilaf–5

PRODUCE

2 lemons–1
1 green bell pepper–3,5
1 red bell pepper–5
1 bag carrots–1
5 cloves garlic–1,4,5
1 tablespoon parsley–1
3 apples–1
3 pears–1
3 onions–1,2,3,4,5
Salad greens for 1 dinner–2
Favorite salad toppings for 1 dinner–2
12 mushrooms–5
6 ears corn on cob–5

BAKERY

2 loaves French bread–2,5

DAIRY

1 cup grated Cheddar cheese–3
2 pounds grated mozzarella cheese–2
2 eggs–2,3
2 cups milk–3
2 oz. processed American cheese–3
2 cups ricotta cheese–2
3 sticks butter–3,5

FREEZER

1 package green beans–4

CHECK YOUR STAPLES

Salt–2,3
Seasoned salt–4
Pepper–2,3
Oregano–2
Basil–2
Parsley–2
Chili powder–5
Dry mustard–5
Garlic powder–2
1/2 teaspoon sugar–2
1/4 cup brown sugar–3
1 cup flour–1,3,4
5 tablespoons Worcestershire sauce–1,3,4,5
6 tablespoons oil–1,2,4
5 teaspoons mustard–3
1 1/2 cups catsup–3,4,5
1 tablespoon steak sauce–4
1/4 cup lemon juice–5
1/4 cup white vinegar–5
2 tablespoons dry bread crumbs–3
Instant rice for 1 dinner–1
1 cup Parmesan cheese–2

Shopping List

MEATS

3 pounds ground beef–1,5
1 4-pound frying chicken–2
8 chicken breasts–4
$\frac{1}{2}$ pound bay shrimp–3
$\frac{1}{4}$ pound crab–3

CANS/JARS

2 10$\frac{1}{2}$-oz. cans tomato soup–1
4 dashes hot sauce–1
1 tablespoon tomato paste–2
2 tablespoons white wine–2
1 cup chicken bouillon or broth–2
10 pimento-stuffed olives–2
$\frac{1}{2}$ cup sliced water chestnuts–3
1 2.8-oz. can French fried onions–4
1 teaspoon prepared mustard–4
1 16-oz. can refried beans–5
1 4-oz. can sliced olives–5
3 tablespoons cooking oil–5

GROCERY

1 package cream of mushroom soup mix–1
8 oz. spaghetti or elbow noodles–1
1 package onion soup mix–1
1 cup soda crackers–1
1 6-oz. package seasoned long grain and
    wild rice mix–4
2 tablespoons herbed stuffing mix–4
Tortilla chips–5
Salsa–5

PRODUCE

$\frac{3}{4}$ pound mushrooms, chopped–1,2
2 eggplants–1
1 green bell pepper–2
1 red bell pepper–2
1 clove garlic–2

4 zucchini–2
2 stalks celery–3
$\frac{1}{2}$ cup bean sprouts–3
3 large tomatoes–4,5
$\frac{1}{4}$ cup onion–4
2 teaspoons parsley–4
$\frac{1}{4}$ head lettuce–5
4 to 5 plums–1
4 to 5 peaches–4

BAKERY

2 loaves French bread–2,3
1 package flour tortillas–5

DAIRY

1 cup grated Cheddar cheese–5
1 stick butter–4

FREEZER

1 9-oz. package peas and pearl onions–3
1 10-oz. package peas–4

CHECK YOUR STAPLES

Salt–2,3
Pepper–2
Seasoned salt–2,4
Parsley flakes–2
Instant minced onion–2
Ground oregano–2
Garlic powder–2
Curry powder–3
1 tablespoon flour–2
2 tablespoons soy sauce–1,3
1$\frac{1}{2}$ tablespoons Worcestershire sauce–1,4
$\frac{1}{2}$ cup olive oil–2
2 tablespoons lemon juice–3
$\frac{1}{3}$ cup mayonnaise–3
$\frac{1}{2}$ cup Parmesan cheese–1

Bulk Shopping List

SUMMER • WEEKS 9–13

MEATS

1 4- to 5-pound frying chicken
3½ pounds ground beef
10 boneless chicken breasts
22 frankfurters

CANS/JARS

Favorite salad dressing for 3 dinners
1 28-oz. can pineapple chunks
5 cups barbecue sauce
1 22-oz. can mandarin oranges
19 oz. white tuna
2 cups barbecue sauce

PRODUCE

11 onions
4 bulbs garlic
2 pounds carrots

BAKERY

Dinner rolls for 5 dinners

DAIRY

1 pound grated Cheddar cheese
6 sticks butter

CHECK YOUR STAPLES

2 cups catsup
15 teaspoons salt
8 teaspoons pepper
3 teaspoon garlic powder
2 tablespoons ground ginger
2 cups sugar
1½ teaspoons seasoned salt
2¾ cups oil
2½ cups mayonnaise
1 cup lemon juice
1½ cups vinegar
4½ teaspoons mustard
1½ cups soy sauce

Shopping List

MEATS

1 pound boneless, skinless chicken breasts–1
6 $\frac{1}{2}$-inch-thick pork chops–2
1$\frac{1}{2}$ pounds bone-in round steak–3
$\frac{1}{2}$ pound ground turkey–4
$\frac{1}{2}$ pound hot Italian turkey sausage links–4
10 frankfurters–5

CANS/JARS

Favorite salad dressing for 1 dinner–1
1 can cream of celery soup–2
1 2.8-oz. can French fried onions–2
3 14$\frac{1}{2}$-oz. cans stewed tomatoes–3,4
1 16-oz. can kidney beans–4
2 16-oz. cans baked beans–5
3 cans chicken broth–4
$\frac{3}{4}$ cup cider vinegar–4,5
1 20-oz. can pineapple tidbits–5
1 jar hot dog relish–5

GROCERY

1 16-oz. spiral pasta–1
1 bag corn chips–5
1$\frac{1}{2}$ cups elbow macaroni–4

PRODUCE

3 onions–1,3,4,5
5 cloves garlic–1,3,4
3 zucchini–1,4
2 yellow summer squash–1
Salad greens for 1 dinner–1
Favorite salad toppings for 1 dinner–1
1 green bell pepper–3
1$\frac{1}{2}$ pounds carrots–3
1 bunch parsley–4

BAKERY

Dinner rolls for 3 dinners–2,3,4
10 hot dog buns–5

DAIRY

2 cups whipping cream–1
3 cups grated Cheddar cheese–1,2
$\frac{1}{2}$ cup milk–2
$\frac{1}{2}$ cup sour cream–2
2 sticks butter–1,3

FREEZER

24 oz. hash brown potatoes–2
1 10-oz. package green beans–2
1 10-oz. package mixed vegetables–4

CHECK YOUR STAPLES

Salt–1,3,4,5
Pepper–1,2,3,4
Basil–1,4
Marjoram–1
Savory–1
Rosemary–1
Sage–1
Seasoned salt–2
Oregano–4
$\frac{1}{3}$ cup flour–3
$\frac{3}{4}$ cup brown sugar–3,5
3 tablespoons lemon juice–3
6 tablespoons olive oil–1,2,3,4
5 tablespoons oil–2,3,4
$\frac{3}{4}$ cup vinegar–4
1 cup catsup–5
2 teaspoons mustard–5

Shopping List

MEATS

3 broiler chickens–1,4
1 pound sirloin beef–2
2 pounds jumbo shrimp–3

CANS/JARS

1 8-oz. jar apricot preserves–1
1 bottle Russian dressing–1
2 teaspoons vermouth–1
2 8-oz. cans pineapple chunks–2,4
1 cup barbecue sauce–3
$\frac{1}{8}$ teaspoon sesame oil–3
1 cup whole cranberries–3
1 8-oz. can crushed pineapple–3
1 8-oz. can sliced water chestnuts–4
1 11-oz. can mandarin oranges–4
1 7-oz. can tuna–5
$\frac{1}{4}$ cup sweet pickle relish–5

GROCERY

1 package dry onion soup mix–1
1 cup chopped walnuts–3
1 cup crushed pecans–1
$\frac{1}{2}$ cup sliced almonds–4
$\frac{1}{2}$ cup herbed stuffing mix–2
$\frac{1}{2}$ package miniature marshmallows–3
1 box won tons–4
1 bag favorite potato chips–5

PRODUCE

24 medium mushrooms–1
2 tablespoons parsley–1,2

6 cloves garlic–1,2
4 medium tomatoes–2
$\frac{1}{2}$ teaspoon basil–2
Ginger root–3
1 green bell pepper–4
6 stalks celery–4,5
1 whole or half watermelon–5
Head of lettuce–4

BAKERY

2 loaves French bread–1,3
8 French sandwich rolls–5

DAIRY

$\frac{1}{2}$ pint whipping cream–3
2 eggs–5
2 sticks butter–1,2,5

CHECK YOUR STAPLES

Salt–1,2,4
Pepper–2,4
Ground ginger–2,3
Garlic powder–2
Onion salt–2
Curry–4
$\frac{3}{4}$ cup sugar–3
1 cup soy sauce–2,3
2 tablespoons lemon juice–2
1 cup mayonnaise–4,5
$\frac{1}{2}$ teaspoon prepared mustard–5
Instant rice for 1 dinner–2
$\frac{1}{4}$ cup brown sugar–2

Shopping List

MEATS

1 pound ground beef–1
12 frankfurters–2
2 chicken breasts–3
6 favorite steaks–4

CANS/JARS

2 16-oz. cans crushed tomatoes–1
2 8-oz. cans tomato sauce–1,2
2 cups red wine–1
Favorite salad dressing for 1 dinner–1
2 15-oz. cans chili beans–2
1 4-oz. can chopped black olives–3
1 20-oz. can pineapple chunks–3
1 11-oz. can mandarin oranges–3
Barbecue sauce–4
1½ cups corn–4
1 tablespoon Dijon mustard–4
½ teaspoon hot pepper sauce–5
1 12-oz. can white tuna–5

GROCERY

4 cups rigatoni–1
1 bag potato chips–2
1 box or bag croutons–3
12 oz. tiny shell pasta–4
1 7-oz. package linguine–5

PRODUCE

3 cloves garlic–1,4
2 onions–1,3
2 green bell peppers–1,3,4
Salad greens for 1 dinner–1
Favorite salad toppings for 1 dinner–1
8 plums–2
1 bunch celery–3
½ cup sliced mushrooms–3
1 cup grapes–3
1 head lettuce–3
1½ cups radishes–4
⅓ cup dill–4
1 bunch green onions–5
2 tomatoes–5
6 peaches–5

BAKERY

2 loaves ready-to-heat garlic bread–1,4
6 croissants–3
Dinner rolls for 1 dinner–5

DAIRY

6 slices American cheese–2
⅓ cup sour cream–4

FREEZER

1 10-oz. package green peas–5

CHECK YOUR STAPLES

Thyme–1
Italian seasoning–1,5
Salt–1,4
Pepper–1,4
Chili powder–2
Cumin–2
Cayenne pepper–2,4
Paprika–4
Seasoned salt–5
2 teaspoons sugar–5
¼ cup lemon juice–5
¼ cup oil–5
1½ cups mayonnaise–3,4
2 teaspoons mustard–3

Shopping List

SUMMER • WEEK 12

MEATS

1 5-pound frying chicken–1,5
1 pound ground beef–3

CANS/JARS

3 tablespoons peanut oil–1
1 10½-oz. can pizza sauce–2
1 small can sliced olives-2
1 4-oz. can chilies–2
1 4-oz. can sliced mushrooms–2
Favorite dressing for 1 salad–2
1 tablespoon red wine vinegar–3
1 16-oz. can spinach–4
1 tablespoon pickled ginger–5
1½ cups rice vinegar–5

GROCERY

2 cans Chinese crispy noodles–1
6-oz. package jumbo pasta shells–4
Vegetable cooking spray–4
2 cups crisp rice noodles–5
½ cup toasted almonds–5
1 tablespoon toasted sesame seeds–5

PRODUCE

1 bulb garlic + 2 cloves–1,3
2 small dried hot red peppers (opt.)–1
Favorite fruit for salad–1,5
Salad greens for 1 dinner–2
Favorite salad toppings for 1 dinner–2
10 carrots–3
3 onions–3,4,5
5 zucchini–3,4
4 yellow squash–3
½ teaspoon basil–3

⅛ teaspoon oregano–3
4 medium potatoes–3
⅓ cup parsley–4
1 scallion–4
1 head lettuce–5
1 bunch spinach–5
8 stalks celery–5
1 tablespoon cilantro–5
1 tomato–5

BAKERY

1 package English muffins–2
Dinner rolls for 1 dinner–4

DAIRY

½ pound grated Cheddar cheese–2
½ pound grated Jack cheese–2
3 eggs–3,4
1 pound ricotta cheese–4
½ cup plain yogurt–4
1 stick butter–3,4

CHECK YOUR STAPLES

Salt–3,4,5
Pepper–3,5
Garlic powder–4
Ground ginger–5
1 tablespoon sugar–5
¾ cup white vinegar–1
½ cup soy sauce–1,5
3 tablespoons honey–1
1¼ cups oil–2,3
2 tablespoons catsup–3
⅔ cup seasoned bread crumbs–3
6 tablespoons Parmesan cheese–4

Shopping List

MEATS

6 hamburger patties–1

1 1/2 pounds ground beef–2

6 boneless, skinless chicken breasts–4

2 pounds cubed steak–3

I pound bacon–5

1 1/2 pounds top sirloin–5

CANS/JARS

2 16-oz. cans ranch beans–1

1/2 cup barbecue sauce–1

1 6-oz. can tomato paste–2

2 8-oz. cans tomato sauce–2

1/2 cup red wine–2

Salad dressing–2,4

1 10 1/2-oz. can cream of mushroom soup–3

1 4-oz. can sliced mushrooms–3

1 jar stuffed green olives–5

1 16-oz. can chicken broth–5

GROCERY

1 package spaghetti sauce mix–2

12 oz. lasagna noodles–2

1 package rice pilaf–4

1/4 cup chopped walnuts–5

PRODUCE

Favorite condiments for hamburgers–1

1 bunch grapes–1

1 cantaloupe–1

1 honeydew–1

1 watermelon–1

2 apples–1

3 white onions–2,3,5

Salad greens for 2 dinners–2,4

Favorite salad toppings for 2 dinners–2,4

3 red bell peppers–5

6 sprigs fresh rosemary–5

2 lemons–5

1 bunch green onions–5

1 dozen Brussels sprouts–5

5 pounds potatoes–3,5

3 pounds fresh green beans–3

6 cloves garlic–2,3,4,5

1 bunch parsley–5

1 carrot–5

BAKERY

1 loaf ready-to-heat garlic bread–4

1 package hamburger buns– 1

1 loaf French bread–2

DAIRY

6 slices American cheese–1

2 pounds mozzarella cheese–2

1 pound ricotta cheese–2

5 eggs–2,5

1/2 cup sour cream–5

1/2 cup milk–3

1 stick butter–2,3

continued on next page

FREEZER

1 bag frozen French fries–1

CHECK YOUR STAPLES

Salt–1,3,5

Pepper–1,4,5

Garlic powder–1,2

Oregano–2

Basil–2, 5

Parsley–2

Thyme–4

Ground mustard–5

Seasoning salt–3

4 tablespoons olive oil–2,5

1 tablespoon oil–3

Sugar–2

2 tablespoons Worcestershire sauce–3

$\frac{1}{2}$ cup mayonnaise–5

Steak sauce–3

Flour–3

3 tablespoons cider vinegar–4

5 tablespoons horseradish–4,5

2 teaspoons brown sugar–4

1 cup catsup–3,4,5

$\frac{1}{2}$ cup grated Parmesan–2

Bulk Shopping List

FALL • WEEKS 1–4

MEATS

24 chicken breasts
5 pounds ground beef

CANS/JARS

Favorite salad dressing for 3 dinners
4 10½-oz. cans cream of mushroom soup
2 10½-oz. cans golden mushroom soup
40 oz. sliced mushrooms
8 oz. green chilies, diced

GROCERY

2 bags tortilla chips

PRODUCE

13 onions
23 carrots
12 garlic cloves, minced
7 zucchini

BAKERY

3 packages flour tortillas

DAIRY

9 cups grated Cheddar cheese
⅓-pound block Cheddar cheese
2 pounds cottage cheese
9 sticks butter

FREEZER

16 oz. mixed vegetables

CHECK YOUR STAPLES

8 teaspoons salt
½ cup pepper
2 teaspoons garlic salt
6 tablespoons flour
2¼ teaspoons cumin
2½ teaspoons oregano
⅔ cup soy sauce
2 cups vegetable oil
2½ pints mayonnaise
38 cups rice
¼ cup vinegar

Shopping List

FALL • WEEK 1

MEATS

1 whole frying chicken–1
1 pound bulk Italian sausage–2
1 pound ground beef–5
6 ½-inch-thick pork chops–3
2 ½-pound turkey breast tenderloin–4

CANS/JARS

¼ cup white wine–1
1 12-oz. can whole kernel corn with sweet
    peppers–2
1 15-oz. can apricot halves–3
¼ cup apple juice–4
1 15-oz. can kidney beans–5
1 8-oz. bottle Catalina salad dressing–5
1 4-oz. can mushroom, stems and pieces–2
2 2.8-oz. cans French fried onions–2
1 40-oz. can whole sweet potatoes–2

GROCERY

Tortilla chips–5
¼ cup slivered almonds–3
½ cup walnuts, chopped–4

PRODUCE

1 bunch parsley–1
¼ teaspoon basil–1
1 bunch Thompson seedless grapes–1
1 red onion–4
1 head iceberg lettuce–5
4 minced garlic cloves–2
3 stalks celery–3
2 heads broccoli–3
4 medium potatoes–4
3 carrots–4
1 bunch green onions–5

4 tomatoes–5
2 cups fresh cranberries–2
1 bunch spinach–4

BAKERY

1 loaf French bread–2
1 package flour tortillas–5

DAIRY

1 cup milk–2
2 eggs–2
1 garlic rondele cheese spread–1
1 herb rondele cheese spread–1
1½ cups grated Cheddar cheese–4,5
4 oz. grated Monterey Jack cheese–2
3 sticks butter–1,2,3,4

FREEZER

1 package mixed vegetables–1

CHECK YOUR STAPLES

Salt–3,4
Pepper–1,3,4
Garlic powder–4
Dried minced onion–4
Ground ginger–3,4
Chili powder–2
¾ cup vegetable oil–2,4
¾ cup lemon juice–4
1 cup flour–2
2 tablespoons brown sugar–2
⅓ cup honey–2
¼ cup golden raisins–3
Instant rice for 1 dinner + 2½ cups–1,3
¼ cup soy sauce–4
1 teaspoon vanilla extract–4

Shopping List

MEATS

2 pounds ground beef–1

3½ pounds beef short ribs–2

6 chicken breasts–3

1½ pounds cooked bay shrimp–5

CANS/JARS

1 28-oz. can tomatoes–1

1 12-oz. can whole kernel corn–1

2 4-oz. cans sliced mushrooms–1,2

Favorite salad dressing for 1 dinner–1

1 10½-oz. can beef soup with vegetables
        and barley–2

1 10½-oz. can cream of mushroom
        soup–3

2 cans chili beans–4

1 6-oz. can crabmeat–5

1 8-oz. can diced water chestnuts–5

2 small cans ripe sliced olives–1,4

1 jar salsa–4

GROCERY

6 oz. narrow noodles–1

Cornbread mix–2

1 envelope dry onion soup mix–2

1 bag corn chips–4

PRODUCE

4 onions–1,3,4,5

4 cloves garlic–1,3

2 green bell peppers–1,3,5

Salad greens for 1 dinner–1

Salad toppings for 1 dinner–1

1½ pounds mushrooms, sliced–3,5

8 stalks celery–3,5

2 tablespoons parsley, minced–3

1 head lettuce–4

2 small tomatoes–4

BAKERY

8 slices white bread–3

French bread–5

Buttered bread crumbs–5

DAIRY

4½ cups grated cheese–1,3,4

2 eggs–3

1½ cups milk–3

½ cup sour cream–4

1 stick butter–3

FREEZER

20 oz. lima beans–2

8 oz. peas–5

8 oz. mixed vegetables–2

CHECK YOUR STAPLES

Salt–1,3

Pepper–1,3

Ground cumin–3

Chili powder–3

Oregano–3

2 tablespoons flour–2

2 pints mayonnaise–3,5

1 tablespoon vegetable oil–3

Instant rice for 1 dinner–3

Shopping List

MEATS

2 pounds ground beef–1,4

3 whole chicken breasts, halved–2

1 large tri-tip or chuck roast (for 2 meals)–3,5

CANS/JARS

1 4-oz. can sliced mushrooms–1

1 16-oz. can sliced potatoes–1

1 10½-oz. can golden mushroom soup–1

2 small cans sliced olives–1,4

⅔ cup sherry–2

2 4-oz. cans button mushrooms–2,3

2 16-oz. cans ranch beans–3

Favorite dressing for 2 dinners–3,4

1 10½-oz. can cream of chicken soup–4

1 4-oz. can chopped green chilies–4

2 17-oz. cans refried beans–4

GROCERY

1 package chicken gravy mix–2

¼ cup vermicelli–3

1 bag tortilla chips–4

PRODUCE

3 onions–1,2,4

1 green bell pepper–1

8 stalks celery–1

Salad greens for 2 dinners–3,4

Salad toppings for 2 dinners–3,4

1 green onion–5

2 cloves garlic–3,5

6 ears corn on cob–5

4 zucchini–2

4 large carrots–2

BAKERY

1 bag dinner rolls–1

1 package flour tortillas–4

DAIRY

2 sticks butter–1,2,3

1 egg–1

1 cup grated Cheddar cheese–1

1⅓ cups milk–1,4

1 cup sour cream–2

2 cups grated Jack cheese–4

CHECK YOUR STAPLES

Pepper–1,3,5

Garlic salt–1

Paprika–1

Seasoned salt–2,3

Cumin–3

Butter flavored sprinkles–3

Chili powder–4

Ground mustard–5

1 bay leaf–1

1½ cups sugar–5

1 cup seasoned bread crumbs–1

6 tablespoons soy sauce–5

2 tablespoons vegetable oil–5

Instant white rice for 2 dinners–2,5

1 cup long grain rice–3

Shopping List

MEATS

6 chicken breasts–1,5
1½ pounds round steak–2
4 Polish sausages–4
4 salmon steaks, 1-inch thick–3

CANS/JARS

1 10½-oz. can cream of mushroom
    soup–5
½ cup red wine–2
1 16-oz. can stewed tomatoes–2
1 4-oz. can sliced or button mushrooms–2
1 4-oz. can diced green chilies–5
1 cup salsa–5
1 17-oz. can refried beans–5
1 small jar capers–3
1 tablespoon sun-dried tomatoes–3
2 10½-oz. cans cream of chicken soup–1

GROCERY

1 package egg noodles–2

PRODUCE

2 heads broccoli–1
2 lemons–1,3
3 onions–2,4
6 tablespoons fresh parsley–2,3
2 tablespoons fresh tarragon–3
1 head cabbage–4
2 medium apples–4
2 pounds medium potatoes–3,4
16 carrots–3,4
1 clove garlic–3

3 zucchini–3

BAKERY

Dinner rolls for 2 dinners–1,4
1 package flour tortillas–5

DAIRY

1 pound cottage cheese–2
4 eggs–2,3
¼ pound Cheddar cheese–2
1¾ cups grated Cheddar cheese–1,5
1 cup plain yogurt–3,5
1 stick butter–1,2

FREEZER

1 10-oz. package chopped spinach–2

CHECK YOUR STAPLES

Garlic salt–2
Salt–3
Pepper–2,3
Oregano–2
Thyme–3
Lemon pepper–3
5 tablespoons flour–2,3
2 tablespoons oil–2
1 tablespoon olive oil–3
White rice for 1 dinner–5
1 cup bread crumbs–3
1 cup mayonnaise–1
5 tablespoons oil–2,3

Bulk Shopping List

MEATS

5 cups crabmeat

10 boneless chicken breasts

CANS/JARS

Favorite salad dressing for 3 dinners

2 cans cream of celery soup

GROCERY

32 oz. noodles

2 envelopes onion soup mix

2 boxes stuffing mix

PRODUCE

11 onions

16 cloves garlic

15 potatoes

3 pounds carrots

BAKERY

3 loaves French bread

Dinner rolls for 3 dinners

DAIRY

5 cups sour cream

14 slices Swiss cheese

$7\frac{1}{2}$ sticks butter

2 cups Parmesan cheese

CHECK YOUR STAPLES

10 teaspoons salt

6 teaspoons pepper

$\frac{3}{4}$ teaspoon thyme

$3\frac{1}{2}$ teaspoons paprika

$1\frac{1}{4}$ tablespoons sugar

$\frac{1}{3}$ cup flour

1 cup vegetable oil

2 cups mayonnaise

5 cups white rice

$2\frac{1}{4}$ cups Parmesan cheese

Shopping List

MEAT

1 4-pound beef roast–2,4

¾ pound bulk Italian sausage–3

6 large boneless, skinless chicken breasts–5

6 slices fully cooked ham–5

4 pork loin chops–1

CANS/JARS

1 10½-oz. can cream of chicken soup–5

1 10½-oz. can cream of mushroom soup–2

Favorite salad dressing for 1 dinner–2

1 15½-oz. can butter beans–3

1 15-oz. can black beans–3

1 14½-oz. can diced tomatoes–3

2 14½-oz. cans beef broth–3,4

½ cup chicken broth–5

1 16-oz. can green beans–5

⅓ cup apricot preserves–1

2 tablespoons Dijon mustard–1

GROCERY

2 tablespoons slivered almonds–1

1 envelope onion soup mix–2

1 package stuffing mix–5

PRODUCE

6 potatoes–2

8 carrots–2

Salad greens for 1 dinner–2

Salad toppings for 1 dinner–2

2 onions–3,4

2 cloves garlic–3,4

1 pound asparagus–1

1 tablespoon basil–3

Fresh mint–3

8 stalks celery–4

1 bell pepper–4

½ teaspoon sage–5

Small bunch fresh parsley–5

3 green onions–1

BAKERY

Dinner rolls for 1 dinner–2

Sliced Italian bread–3

DAIRY

4 slices mozzarella cheese–3

3 eggs–3

½ cup milk–3

6 slices Swiss cheese–5

1 stick butter–2

1 cup grated Parmesan cheese–3,5

CHECK YOUR STAPLES

Italian seasoning–3

Garlic salt–3

Cornstarch–4

Sugar–1,4

Pepper–1,4,5

Paprika–5

Salt–1

¼ cup flour–5

¼ cup vegetable oil–5

5 tablespoons corn oil–4

4 tablespoons soy sauce–4

1 teaspoon lemon juice–1

White rice for 2 dinners–1,4

⅔ cup Italian seasoned bread crumbs–3

4 teaspoons olive oil–1

½ cup grated Parmesan cheese–3,5

Shopping List

FALL • WEEK 6

MEATS

1 3-pound boneless beef chuck pot roast–1
6 to 8 turkey breasts–2
3 cups crabmeat–4
8 pork chops–5
1¼ pounds large shrimp, peeled and deveined–3

CANS/JARS

½ cup German-style mustard–1,3
2 large Kosher-style dill pickles–1
¾ cup dry red wine or beef broth–1
1 cup Italian dressing–3
1 17-oz. can asparagus–4
3 tablespoons sweet relish–3
1 teaspoon Dijon mustard–3

GROCERY

1 package egg noodles–1
1 package crackers–4,5
1 cup corn flakes crumbs–3

PRODUCE

3 onions–1,3,5
2 stalks celery–1
6 cloves garlic–2
5 medium potatoes–2
1 bunch green onions–2
1 pound green beans–2
1 bunch parsley–3,5
3 zucchini–3
8 large tomatoes–3,4
1 head lettuce–4
1 lemon–5
3 pounds carrots–1,5

BAKERY

1 loaf French bread–5

DAIRY

1½ sticks butter–3,5
2 cups cottage cheese–2
1 cup sour cream–2
1 cup grated Swiss cheese–3
4 eggs–3,4
½ cup grated Cheddar cheese–2

FREEZER

1 16-oz. package vegetable combination–1
1 10-oz. package whole kernel corn–3

CHECK YOUR STAPLES

2 teaspoons hot pepper sauce–3
Pepper–1,2,5
Salt–2,3,4,5
Ground cloves–1
1 leaf sage–2
Paprika–2,5
Thyme–5
Garlic salt–2
Minced onion–5
1¼ cups catsup–4,5
½ teaspoon oregano–2
8 tablespoons brown sugar–5
2 tablespoons flour–1
4 bay leaves–1,5
2 tablespoons vegetable oil–1,2
2¼ cups mayonnaise–3,4,5
1¼ cups lemon juice–4
1 tablespoon prepared horseradish–5
¼ cup dry bread crumbs–3
¼ cup grated Parmesan cheese–3

Shopping List

MEATS

1½ pounds ground beef–1
1 pound sirloin or roast–1
1½ pounds round steak–3
4 boneless, skinless chicken breasts–5

CANS/JARS

1 16-oz. can pinto beans–1
1 16-oz. can kidney beans–1
2 16-oz. cans stewed tomatoes–1
1 28-oz. can tomatoes–1
1 cup red wine–1,3
2 4-oz. cans sliced mushrooms–2,3
1 10½-oz. can cream of celery soup–2
1 6-oz. can tuna–2
2 16-oz. cans peas–2,3
1 10½-oz. can golden mushroom soup–3
3 6½-oz. cans clams–4
1 jar salsa–5
1 16-oz. can refried beans–5
Favorite salad dressing for 1 dinner–5
½ cup red wine–3
1 8-oz. can tomato sauce–5

GROCERY

2 packages chili mix–1
1 box corn bread mix–1
24 oz. noodles–2,3
1 envelope onion soup mix–3
Oyster crackers–4
Tortilla chips–5

PRODUCE

3 onions–1,2,4,5
3 bell peppers–1,4
3 cloves garlic–1,5
2 bunches celery–2,4
8 to 10 peaches–3
3 potatoes–4
Salad greens for 1 salad–5
Favorite toppings for 1 salad and chicken
    tacos–5

BAKERY

1 loaf French bread for 1 dinner–2
Dinner rolls for 1 dinner–3

DAIRY

½ cup grated Jack cheese–2
5½ cups milk–2,4
Favorite toppings for chicken tacos–5
2 sticks butter–2,4

CHECK YOUR STAPLES

Thyme–4
Salt–4
Pepper–4
Cumin–5
¾ cup flour–4
1 tablespoon vegetable oil–5
2 beef bouillon cubes–5
1½ cups long grain rice–5

Shopping List

MEATS

1 5-pound turkey–1,4
12 oz. fully cooked smoked sausage
    links–2
2 cups crabmeat–3

CANS/JARS

2 8-oz. jars cheese spread–2
1 10½-oz. can cream of celery soup–4
Favorite dressing for 1 dinner–5
1 6-oz. can tomato paste–5
3 cubes chicken bouillon –5
1 4-oz. can chopped green chilies–5

GROCERY

3 cups herb-seasoned stuffing croutons–1
⅓ cup blanched almonds–3

PRODUCE

6 pears–4
12 medium potatoes–2
4 yams–1
1 celery stalk–3
1 bunch scallions–2
1 green bell pepper–3
1 large pimento–3
1 head lettuce–3
1 pound small white potatoes–4
5 cloves garlic–4,5
1 bunch parsley–4
2 onions–5
2 pounds tomatoes–3
6 large tomatoes–5
Salad greens for 1 dinner–5
Salad toppings for 1 dinner–5
2 tablespoons basil–5

4 teaspoons thyme–5

BAKERY

8 dinner rolls–2
1 loaf sliced French bread–3
4 baguettes–5
1½ cups soft bread crumbs–2

DAIRY

5 cups milk–1,3,4
1 cup grated sharp American cheese–1
8 eggs–1,3
3 cups sour cream–2
1 package sliced Swiss cheese–2
½ cup whipped topping–4
½ pound grated Monterey Jack cheese–5
3 sticks butter–1,2,3,4,5

FREEZER

2 10-oz. packages chopped broccoli–1,4
3 10-oz. packages string beans–2

CHECK YOUR STAPLES

Salt–1,3,4
Pepper–1,4
Paprika–1,2
Parsley–2
Instant minced onion–2
¼ cup brown sugar–1
1 cup flour–2,3
1 teaspoon sugar–2
1½ cups mayonnaise–4,5
1 tablespoon Worcestershire sauce–4
6 tablespoons olive oil–4,5
1 cup Parmesan cheese–4

Bulk Shopping List

FALL • WEEKS 9–13

MEATS

28 boneless, skinless chicken breasts

8½ pounds ground beef

12 slices bacon

1½ pounds crabmeat

CANS/JARS

2 10½-oz. cans cream of tomato soup

4 cans cream of mushroom soup

3 2.8-oz. cans French fried onions

2 8-oz. cans tomato sauce

1 8-oz. can Italian-seasoned tomato sauce

GROCERY

2 packages wide noodles

1 box crackers

PRODUCE

11 cloves garlic

6 pounds carrots

4 pounds onions

2 lemons

18 potatoes

BAKERY

5 loaves French bread

2 loaves ready-to-serve garlic bread

DAIRY

7 cups sour cream

1¾ pounds Jack cheese

1 16-oz. container cottage cheese

6 cups grated Cheddar cheese

1¼ cups Swiss cheese

10 sticks butter

FREEZER

50 oz. chopped spinach

CHECK YOUR STAPLES

1 cup vegetable oil

½ cup olive oil

1 cup soy sauce

3½ cups mayonnaise

8½ teaspoons salt

11 teaspoons pepper

1¼ teaspoons oregano

2 teaspoons basil

2½ teaspoons ground ginger

1¼ teaspoons dry mustard

1 cup Italian seasoned bread crumbs

1 cup seasoned bread crumbs

1⅓ cups bread crumbs

5 tablespoons Worcestershire sauce

7½ cups instant rice

1 cup Parmesan cheese

Shopping List

MEATS

12 oz. Italian sausage–1
1 pound sirloin steak–2
4 thick pork chops–3
4 boneless, skinless chicken breasts–4
4 large halibut fillets–5

CANS/JARS

1 8-oz. can tomato sauce–1
1 12-oz. jar spaghetti sauce with mush-
    rooms–1
2 10½-oz. cans cream of mushroom
    soup–2,3
1 4-oz. jar chopped pimento–2
2 2.8-oz. cans French fried onions–2,3
1 small can sliced pineapple–3
1 small jar maraschino cherries–3
½ cup apricot preserves–3
¼ cup white wine–3
1 jar applesauce–3
1 jar bacon bits–5
Favorite salad dressing for 1 dinner–1
Red wine or poppy seed dressing–5

GROCERY

2½ cups spiral or wagon wheel noodles–1
1 package angel hair pasta (fresh)–5

PRODUCE

Salad greens for 1 dinner–1
Favorite salad toppings for 1 dinner–1
¼ cup green onions–1
2 cloves garlic–1
2 oranges–3
1 bunch watercress–3
1 lemon–5
1 bag spinach salad–5
1 red onion–5
1 bunch carrots–5

3 zucchini–5
6 to 8 potatoes–2

BAKERY

Dinner rolls for 1 dinner–2
2 loaves ready-to-heat garlic bread–1,5

DAIRY

1 cup grated mozzarella cheese–1
1 cup grated Swiss cheese–2
⅓ cup light sour cream–2
¾ cup milk–3
2 eggs–5
2 sticks butter–2,4,5

FREEZER

1 16 oz. package broccoli, carrots, cauli-
    flower mix–2
18 oz. cut green beans–3
3 cups cut broccoli or Italian mixed
    vegetables–4

CHECK YOUR STAPLES

Salt–1,2
Pepper–1,2,3
Paprika–4
Parsley flakes–4
Crushed thyme–4
Lemon and herb seasoning–5
1 teaspoon olive oil–1
½ cup vegetable oil–2,3
¼ cup soy sauce–3
2 tablespoons mayonnaise–4
⅓ cup Italian seasoned bread crumbs–4
1½ cups instant rice–4
1 teaspoon instant chicken bouillon
    granules–4
3 tablespoons Parmesan cheese–4,5

Shopping List

MEATS

1 8-pound bone-in ham–1,3,5
4 slices bacon–1,2
4 veal or turkey cutlets–2
1 pound crabmeat–4

CANS/JARS

1 12-oz. can beer–1
1 10½-oz. can Cheddar cheese soup–1
2 11-oz. cans mandarin oranges–2
½ cup orange marmalade–3
1 10½-oz. can cream of mushroom
      soup–4
¼ cup dry sherry-4
Favorite salad dressing–4
Italian tomato sauce–2
1 28-oz. can peeled tomatoes–5

GROCERY

4 tablespoons chopped pecans–3
8 crackers–3
1 cup elbow macaroni–5

PRODUCE

3 pounds carrots–1,3,5
4 onions–1,2,3,5
7 cloves garlic–5
1½ pounds zucchini–2,5
1 bunch parsley–3
Salad greens–4
Favorite salad toppings–4
1 head savory cabbage–5
1 stalk celery–5
1 turnip–5
1 bunch green onions–3

BAKERY

Sliced French bread for 4 meals–2,3,4,5

DAIRY

2 sticks butter–2,3,4,5
¼ cup milk–1
¼ pound sliced Monterey Jack cheese–2
2 eggs–2
2 cups grated Cheddar cheese–4
¼ cup cream–4

FREEZER

4 10-oz. packages chopped spinach–1,4

CHECK YOUR STAPLES

Salt–2,3,5
Pepper–2,3,4,5
Italian herb seasonings–2
Ground ginger–3
Paprika–3,4
Basil–5
1 bay leaf–5
2 cups mayonnaise–3
2 tablespoons lemon juice–3
1 tablespoon prepared horseradish–3
1 teaspoon Worcestershire sauce–4
Dash olive oil–5
4 cups rice–1,3
1 cup dry bread crumbs–2,4
2 teaspoons grated Parmesan cheese–2

Shopping List

MEATS

8 boneless chicken breasts–1
4 slices bacon–1
2 pounds ground beef–2,5
1½ pounds kebab meat–4

CANS/JARS

2 10½-oz. cans cream of tomato soup–1
2 4-oz. cans mushrooms–1
1 10½-oz. can cream of mushroom soup–1
2 16-oz. cans any style green beans–1
1 2.8-oz. can French fried onions–1
1 6-oz. can tomato paste–2
1 8-oz. can tomato sauce–2
Salad dressing for 1 dinner–2
1 can sliced fruit–3
1 20-oz. can unsweetened pineapple
    chunks–4
1 16-oz. can refried beans–5
½ cup dry white wine–2

GROCERY

1 package wide egg noodles–1
Spaghetti noodles–2
1 package rice pilaf–4
1 package taco seasoning–5
Tortilla chips–5

PRODUCE

2 medium onions–2,4
1 clove garlic–2
Salad greens–2
1 head lettuce–3,5
2 large green peppers–4
16 fresh mushrooms–4
16 cherry tomatoes–4
Corn on the cob for 1 dinner–4
1 tomato–5
Salad toppings–2

BAKERY

2 loaves French bread–2,4
1 dozen corn tortillas–5

DAIRY

1 stick butter–2
2 cups sour cream–1
1½ pounds Jack cheese–1
½ cup milk–1
1 container cottage cheese–3
2 cups grated Cheddar cheese–5

FREEZER

1 box fish sticks–3
1 bag French fries–3

CHECK YOUR STAPLES

Salt–2
Pepper–1,2,4
Oregano–2
Basil–2
Parsley–2
Ginger–4
Garlic powder–4
Dry mustard–4
½ teaspoon sugar–2
¼ cup vegetable oil–5
¼ cup olive oil–2,4
¾ cup soy sauce–1,4
1 tablespoon brown sugar–4

Shopping List

MEATS

14 chicken breasts–1,4

4 bacon slices–1

4 pounds ground beef–2,5

$\frac{1}{2}$ pound crab–3

CANS/JARS

1 tablespoon sherry–3

1 cup white wine–4

1 16-oz. can sliced peaches–5

1 15-oz. can red kidney beans–5

1 14$\frac{1}{2}$-oz. can tomatoes, cut up–5

1 10$\frac{3}{4}$-oz. can condensed tomato soup–5

GROCERY

$\frac{1}{4}$ cup oats–2

1 package egg noodles–4

Crackers–5

PRODUCE

1 lemon–1

2 pounds yellow squash or zucchini–1

5 medium zucchini–4

Favorite fruit for salad–1

3$\frac{1}{2}$ pounds onions–2,5

6 large potatoes–2

12 carrots–2

30 asparagus spears–3

4 tomatoes–3

8 oz. sliced fresh mushrooms–4

1 green bell pepper–5

1 clove garlic–5

BAKERY

3 slices wheat bread–2

1 loaf French bread–5

DAIRY

2 sticks butter–1,3,4

5 eggs–1,2,3

1$\frac{3}{4}$ cups grated Cheddar cheese–1,3

2$\frac{1}{3}$ cups milk–2,3

$\frac{1}{4}$ cup grated Swiss cheese–3

1 16-oz. tub sour cream–1,5

FREEZER

1 10-oz. chopped spinach–3

CHECK YOUR STAPLES

Lemon pepper–1

Celery salt–2

Pepper–2,3,4

Sage–2

Garlic salt–2

Dry mustard–2

Salt–3,4

Onion powder–3

Crushed oregano–3

Tarragon–4

Chili powder–5

1 bay leaf–5

1 tablespoon Worcestershire sauce–2

$\frac{1}{3}$ cup bread crumbs–1

$\frac{1}{4}$ cup Italian dry bread crumbs–3

5 tablespoons flour–1,3,4

$\frac{1}{2}$ cup Parmesan cheese–3

Shopping List

MEATS

2½ pounds ground beef–2,4

1 5-pound canned ham–1

12 oz. sirloin steak–3

1 pound boneless, skinless chicken breast
strips–5

CANS/JARS

½ cup green olives, chopped–2

5 4-oz. cans sliced mushrooms–3,4

2 cups beef broth–3

½ cup tomato sauce–3

1 16-oz. can sliced potatoes–4

1 10½-oz. can golden mushroom soup–4

1 4-oz. can sliced olives–4

2 16-oz. cans creamed corn–3

1 tablespoon Dijon mustard–5

GROCERY

⅛ cup slivered almonds–3

½ cup cracker meal–5

PRODUCE

12 russet potatoes–1

6 carrots–1

3 onions–3,4

6 potatoes–5

1 green bell pepper–4

1 bunch celery–4

1 tablespoons chopped parsley–5

BAKERY

Dinner rolls for 2 dinners–2,4

DAIRY

3 sticks butter–1,4,5

2 eggs–2,4

2 slices mozzarella cheese–2

½ cup sour cream–3

2 cans refrigerator biscuits–1

1 cup grated Cheddar cheese–4

1 cup milk–4,5

FREEZER

1 package mixed vegetables–2

1 package green beans–3

1 package corn on cob niblets–5

CHECK YOUR STAPLES

Salt–1,2,5

Pepper–1,2,4,5

Paprika–3,4,5

Garlic salt–4

Ground red pepper–5

Powdered butter substitute–5

1 bay leaf–4

3 tablespoons Worcestershire sauce–3,5

2 tablespoons mayonnaise–5

Seasoned bread crumbs–4

2 tablespoons lemon juice–5

2 tablespoons corn oil–3

2 cups instant rice–3

Bulk Shopping List

WINTER • WEEKS 1–4

MEATS

30 boneless chicken breasts

4½ pounds ground beef

CANS/JARS

2½ cans tomato soup

Salad dressing for 4 dinners

3 16-oz. cans chicken broth

2 10½-oz. cans cream of chicken soup

PRODUCE

2½ pounds carrots

13 cloves garlic

12 onions

13 potatoes

BAKERY

3 loaves French bread

Dinner rolls for 3 dinners

20 flour tortillas

DAIRY

3 tubs sour cream

5 cups grated Cheddar cheese

13 sticks butter

FREEZER

30 oz. peas

20 oz. green beans

4 pounds hash browns

CHECK YOUR STAPLES

1 cup vinegar

7 teaspoons salt

6 teaspoons pepper

1 teaspoon paprika

3 cups flour

13 cups instant or long grain rice

2 cups mayonnaise

¾ teaspoon oregano

1 cup honey

2 cups bread crumbs

2 cups Parmesan cheese

1½ cups vegetable oil

½ cup mustard

1 cup brown sugar

1½ teaspoons dry mustard

Shopping List

WINTER • WEEK 1

MEATS

12 chicken breasts–1,3
2 slices bacon–1
Chuck or tri-tip roast–2,4

CANS/JARS

1 16-oz. can chicken broth–1
1/4 cup dry white wine–1
2 16-oz. cans green beans–1
3 4-oz. cans whole green chilies–3,4
2 16-oz. jars salsa–3,4,5
1 16-oz. can refried beans–4
1 8-oz. can tomato sauce–4
Salad dressing for 2 dinners–4,5

GROCERY

1 envelope taco sauce mix–4
1 bag tortilla chips–4
1 package onion soup mix–2

PRODUCE

1 bunch parsley–1
1 bunch oregano–1
1/2 large onion–1,4
1 bag baby carrots–2
6 potatoes–2
2 cloves garlic–4
Salad greens for 2 dinners–4,5
Salad toppings for 2 dinners–4,5

BAKERY

Dinner rolls for 2 dinners–1,2
16 8-inch flour tortillas–4

DAIRY

3 sticks butter–1,2,3
2 slices Swiss cheese–1
20 oz. Monterey Jack cheese–3,4
1 cup sour cream–4
1 tub guacamole–4

FREEZER

1 bag vegetable medley–3
1 1/2 pounds fish fillets–5
1 large package hash browns–5

CHECK YOUR STAPLES

Pepper–1,2,3
Oregano–1
Chili powder–3
Garlic salt–3
Basil–5
Garlic powder–2
Salt–2
Cumin–2,3,4
2 tablespoons flour–1
1/2 cup bread crumbs–3
2 beef bouillon cubes–4
1 tablespoon oil–4
2 tablespoons honey–5
2 tablespoons mustard–5
Kitchen string–1
2 tablespoons mayonnaise–5
1/4 cup grated Parmesan cheese–3
White rice for 2 dinners–1,3
Long grain rice for 1 dinner–4

Shopping List

WINTER • WEEK 2

MEATS

1½ pounds cubed beef–1
8 boneless chicken breasts–2,4
3 turkey breast fillets–3
1 pound prawns–5

CANS/JARS

1 10½-oz. can condensed tomato soup–1
1 cup chicken broth–1,2
1 10½-oz. can cream of potato soup–2
2 10½-oz. cans cream of mushroom soup–2,4
½ cup apricot jam–3
¼ cup chili sauce–3
1 10½-oz. can cream of chicken soup–4
1 small jar processed cheese–4
2 tablespoons white wine–5
1 tablespoon brandy–5
1 5-oz. can water chestnuts–5
1 5-oz. can sliced mushrooms–5
⅓ cup apple juice–2

GROCERY

Corn bread mix–1
⅛ cup sliced almonds–5

PRODUCE

4 stalks celery–1,4
2 shallots–5
4 carrots–1
3 potatoes–1
3 onions–1,2,3,4,5
Favorite fruit for salad–1
1 lemon–2,5
3 tablespoons fresh basil–2
1 green bell pepper–2
1 apple–2

2 acorn squash–3
1 bunch parsley–2,3,5
5 oranges–4
5 grapefruit–4
6 cloves garlic–5

BAKERY

1 loaf French bread–3

DAIRY

5 sticks butter–2,3,4,5
2 cups sour cream–2,3
1⅓ cups grated Cheddar cheese–2,5
1 egg–3
1¼ cups milk–3,5

FREEZER

2 pounds hash browns–2
3 cups peas–2
2 10-oz. packages chopped broccoli–4
1 10-oz. package French-style green beans–5

CHECK YOUR STAPLES

Salt–1,3,5
Pepper–1,3,5
Basil–1
Dash paprika–2
Cinnamon–3
1 tablespoon vinegar–3
⅔ cup flour–3,5
2 teaspoons cornstarch–2,3
½ cup brown sugar–3
2 tablespoons olive oil–5
1 teaspoon soy sauce–5
1¼ cups bread crumbs–3
Rice for 1 dinner + 4 cups–4,5

Shopping List

MEATS

4 boneless chicken breasts–1
1 canned or boneless ham–2,4
2 pounds ground beef–3,5

CANS/JARS

1 4-oz. can chopped green chilies–1
1 14-oz. can chicken broth–1
1 14½-oz. can diced tomatoes–1
2 16-oz. cans corn–1
2 tablespoons salsa–1
1 16-oz. can refried beans–1
1 17-oz. can baked beans–2
1 jar homestyle applesauce–2
1 large jar pizza sauce–3
Salad dressing for 1 dinner–3
1 10½-oz. can cream of chicken soup–4
1 16-oz. can sliced peaches–5

GROCERY

1 can beer–2
2 tablespoons orange juice–2
1 box mac 'n' cheese–2
1 can crescent rolls–3
Favorite pizza toppings–3
2 cups corn flakes–4
1 bag corn chips–5

PRODUCE

1 clove garlic–1
2 onions–1,4,5
Salad greens for 1 dinner–3
Salad toppings for 1 dinner–3

1 head cauliflower–4
4 zucchini–5

BAKERY

1 package small flour tortillas–1
Dinner rolls for 1 dinner–4

DAIRY

2 sticks butter–1,4
3 cups grated mozzarella cheese–1,3
2 tubs sour cream–1,4
8 oz. cream cheese–1
3½ cups grated Cheddar cheese–1,4,5
1 egg–5

FREEZER

1 32-oz. bag hash browns–4
1 10-oz. package peas–4

CHECK YOUR STAPLES

Dry mustard–2
Garlic salt–4,5
Thyme–5
Salt–5
Pepper–5
1 tablespoon cornstarch–1
1 tablespoon flour–1
½ cup brown sugar–2
½ cup bread crumbs–5
½ cup mayonnaise–4
1 teaspoon prepared mustard–4
½ teaspoon grated Parmesan cheese–3

Shopping List

MEATS

6 chicken breasts–1
2½ pounds ground beef–3,4

CANS/JARS

Favorite salad dressing for 1 dinner–1
2 10½-oz. cans cream of celery soup–2
1 10½-oz. can tomato bisque soup–2
2 cans evaporated milk–2
1 6-oz. can shrimp–2
1 6-oz. can crab–2
1 6-oz. can clams–2
2 tablespoons sherry–2
1 16-oz. jar spaghetti sauce–3
1 10½-oz. can condensed tomato soup–3
1 16-oz. can stewed tomatoes–4
¼ cup white wine–4
1 8-oz. can tomato sauce–4
1 16-oz. can sliced peaches–1

GROCERY

8 manicotti shells–3
1 8-oz. package egg noodles–4

PRODUCE

2 pounds carrots–1,3
Salad greens for 1 dinner–1
Favorite salad toppings for 1 dinner–1
1 bunch asparagus–2
4 cloves garlic–3,4
2 green bell peppers–3,4
5 onions–3,4,5
1 bunch parsley–3
4 potatoes–5
1 stalk celery–5
1 bunch Romaine lettuce–1

BAKERY

1 loaf French bread–3

Breadsticks–4
10 slices bread–5

DAIRY

½ cup grated American cheese + 5 slices–1,5
1 small carton half and half–2
½ cup sour cream–2
2 cups milk–2,5
16 oz. cottage cheese–1,3
1 cup grated mozzarella cheese–3

FREEZER

1 10-oz. package peas–4
1 10-oz. package green beans–4

CHECK YOUR STAPLES

½ cup honey–1
Curry powder–1,2
Salt–1,2,3
Pepper–1
Thyme–1
Paprika–2
Dry mustard–3
Nutmeg–5
Oregano–3
2 cups flour–2
3 sticks butter–1,3,4,5
3 teaspoons baking powder–2
1 cup sugar–3
¼ cup prepared mustard–1
1 cup mayonnaise–2,3,5
1¼ teaspoons lemon juice–2
1¼ cups vegetable oil–2,3
¾ cup vinegar–3
1 teaspoon Worcestershire sauce–3
Dash hot pepper sauce–5
1½ cups rice–1
3 tablespoons instant chicken bouillon
    granules–1,5
1½ cups Parmesan cheese–3,4

Bulk Shopping List

WINTER • WEEKS 5–8

MEATS

6 pounds ground beef
2 pounds boneless chicken breasts
8 strips bacon

CANS/JARS

8 8-oz. cans tomato sauce
Salad dressing for 5 dinners

GROCERY

2 bags tortilla chips
2 bags corn chips

PRODUCE

14 onions
2 bags carrots
13 cloves garlic
13 potatoes

BAKERY

3 loaves French bread

DAIRY

2 pints sour cream
1½ cups grated mozzarella cheese
23 oz. ricotta cheese
32 oz. Monterey Jack cheese
6 sticks butter

CHECK YOUR STAPLES

12 teaspoons salt
9 teaspoons pepper
6½ cups rice, instant or long grain
5 tablespoons flour
2 cups vegetable oil
2 tablespoons Worcestershire sauce
1 pound + 2 cups brown sugar
2 cups vinegar
2 cups catsup

Shopping List

MEATS

1 pound boneless, skinless chicken breasts–2
$\frac{1}{2}$ pound round steak–1
1 pound ground beef–3
2 slices bacon–3
1 pound lean beef chuck or stew meat–4

CANS/JARS

1 16-oz. can chicken broth–2
1 jar chili sauce–1
1 8-oz. can kidney beans–1
Salad dressing for 2 dinners–1,5
3 8-oz. cans tomato sauce–3,5
1 large can pork and beans–3
2 teaspoons reduced-sodium tomato paste–4
1 16-oz. can beef broth–4

GROCERY

$\frac{1}{4}$ cup orange juice–2
1 bag tortilla chips–1
1 bag corn chips–3
9 lasagna noodles–5

PRODUCE

4 cloves garlic–2,4,5
$1\frac{1}{2}$ cups snow peas–2
1 red bell pepper–2
1 bunch green onions–2
1 bag carrots–1,2,4
1 bunch celery–1,3
4 onions–1,3,4
2 green bell peppers–1,3
Salad greens for 2 dinners–1,5
Salad toppings for 2 dinners–1,5
3 jalapeno peppers–1
1 pound mushrooms–4
2 potatoes–4
1 cup green beans–4
1 bunch parsley–4,5

BAKERY

2 loaves French bread–5
1 package hamburger buns–3

DAIRY

1 stick butter–1
1 pound processed American cheese–1
1 15-oz. container ricotta cheese–5
1 cup grated mozzarella cheese–5
2 cans refrigerator biscuits–4

FREEZER

2 10-oz. packages chopped
broccoli–2,5

CHECK YOUR STAPLES

Ground ginger–2
Cumin–1
Pepper–1,3
Thyme–5
Marjoram–5
Paprika–5
Chili powder–1
Mustard–3
Oregano–5
Salt–1,3
Instant rice for 2 dinners–1,2
$2\frac{1}{2}$ tablespoons cornstarch–2,4
$1\frac{1}{2}$ tablespoons soy sauce–2
3 tablespoons flour–1,4
1 cup oil–1,2,4
$\frac{1}{2}$ cup catsup–3
1 tablespoon vinegar–3
1 tablespoon sugar–1,3
$1\frac{1}{2}$ teaspoons Worcestershire sauce–3
$\frac{1}{4}$ cup brown sugar–3
2 teaspoons olive oil–5
$\frac{1}{2}$ cup grated Parmesan cheese–5

Shopping List

MEATS

1 4- to 5-pound ham–1,3,4
4 pounds chicken–2
1/2 pound ground beef–5

CANS/JARS

2 cups apple cider–1
3 tablespoons sherry–1
1 10½-oz. can cream of chicken soup–2
Favorite salad dressing for 3 dinners–2,4,5
1 can whole green chilies–4
2 8-oz. cans tomato sauce–4
1 6-oz. can tomato paste–5

GROCERY

2 tablespoons Knox gelatin–1
2 cups corn flakes–2
1 package Italian salad seasonings mix–4
1 envelope spaghetti sauce mix–5
1 package refrigerated pizza dough–5
1 pound split green peas–3

PRODUCE

8 oranges–1
3 onions–2,3,4
Salad greens for 3 dinners–2,4,5
Salad toppings for 3 dinners–2,4,5
4 celery stalks–3
4 carrots–3
3 cloves garlic–3
3 zucchini–4
3 yellow squash–4
8 mushrooms–4
Favorite fruit–5

BAKERY

1 loaf French bread–3
12 crepes–4

DAIRY

2 sticks butter–2,3
4 eggs–1
1/2 pint whipping cream–1
5 cups grated Cheddar cheese–2,4
1 pint sour cream–2
12 slices Monterey Jack cheese–4
1/2 cup grated mozzarella cheese–5

FREEZER

1 6-oz. can orange juice–2
2 pounds hash brown potatoes–2

CHECK YOUR STAPLES

1 cup vinegar–1,4
1 pound dark brown sugar–1
Dry mustard–1
Salt–1,2,3
Pepper–1,2,3
Turmeric–1
Onion salt–2
Sesame seeds–2
4 whole cloves–3
Savory–3
Marjoram–3
1 bay leaf–3
3/4 cup sugar–1
1/4 cup vegetable oil–4

Shopping List

MEATS

1 pound thinly sliced pork chops–1
3½ pounds ground beef–2,4
4 chicken breasts–3
4 beef rib eye steaks–5
6 bacon strips–5

CANS/JARS

1 can stewed tomatoes–2
3 8-oz. cans tomato sauce–2,4
2 cans green beans–2
2 tablespoons pimentos–3
1 4-oz. can chopped green chilies–4
1 16-oz. can refried beans–4
Salad dressing for 1 dinner–4
1 can sliced water chestnuts–5

GROCERY

Fettuccine noodles–1
3 cups corn flakes–2
½ cup slivered almonds–3
1½ cups potato chips–3
1 bag tortilla chips–4
1 package taco seasoning mix–4
1 box rice pilaf–5

PRODUCE

3 oranges–1,5
6 potatoes–2
1 bunch celery–3
Salad greens for 1 dinner–4
Salad toppings for 1 dinner–4
6 baking potatoes–5
1 bunch spinach–5
2 cups fresh bean sprouts–5
2 onions–2,3,5

BAKERY

Dinner rolls for 1 dinner–3
1 package corn tortillas–4
1 loaf ready-to-heat garlic bread–1

DAIRY

1 stick butter–1,2
½ cup milk–2
10 eggs–3,4,5
¾ cup sour cream–3
2 cups grated Jack cheese–3,4
8 oz. ricotta cheese–4

FREEZER

1 bag California blend vegetables–1

CHECK YOUR STAPLES

Rosemary–1
Lemon pepper–1,5
Salt–1,2,3,5
Pepper–2,5
Garlic powder–5
Paprika–5
Thyme–5
Oregano–5
Ground red pepper–5
Seasoned salt–4
2 tablespoons flour–2
1 teaspoon sugar–2
2 tablespoons lemon juice–3
¾ cup mayonnaise–3
1 tablespoon olive oil–5
½ cup brown sugar–5
½ cup oil–5
⅓ cup vinegar–5
⅓ cup catsup–5
1 tablespoon Worcestershire sauce–5

Shopping List

WINTER • WEEK 8

MEATS

1 4-pound pot roast–1
1 pound ground beef–2
1 pound pork sausage–4
2 pounds center-cut boneless pork loin
   roast–5

CANS/JARS

2 teaspoons Dijon mustard–1
¼ cup dry red wine–1
1 15-oz. can pinto beans–2
1 10-oz. can enchilada sauce–2
2 8-oz. cans tomato sauce–2,4
Favorite salad dressings for 1 dinner–3
4 oz. chopped black olives–4
4 oz. chopped mushrooms–4
1 6-oz. can chopped green chilies–4

GROCERY

1 envelope brown gravy mix–1
6 oz. package corn chips–2
2 packages instant mashed potatoes–3
1 cup herb-seasoned stuffing mix–3

PRODUCE

5 onions–1,4
20 carrots–1,4,5
5 potatoes–1
Favorite fruit for fruit salad for
   2 dinners–2,4
2 lemons–3
Favorite salad toppings for 1 dinner–3
Salad greens for 1 dinner–3
8 stalks celery–4
4 cloves garlic–5
1 bunch parsley–5

1 tablespoon rosemary–5
1 tablespoon sage–5
6 apples–5

BAKERY

Dinner rolls for 1 dinner–1
Breadsticks–2

DAIRY

2 sticks butter–1,3,5
2 cups grated American cheese–2,5
2 cups sour cream–2,3
½ cup milk–3
2 cups grated Jack cheese–4
1 egg–5

FREEZER

20 oz. chopped spinach–3
32 oz. perch fillets–3
1 loaf bread dough–4

CHECK YOUR STAPLES

Salt–1,4,5
Pepper–1,3,4,5
Garlic powder–1
Oregano–4
Thyme–5
Instant onion–2
¼ cup catsup–1
1 teaspoon Worcestershire sauce–1
2 cups bread crumbs–5
1 tablespoon instant chicken bouillon
   granules–5
1½ cups rice–5
Kitchen string–5

Bulk Shopping List

WINTER • WEEKS 9–13

MEATS

21 boneless chicken breasts

18 boneless pork chops

6 pounds ground beef

CANS/JARS

Salad dressing for 7 dinners

2 jars spaghetti sauce

32 oz. tomato sauce

2 jars salsa

2 16-oz. cans refried beans

2 2.8-oz. cans French fried onions

2 10½-oz. cans cream of chicken soup

GROCERY

2 packages elbow macaroni

PRODUCE

12 onions

15 cloves garlic

BAKERY

Dinner rolls for 3 dinners

2 loaves French bread

DAIRY

4 cups sour cream

6⅓ cups grated Cheddar cheese

4 cups grated Monterey Jack cheese

12½ sticks butter

FREEZER

30 oz. green beans

CHECK YOUR STAPLES

8½ teaspoons salt

8½ teaspoons pepper

2 cups flour

1 cup honey

1 cup vegetable oil

1¾ cups Worcestershire sauce

1 cup grated Parmesan cheese

1¼ cups soy sauce

1 cup catsup

1 teaspoon ground ginger

2 teaspoon cumin

9½ cups instant rice

1½ cups brown sugar

1 cup mustard

Shopping List

MEATS

12 oz. Italian sausage–1
8 boneless chicken breasts–2,5
1½ pounds cubed steak–3
6 pork chops, boned–4

CANS/JARS

1 12-oz. jar spaghetti sauce–1
2 8-oz. cans tomato sauce–1,5
1 can cream of chicken soup–2
1 10½-oz. can golden mushroom soup–3
1 4-oz. can sliced mushrooms–3
½ cup Burgundy or red wine–3
1 16-oz. can chicken broth–4
1 jar old-fashioned–style applesauce–4
1 jar salsa–5
1 16-oz. can refried beans–5
Salad dressing for 2 dinners–1,5

GROCERY

2½ cups spiral noodles–1
1 box herb stuffing mix–2
2 large cans flaky biscuits–2
1 envelope onion soup mix–3
Tortilla chips–5

PRODUCE

Green onions–1
5 cloves garlic–1,4,5
Salad greens for 2 dinners–1,5
Salad toppings for 2 dinners–1,5
1 head lettuce–5

1 tomato–5
1 onion–5

BAKERY

1 loaf ready-to-heat garlic bread–1
Dinner rolls for 1 dinner–3
1 package flour tortillas–5

DAIRY

1 cup grated mozzarella cheese–1
1 stick butter–2,3
2 cups grated Jack cheese–2,5
1 cup sour cream–5
1 container guacamole–5

FREEZER

1 bag green beans–2
1 bag peas–3
1 bag California blend vegetables–4

CHECK YOUR STAPLES

Instant rice for 2 dinners–3,4
1½ cups long grain rice–5
⅓ cup honey–4
¼ cup soy sauce–4
2 tablespoons catsup–4
¼ teaspoon ground ginger–4
1½ teaspoons cumin–5
2 beef bouillon cubes–5
1 tablespoon oil–5
1 teaspoon olive oil–1

Shopping List

MEATS

5 pounds boneless cooked ham–1,5

6 pork chops, 3/4-inch thick–4

1 1/2 pounds top round–3

CANS/JARS

Favorite salad dressing for 2 dinners–2,4

1 2.8-oz. can French fried onions–2

1 10 1/2-oz. can cream of chicken soup–4

1 16-oz. can sliced pears–5

1 10 1/2-oz. can condensed Cheddar cheese
    soup–3

1 6-oz. can tomato paste–3

1 16-oz. can sliced carrots–3

GROCERY

1 package Italian salad seasoning mix–1

1 package elbow macaroni–5

4 oz. spaghetti–2

9 oz. fettuccine–3

PRODUCE

4 zucchini–1

18 mushrooms–1,3

2 onions–1,4

Salad greens for 2 dinners–2,4

Salad toppings for 2 dinners–2,4

3 tablespoons chives–4

1 orange–4

2 apples–5

8 sweet potatoes–4

BAKERY

Dinner rolls for 1 dinner–1

2 slices bread–5

DAIRY

2 1/2 sticks butter–1,5

2 cups milk–5

2 cups grated Monterey Jack cheese–2

1 egg–2

1 1/2 cups sour cream–2,4

1/2 cup (12 oz.) buttermilk–3

FREEZER

10 oz. chopped spinach–2

10 oz. green beans–5

9 oz. Italian green beans–3

CHECK YOUR STAPLES

Salt–4,5

Pepper–4,5

Garlic powder–2

Minced onion–3

Lemon pepper–3

1 cup brown sugar–1,5

3/4 cup flour–4,5

1/2 cup prepared mustard–1,5

2 tablespoons honey–1

1/2 cup vegetable oil–1,4

2 tablespoons vinegar–1

1/4 cup catsup–4

3 teaspoons Worcestershire sauce–4

1/2 cup grated Parmesan cheese–2

Shopping List

WINTER • WEEK 11

MEATS

3 pounds boneless spareribs–1
6 pork loin chops–2
1½ pounds ground beef–3
6 boneless, skinless chicken breasts–4

CANS/JARS

1 6-oz. can pineapple juice–1
1 10½-oz. can cream of celery soup–2
1 2.8-oz. can French fried onions–2
1¼ cups tomato sauce–3
1 jar old-fashioned–style applesauce–3
1 jar spaghetti sauce–4
Salad dressing for 2 dinners–1,4
3 6½-oz. cans clams with juice–5

GROCERY

¾ cup oats–3
1½ cups elbow macaroni–3
1 pound spaghetti noodles–4

PRODUCE

4 cloves garlic–1
2 medium potatoes–5
3 onions–3,5
1 green bell pepper–3,5
Salad greens for 2 dinners–1,4
Salad toppings for 2 dinners–1,4
1 bunch celery–5

BAKERY

Dinner rolls for 1 dinner–2
1 loaf crusty French bread–5

DAIRY

5 sticks butter–2,3,4,5
7½ cups milk–2,3,5
½ cup sour cream–2
2 cups grated Cheddar cheese–2,3
1 egg–3
1 pound sliced mozzarella cheese–4
2 oz. processed American cheese–3

FREEZER

24 ounces frozen hash brown potatoes–2
1 bag frozen green beans–2
1 bag corn on cob–4

CHECK YOUR STAPLES

Pepper–2,3,5
Seasoned salt–2
Salt–3,5
½ cup vinegar–1
½ cup brown sugar–1,3
½ cup soy sauce–1
2 tablespoons cornstarch–1
1 tablespoon vegetable oil–2
1 cup sugar–3
1 cup flour–3,5
1½ tablespoons mustard–3
¼ cup catsup–3
3 teaspoons Worcestershire sauce–3
2 tablespoons dry bread crumbs–3
¾ cup fine dry Italian seasoned bread
    crumbs–5
½ teaspoon thyme–5
Instant rice for 1 dinner–1

Shopping List

MEATS

4 pounds pork roast or pork loin roast–1
2 cups bite-sized beef steak pieces–2
1½ pounds ground beef–4,5
3 boneless, skinless chicken breasts–3

CANS/JARS

1 can cream of mushroom soup–1
1 8-oz. jar processed American cheese–1
2 tablespoons chopped pimento–2
1 4-oz. can chopped black olives–5
1 large can enchilada sauce–5
1 jar salsa–5
1 16-oz. can refried beans–5

GROCERY

1 small bag coconut–4
1 package dry chicken soup mix–3
Nuts for fruit salad–4

PRODUCE

1 cup cranberries–1
1 orange–1
5 onions–2,3,5
1 green bell pepper–2
1 bunch parsley–2
1 bunch spinach–2
1 basket strawberries–4
3 bananas–4
8 apples–1,4
1 pineapple–4
1 bunch grapes–4
1 bunch celery–3
3 carrots–3
2 potatoes–3

1 clove garlic–3

BAKERY

Breadsticks–2
1 loaf French bread–3
12 corn tortillas–5
1 package hamburger buns–4

DAIRY

1 stick butter–2
1 cup sour cream–2
2 eggs–2
1⅓ cups grated Cheddar cheese–5

FREEZER

10 oz. chopped broccoli or cauliflower
    mix–1
1 9-inch pastry shell–2

CHECK YOUR STAPLES

Salt–1,2,3
Pepper–1,2,3
Ground cloves–1
Ground nutmeg–1
Cumin–3
¼ cup flour–2
½ cup honey–1,4
½ cup vegetable oil–3,5
¼ cup red wine vinegar–2
½ cup Worcestershire sauce–4
1½ cups instant white rice–1,3
Long grain rice for 1 dinner–5
2 chicken bouillon cubes–3

Shopping List

MEATS

3 pounds ground beef–1,2
1½ pounds round steak–3
2 slices bacon–3
1½ pounds sausage–4
4 boneless chicken breasts–5

CANS/JARS

1 6-oz. can tomato paste–1
½ cup dry white wine–1
1 8-oz. can tomato sauce–1
Salad dressing for 1 dinner–1
2 16-oz. cans corn–2
1 16-oz. can sliced peaches–2
1 10½-oz. can cream of mushroom soup–3
1 4-oz. can sliced mushrooms–3
2 16-oz. cans green beans–3
1 4-oz. can diced chilies–4
1 tablespoon capers–4

GROCERY

1 package spaghetti noodles–1

PRODUCE

1 onion–1,2,3
5 cloves garlic–1,3,4
Salad greens for 1 dinner–1
Salad topping for 1 dinner–1
14 potatoes–2,3
1 head lettuce–2
5 carrots–4
3 zucchini–4
Freeze-dried onion–3

BAKERY

1 loaf ready-to-heat garlic bread–1

4 slices sourdough bread–4

DAIRY

3 sticks butter–2,3,4,5
2½ cups grated Cheddar cheese–2,4
1 tub cottage cheese–2
3 cups milk–3,4
3 eggs–4

FREEZER

3 cups cut broccoli–5

CHECK YOUR STAPLES

Thyme–5
Salt–1,2,3,4
Pepper–1,2,3,4
Oregano–1
Basil–1
Parsley–1,5
Rosemary–4
Paprika–5
1 tablespoon olive oil–1
1 tablespoon vegetable oil–3
½ teaspoon sugar–1
3 tablespoons flour–3
2 tablespoons Worcestershire sauce–3
1 teaspoon catsup–3
1 teaspoon steak sauce–3
½ teaspoon chili powder–4
2 tablespoons mayonnaise–5
⅓ cup dry Italian seasoned bread
    crumbs–5
1½ cups instant rice–5
1 teaspoon chicken bouillon granules–5
3 tablespoons Parmesan cheese–5

Index